Abelard
Sat. Oct 5/96

W9-BES-122

# IS IT
# GENUINE?

# IS IT
# GENUINE?

## HOW TO COLLECT ANTIQUES WITH CONFIDENCE

GENERAL EDITOR
### John Bly

Stoddart

# CONTENTS

IS IT GENUINE?
General Editor: John Bly

Edited and designed by
The Cooper Dale Partnership for
Mitchell Beazley International Limited,
Artists House,
14-15 Manette Street,
London W1V 5LB.

Copyright © Mitchell Beazley
Publishers Ltd 1986

First published in Canada in 1986 by
Stoddart Publishing Co. Limited,
34 Lesmill Road,
Toronto,
Canada M3B 2T6.

**Canadian Cataloguing
in Publication Data**
Bly, John
   Is it genuine?: how to collect antiques
   with confidence

ISBN 0-7737-2088-X

1. Antiques—Collectors and collecting.
2. Art objects—Collectors and collecting.
I. Title.

NK1125.B58 1986     745.1     C86-093622-8

Printed and bound in England

The title page illustration is of a
1750s Chelsea "billing doves"
tureen, as reproduced at the Paris
factory of Emile Samson in the late
19th century.
   Samson's was not the only factory
to reproduce these very desirable
items: they had previously been
copied at Worcester in the 1760s,
though with imperfect accuracy.
The only surviving Worcester copy
reproduces a Chelsea mark, but of
the wrong period. See page 162.

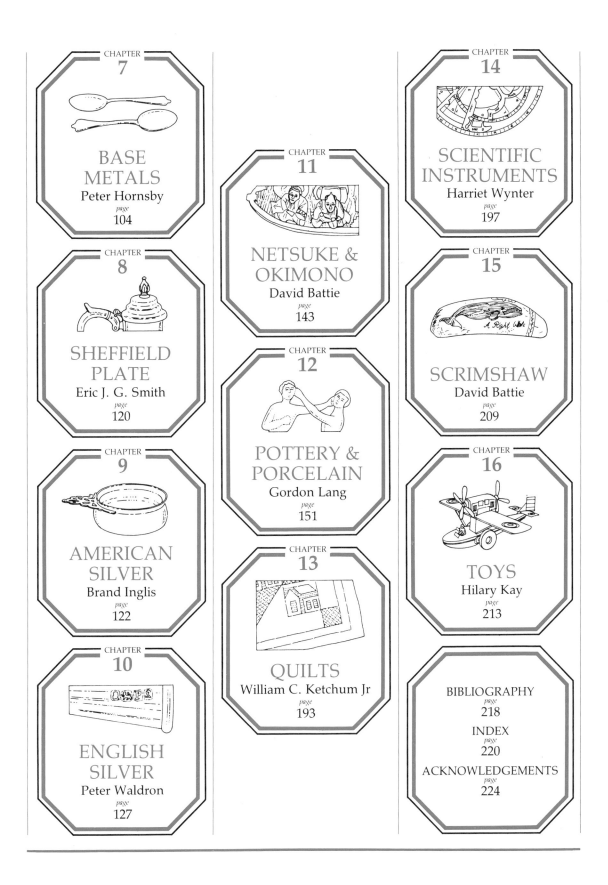

# PREFACE

I WAS DELIGHTED TO BE ASKED, as President of the British Antique Dealers' Association, to write a preface to this book, compiled by one of our members.

Those of us who are engaged professionally with antiques are always beset by questions of authenticity. Our assessment of whether a piece is genuine has to be carefully done. Errors in buying can be the ruin of our businesses. We also owe a duty of care to the collecting public—a duty to ensure that our descriptions of the antiques we sell are as accurate as they can be. Indeed, it is a condition of membership of this Association that if a buyer should discover that a piece does not conform to the description of it given by one of our members, that member must refund the purchase price on request.

Faking does go on, of course, though there is no reason to believe that it is any more prevalent now than it has been in the past. What concerns collectors, dealers and experts far more frequently is alteration and reproduction—matters on which the contributors to this book rightly dwell at some length.

At the end of the day, there is no substitute for long experience and daily handling of antiques when it comes to assessing their authenticity. That said, however, we all of us have to learn, and that is why this book could prove very valuable to many people, be they dealers or collectors. A thorough airing of this subject will be of service to us all.

**David Pettifer**

President, The British Antique Dealers' Association

*An English silver cigarette box. Its hallmark dates it to 1803, but its maker neglected to discover that no-one required such articles at that date, cigarettes being quite unheard of . . . See ''English Silver'' on pages 127-142.*

# FOREWORD

THE SUBJECT OF FAKES, forgeries and deceptions is intriguing enough by itself to pique the curiosity of those who have only the most passing of interest in the antiques and art worlds. However, even after the briefest perusal the reader rapidly becomes aware of the breadth and depth of knowledge to be gleaned from this volume.

Fourteen experts from various fields have been brought together to discuss their particular expertise. Their contributions will, no doubt, make everyone in the antiques field— dealers, collectors and curators—more knowledgeable, and therefore we welcome them. The concise way in which the information is presented, together with the number and quality of the illustrations—particularly the photographs of various details that one does not normally see—set this book apart from many others issued each year.

Among the plethora of volumes, large and small, some narrowly written for the scholar, others taking a broader view for the coffee table, this is a pleasing and welcome addition to one of the more prolific fields of publishing. John Bly is indeed to be congratulated on his energy and enthusiasm for this project which, I am sure, were of no small importance in getting from drawing board to the printed page.

The National Art & Antique Dealers Association of America, Inc. is most pleased heartily to recommend this volume.

**Lee Howard Beshar,**

President, The National Art & Antique Dealers
Association of America, Inc.

*An American ''Chippendale'' corner chair. It came on the market with a provenance tracing it back to the 18th century, but the provenance was every bit as spurious as the chair. See ''American Furniture'' on pages 22-27.*

# INTRODUCTION

Fakes, frauds and forgeries are all fascinating—until you get caught by one. The blow then is not just to the pocket, for self-esteem can suffer just as much.

Outright fakes are however rare by comparison with not-quite-genuine pieces. These abound and include utterly honest copies whose origins may get lost in the mists of memory, copies whose provenance was forgotten at the work-shop door and altered items. Almost anything can be altered to update it, make it more useful or more saleable. Whatever the motive for alteration might have been, the artifact may now deceive. It behoves buyers to be aware of what might have happened to standard items and to be able to judge if it did.

In principle, the immorality of passing off dud antiques is utterly clear. In practice however the view from the saleroom floor is not quite the same as from the pulpit. The best dealers, like the best collectors, are extremely knowledgeable, but anyone can be fooled—and most of us have been. There remains however a world of difference between making an honest mistake and deliberately perpetrating a deception.

Many people have assisted in ways great and small with the preparation of this book and I am grateful to them all. My principal acknowledgement however must be to the outstand-ing group of experts who agreed to contribute their special stores of knowledge. Their names are recorded in the table of contents, but not their years of learning or the efforts they made to share their knowledge so freely and with such lucidity. If readers find reason to be grateful for the protection this book offers, as I hope they will, it is to my colleagues in this enterprise that their gratitude is due.

I owe a further debt which I would not wish to express only in the list of acknowledgements at the back of the book: it is to my family for their support, and most especially to my father, from whom I learned so much about antiques and whose knowledge has safeguarded me from being caught out on more occasions than I care to remember, but all of which I am happy to acknowledge.

**John Bly**
Tring, Hertfordshire

*Beneath the pleasant exterior of this English cabinet lies an older and prettier piece. The story is told on page 65 in "English Furniture".*

# 1 : C L O C K S

THIS CHAPTER IS NOT INTENDED to describe the variety of antique clocks most frequently found or how to go about buying them: its purpose is to alert collectors to the commoner alterations or deceptions which, if they go unnoticed, can cost the buyer dearly.

Most clocks have the following elements: the dial and its fittings, the movement and the escapement. We shall look at each in turn, before considering particular points about certain familiar types of clock.

1 *below, left*
A tavern clock in black and gold lacquer dating from the mid-18th century. Note how the contraction of the timber has separated the panels of the dial. The absence of signs of contraction on the front would indicate heavy restoration, and if the back was in similar condition it should be a cause for anxiety.

## Dials and Their Fittings

Dials fall into the following categories: painted metal, painted wood, enamel on metal, and engraved metal.

**Painted metal dials** This was a popular form of decoration for bracket, long case and wall clocks of the late 18th and early 19th centuries. It was relatively cheap and is therefore found particularly on provincial clocks. Tin was the metal most commonly used, for reasons of cost.

An authentic example will almost certainly show crazing, similar to that found on old oil paintings. If the dial has been cleaned or restored the crazing will be less obvious, but will show as hairline cracks or small indentations respectively.

Most dials bear a signature (probably that of the clock seller, rather than that of the maker) and it is quite possible to alter these to more famous names. The test here is that the quality

2 *above*
A late 18th-century English dial clock. The painted metal dial has been carefully cleaned, but still shows traces of hairline cracking where the paint has crazed.

[2]
Back view of a long case clock dial, dating basically from the early 18th century. The dial pillars have all been moved to enable a different movement to be fitted: the original holes, which have not been blocked, can be seen slightly above the present fittings. The centre hole and the smaller seconds aperture have been ovalized to line up with the new arbors.

Repositioning the pillars like this has necessitated cutting into the calendar ring so that it can no longer revolve. This was an amateurish alteration.

[1]
A mahogany cased dial clock dating from the latter part of the 18th century, with silvered brass dial, typical period pierced hands of blued steel and a substantial cast bezel. Its overall appearance and quality immediately suggest an authentic item.

of the clock, in all its parts, should match the importance of the signature. Local interest can add a premium and so it is not unknown for an appropriate signature to be contrived.

**Painted wooden dials** The quality and signature criteria applicable to painted metal dials are equally relevant here. Further, the wood of an authentic dial will certainly have contracted and cracks should show. If they appear on the back of the dial but not on the face the dial has been restored.

**Enamelled metal dials** Make sure that the dial is original to the clock by checking that the dial feet fit into their original fixing holes and that the winding squares are properly centred in the winding holes.

The signature will usually be underneath the glaze and will not therefore show signs of wear. However certain clocks, especially those of the later 19th century, were retailed by jewellers and large stores, who painted their names on top of the enamel. The presence of such a signature does not add to the value nor does wear to the signature detract from it.

**Engraved dials** Throughout the 18th century the standard form of dial for better quality long case and bracket clocks was engraved brass, often enhanced with applied spandrels and a separate chapter ring. The backs of metal dials are generally brownish, partly because of oxidation and partly because they were not highly finished. This appearance can be simulated chemically—a deception that is very difficult to spot if it has been done well.

Simple brass dials have sometimes been later engraved with scrollwork or flowers, for example, to enhance their charm or value. If the style of the added decoration is compatible with the period of the clock, this too can be difficult to tell (though see Chapter 14 for some tell-tale signs of later engraving). A good general rule for initial assessment is that a plain dial goes with a plain looking case and one would expect to find an elaborate dial ornately cased. Similarly, the spandrels should balance the rest of the engraving and the size of the dial plate. For example, the more elaborate the half-hour marks on the chapter ring, the more ornate the spandrels should be.

It is also important to examine the mounts of brass dials with applied decoration and chapter rings. The back of the dial should show no signs of additional or blocked holes indicating that the screw fixings have been changed.

From about 1700 to about 1740 winding apertures were often ringed. However, rings have sometimes been added later to cover up damage caused by clumsy winding and, more seriously, they may have been applied to disguise minor movement of the winding holes. When a dial has been transferred from one clock to another and the apertures do not coincide exactly with the winding squares, new holes have to be bored and the old openings blocked or partly blocked. The metal is then matted flush with a punch and finished off with rings to complete the disguise.

It is very difficult to spot a signature that has been added to a previously unsigned clock. If it conforms in style to the period of the clock the only test is that for later engraving. The only way to alter an existing signature however is to file it away and hammer fresh metal forward from the back for re-engraving. When a dial has been signed at the base the back can be examined and signs of hammer marks or thinning will probably show. If the original signature was on the chapter ring the only sure way of checking is to remove it.

**Chapter rings** Engraved chapter rings were normally silvered, though the silvering may have worn away in part or in whole. Some rings therefore are now found polished. Re-silvering is a normal part of restoration, but it can disguise a blocked hole. It is important therefore to examine the back of the ring if at all possible, as it is much more difficult to disguise a blocked hole from the reverse.

Chapter rings vary enormously both in the size of the numerals and the decoration of the half-hour marks. The guide is that the decoration should be of the right form and style for the period of the clock, and to determine this there is no substitute for looking at as many clocks and reading as much about them as you can.

Chapter rings are fixed to the clock by feet that pass through the dial plate, where they are pinned. The feet should be in their original holes and should fill them adequately.

**Calendar rings** Many long case and some bracket clocks are fitted with calendar rings that show the date through an aperture. The ring is usually designed to run in rollers, but friction has often taken its toll and the wheel that carries the advancing pin has been removed or had the pin cut off.

**Hands** Replaced hands do not necessarily detract from the value of a clock. If the hands are of the correct style for the period and of a matching quality with the rest of the clock there should be little cause for concern except on the most elaborate and costly pieces.

## Movements

It is not often that one finds a movement which has had the planting of the trains altered to fit another dial. However, if the clock has not been cleaned and polished recently it is often possible to detect blocked holes by looking at the back plate. Blocked holes are warning signs, but do not automatically indicate a transferred movement. A clockmaker is unlikely to scrap an entire movement just because he made a small mistake in planting a wheel. Although a clever restorer will use contemporary brass to make a plug so that there is no (or virtually no) disparity in the colour of the metal, it is possible to see small circles of slight discoloration where the plugs have been inserted. If modern brass has been used the discontinuity in colour will be obvious.

3 *above and below*
The front plate of a late 17th-century bracket clock movement, showing the large-toothed calendar wheel in place complete with its advancing pin.

As this movement has not been cleaned for many years it is possible to see some blocked holes—for example the two dark spots one above the other on the left-hand side, opposite the centre wheel (detail, below). In this instance they are explicable as mistakes, but if a rational explanation cannot be found for blocked holes one should examine the clock with particular care.

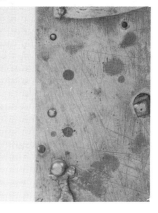

The back plate of a late 18th-century bracket clock showing a very badly punched and plugged barrel arbor hole bottom right. As the back plate is plain it should be possible to disguise the damage quite successfully; had it been engraved, restoration would have been considerably more difficult.

2
The movement and dial of a long case clock that is essentially early 18th century. The anchor is a 19th-century replacement, as its form shows; it is also secured to the collet by screws, which was standard practice in the 19th century but rare in the 18th. The collet on the last wheel in the striking train is also a replacement—the result of wear.

In obedience, no doubt, to the dictates of fashion, an arch has been added to the dial plate, probably about 1730; the fixing brackets are clearly visible. The case would have been altered to match.

The back plates of bracket clocks made in the 17th and 18th centuries are often engraved (those of long case clocks are almost invariably plain), so jobbers' repairs and bad hammering become more difficult to remove. Huffing on the back plate will often reveal signs of damage or blocked holes.

Spare holes are another matter. Bracket clocks often had repeating trains which, when they became worn, were sometimes removed rather than repaired. Removal leaves a series of spare (but legitimate) holes down one side of the plate.

Uniformity in the colour of the parts of a movement is a useful guide to originality, though one must be prepared for the replacement of those parts that move the most or the fastest—the fly pinion (or regulator) on the striking train and the escapement. Similarity in style of pillars, arbors and collets can also point towards or away from originality.

Signs of wear Certain types of repair, which may have been carried out a long time ago, should be treated with care. In particular there is the clock jobbers' tendency to try and close worn pivot holes with a punch—the proper technique is to use a bush—but it is often possible to cover up this form of bad workmanship by restoring with a bush.

Bushing of holes, particularly of those whose wheels turn rapidly, is to be expected. Another good sign is a certain degree of ovalizing of the barrel arbor holes—a result of the considerable pull exercised by the weights.

Always examine pinions for signs of wear. This is to be expected as dust and oil become impacted into the teeth, where they form an abrasive sludge which wears away the steel of the pinions. Some wear is a good sign of age, but excessive wear can be very expensive to repair.

Bells can crack and need replacement. Old bells have a silvery colour, a sweet sound and they resonate after the strike. The metal of modern bells tends to have a pinkish tinge and the ring is more strident.

## Escapements

Long case clocks The escapement on a long case clock will almost certainly be one of two types—anchor or dead beat. The anchor escapement was introduced in the third quarter of the 17th century and continued in general use through to the decline of the long case clock in the mid-19th century. As it is continually in motion, the steel pallets wear and have often been replaced. The simplest way to identify a replacement is to look at the brass collet on which the anchor is fixed—in most cases it will be in a different style to the other collets in the clock. One way of repairing worn pallets was to solder slips of spring steel to the faces, but it may not be possible, once these have been removed, for the original pallets to be kept.

Dead beat (or Graham) escapements are more rarely found, being generally reserved for regulators and precision timekeepers. Dead beat escapements should always be examined carefully for wear as the cost of restoration will be high.

It is always desirable to have original weights and pendulum, but many have gone astray, quite legitimately, and their absence does not immediately imply that a clock is "wrong".

Bracket clocks The standard form of escapement for bracket clocks throughout the 17th and 18th centuries was the verge, although in the latter part of the 18th century precision clocks tended to use the anchor with a short pendulum. It was common practice in the 19th century for clockmakers to replace a worn verge escapement with an anchor, which could be bought off the shelf and fitted easily. This is a perfectly genuine alteration and the argument has raged for years as to whether one should re-convert or leave the modified escapement as part of the clock's history. Many experts now accept that the returning of a clock to verge escapement is a permissible, even desirable, restoration, justified by the softer "tick" and the aesthetic improvement.

Conversion from verge to anchor is easy to spot. The anchor escapement requires a large, flattish bob which, in the case of a clock with an engraved back plate, will cover a considerable portion of the engraving as it swings. By contrast, the small bob of the verge balances the design and shape of the back plate much more closely.

The verge requires a top and bottom block (potence) to fix the crown wheel. These blocks are removed when the escapement is converted and the holes they occupied are left open or may still be visible if they have been blocked. On original verge escapement clocks the pendulum bob was normally drilled out so that a plug of wood could be inserted into which the pendulum rod was screwed. This made a tight fit for the threads of the rod, lessening the likelihood that it would unscrew itself with the motion of the pendulum. Restorers frequently forget this detail.

If a clock has been reconverted recently, there will be little wear to the crown wheel and pallets. Another sign may be that the back cock or keeper, which on an original escapement would have been engraved, does not have decoration of a quality to match the backplate.

Most bracket clocks made during the 18th century are fitted with fusees to compensate for the varying force of the main spring as the clock runs down. The cord connecting the fusee to the main spring was usually of gut; less frequently it was a chain, constructed like a miniature bicycle chain. If the clock was designed for gut lines, the grooves will be semi-circular—chains ran in square-section grooves. If broken chains have been replaced with gut the wrong shape of the groove will be obvious.

Recently, gut has begun to be replaced by wire, but this tends to scratch or cut the barrels—the kind of damage it can cause is shown in *Ill. 1* on the next page. Nylon-coated fishing line is a more satisfactory replacement. Badly worn gut in a fusee train should always be replaced immediately: if a cord breaks it will release massive power from the mainspring and this could result in serious damage to the movement.

3 *above*
The back plate of an early 18th-century bracket clock, showing a group of empty holes top left where a repeat train was originally fitted (compare *Ill. 4*, below). This clock has further been converted to anchor escapement. A heavy back cock partially masks the original engraving and the large bob is out of both sympathy and proportion.

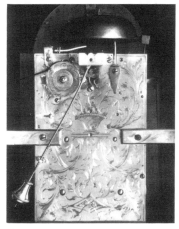

4
The back plate of a mid-18th century bracket clock, with original alarm mounted in the repeat train position (compare *Ill. 3* above). The clock is still fitted with a verge escapement and original small bob. The feet of the back cock are engraved but the back is plain, indicating that it probably had an engraved keeper at one time.

## Long case clocks

The cases of long case clocks were made by cabinetmakers, and therefore should be assessed as antique furniture. What particularly concerns us here however is establishing whether the clock belongs with the case.

In a small group of exceptionally rare and valuable 17th-century clocks the hood was originally of the rising type, but due to the inconvenience of this design, they were often converted to a conventional opening door. Signs of this conversion will not appear on any modestly priced long case clock.

The dial should be an adequate fit inside the mask of the hood door, which should neither conceal the decoration of the dial nor reveal its edge.

When you remove the hood, examine the seat board on which the movement rests. Ideally the seat board will be original, showing age in the timber compatible with the rest of the case, but seat boards do have a heavy weight to carry and some have broken and therefore been replaced, quite legitimately. However, any indication of a non-original seat board should immediately raise suspicions.

The movement of a long case clock is usually secured to the seat board by hooks that pass over the bottom pillars of the movement or by bolts drilled up through the seat board into the pillars. If the movement and the seat board belong together there should be only one set of aligning holes, whichever fixing method was used.

A seat board should be neither clumsily thick nor apparently too thin to support the weight of the movement. If the board is raised on blocks it is possible that there has been an alteration. Seat boards were normally nailed or screwed straight down into the cheeks, therefore any holes in the seat board should have corresponding holes in the trunk side panels below. A line was often scored across the backboard when the original seat board was fitted. If the existing seat board does not conceal or coincide with this line, it is quite possible that it has been moved to accommodate a transferred movement.

The back board can be revealing in another way. The one-second pendulum has a virtually standard length of $39\frac{1}{2}$ in. (1m). If the pendulum has knocked against the back or the sides for any length of time, there will be scrape marks. If these marks do not correspond with the present position of the bob the likelihood is that the seat board has been moved up or down to accommodate a transferred movement.

## Wall Clocks

The earliest form of English wall clock is the lantern, dating from c. 1620. Their age, simple construction and desirability mean that they are one of the most faked types of clock.

Early lantern clocks were fitted with balance wheel escapements, but surviving examples are almost unknown. In general, any lantern clock with a balance wheel has had its escapement restored. Many early lantern clocks were con-

[1]
Side view of the movement of an 18th-century timepiece wall clock, showing the verge escapement complete with original keeper on the back cock. Scratch lines are starting to appear on the barrel, caused by fitting unsheathed wire to the fusee. Rawhide, gut or nylon coated fishing line would be preferable.

verted to short pendulum verge escapements later in the 17th century and were often further converted to long pendulum anchor escapements at a later date. Redundant holes in the top plate are the usual evidence of such conversions.

Lantern clocks originally ran on woven ropes, which were threaded over spikes on the ratchet wheels. They were often converted to run on chains; if so, the ratchet wheels will have had their points filed down.

Pierced frets at the top of lantern clocks have sometimes been damaged and required replacement. These frets are cast in one piece with their feet: if a replacement has been fitted its feet may not match the original holes, which will be detectable. Any signature that appears at the base of the front fret should be checked for authenticity.

In recent years the increasing value of lantern clocks has led to the production of many counterfeits, some using movements taken out of simple 30-hour country long case clocks. Others, such as the large number of examples signed "Thomas Moore, Ipswich", are brand new though given the appearance of age by being chemically treated or buried in earth for a while.

## Act of Parliament Clocks

These large wall clocks take their name from the Act of 1797 which put a sales tax on clocks, though similar items had been made since the early 18th century. They were made for public places, such as inns, and were often lacquered. Recently a number of copies have been made that are very convincing at first sight, though a close inspection will often reveal inappropriate and inferior materials, such as plywood.

2 *above, left*
A 17th-century weight-driven lantern clock with original alarm disc, dial and single hand.

3 *above, centre*
A lantern clock case that is basically 17th century, now fitted with a later chapter ring, a Victorian fusee movement (note the winding holes) and two hands.

4 *above, right*
A Victorian "copy" of a 17th-century lantern clock. Note the revealing lack of symmetry in the dial-centre engraving.

[1] *above*
A mid-19th century skeleton clock exhibiting all the features of an authentic quality piece, notably: delicate wheelwork, an elaborate chapter ring, and a marble base compatible with the correctly proportioned dome.

[2]
A fine quality French carriage clock, dating from *c.* 1860. The signature—that of Aubert & Co, London—is the retailer's, added by the shop after the dial was enamelled and therefore vulnerable to wear. Erosion of the signature, as here, does not affect the clock's value.

## Dial Clocks

Dial clocks were introduced into Britain in the mid-18th century and were popular until the early part of this century. Although they are not much faked yet, early examples are now sufficiently valuable to merit careful scrutiny.

The first examples had painted wood or engraved and silvered dials similar to those of long case and bracket clocks. They were usually signed by a London maker. The movements had short pendulum verge escapements with a fusee in the train. The cases were generally a rich, dark mahogany with a broad turned bezel and a substantial wood or brass ring securing the glass. The hands were of pierced blued steel or, very occasionally, brass, and were similar in design to those of contemporary bracket and long case clocks.

During the early part of the 19th century the number of examples increased dramatically and the silvered dial passed out of fashion, being supplanted by painted metal—usually tin. Examples do exist in which original painted dials have been exchanged for engraved, signed, silvered or brass dials to give the impression of an earlier date.

Later in the 19th century these clocks changed very little in detail, but just enough to make them less valuable. The dials and glass became flat and the brass bezel less substantial. Hands became plainer, sometimes with simple spade ends; minute hands might have no decorative shaping at all.

Check that the clock belongs in the case by examining the retaining screws in the edge of the dial. All three or four of them should align with holes in the frame and there should be no redundant holes.

## Skeleton Clocks

There is no simple guide to establishing whether a skeleton clock is genuine, made up from old parts or an outright fake. Many examples were produced during the 19th century as it was common practice for provincial clockmakers to contrive a skeletonised clock as a window display. These clocks were readily made up by taking the wheels from an old dial or bracket clock and replanting them within a set of pierced, skeletonised plates. Such clocks often had painted metal dials, whereas their more sophisticated contemporaries were likely to have their dials engraved and silvered.

Skeleton clocks are as easy to make up now as they were then, and their increase in value has made it a commercially viable proposition to produce them. Timepiece clocks are the most often faked.

All the wheels of superior skeleton clocks are finely pierced, normally with four, five or six spokes. Bracket clocks rarely had more than four spokes as the wheel work was not on display. The under-dial wheels driving the hands of a cased clock are almost never pierced, though the copier with an eye for detail will rectify this when using them to make up a skeleton clock.

The base can sometimes reveal more than the wheel work. A new wooden base should always be regarded with suspicion. Odd-looking feet supporting the clock frame should be examined, as should the studding that holds the clock to the base: a common sign of replacement or alteration is the fitting of over-large feet to add height to a clock that has been placed under a non-original dome.

Skeleton clocks are not usually signed on the movement because of lack of space. When a signature appears engraved on a plaque fitted to the base it is very important to establish that the entire assembly belongs together.

## Carriage Clocks

Carriage clocks were introduced early in the 19th century and are traditionally held to be modelled on the *pendules d'officiers* used by Napoleon's commanders. It was the perfection of the lever escapement and the low cost of manufacture, combined with their exceptional accuracy, that led to the mass production of these clocks.

English examples are rare by comparison with their French counterparts, of which hundreds of thousands were made between 1850 and 1920. In the last ten years several French and Swiss companies have recreated them, not as forgeries but simply as copies of a continuously popular style. They are obviously new, although a small number are around that have been "aged" by dirtying the case and the movement.

The clock is very likely to be modern if the dial, which should be enamel and very smooth, is thin and slightly corrugated, with the white very white and the back very black. Some clocks are stamped with serial numbers on the back plate, and if these are composed of more than five digits the clock is unlikely to be old.

Beware of alterations to carriage clocks. A recent modification has been the replacement of the side glasses with modern electrotyped metal or porcelain panels. They are inferior in quality, being decorated in acrylic or cellulose paints which have a soft and greasy appearance, and sit ill with an original plain white dial.

Although mass-produced, carriage clocks were finely if not heavily gilded and some signs of wear should be expected if the gilding is claimed as original. The best quality examples were fire gilded and can occasionally be found still in perfect condition. Original gilding should be preserved if possible.

One particular "enhancement" to be aware of is the alteration of a quarter-striking (*petite sonnerie*) clock to a full *grande sonnerie*. It is not technically difficult to lengthen the slide on a quarter-striking clock or to fit the complete mechanism and to turn such a clock into a grande sonnerie. However, the modification means that the clock will not strike in the grande sonnerie mode throughout a full seven-day period—the barrel on a grande sonnerie clock is larger than its quarter-striking contemporary. The *ideal* way to buy a grande sonnerie carriage clock of doubtful history is therefore on eight days' approval.

[3] *above and below*
An alteration that can affect the value of carriage clocks is the replacement of the original platform escapement. The example above is original, being well proportioned, with a silvered finish and secured by blued-steel screws through polished washers. Below is a modern replacement, distinguishable by its size, gilt finish and pragmatic but inelegant construction.

**1** *left*
A month-going walnut long case
clock by Joseph Knibb of London,
*c*. 1685. It was originally made with
a flat top and bun feet, but a caddy
top was superimposed and the feet
were replaced by a plinth, probably
early in the 18th century.

Notice the shutters covering the
winding apertures. Pulling a cord
on the side of the movement reveals
the winding squares and also
provides maintaining power during
the winding of the clock. This
simple mechanism has often been
removed.

**2** *above*
A fine mid-18th century "Act of
Parliament" clock, with red and
gold decoration on a black ground.
The door is applied with a coloured
and varnished print. The condition
is very good, given the age and
delicate nature of the decoration,
but shows chipping and foxing
consistent with its date.

The dial is made in two parts,
joined horizontally, and has been
exceptionally well conserved. In this
instance the two boards show little
sign of movement, but tell-tale
cracks in the black rim just below 9
o'clock and 3 o'clock are reassuring.

1 *left*
Eider decoys are among the more spectacular of wildfowl lures and among those most often faked. A single coat of paint with little sign of wear or loss indicates that this is a recent construction.

2 *below*
Since they are both interesting in appearance and popular with collectors, Canada Geese are often faked. One trick is to build a new body to go with an old head, since the latter were often made up in quantity and may be found in old shops or among hunters' stores. The crackled paint on this canvas body however indicates clearly that this is not a recent reproduction.

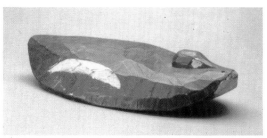

3 *above*
Crude, old and wonderful, this White Winged Scoter decoy shows the sort of age and wear appropriate to its 1885–1900 vintage. The folk quality of this piece is too idio-syncratic to be reproduced easily.

4 *below*
Other folky and desirable decoys include Mergansers. This matching pair was made in Maine at the turn of the century. The longitudinal crack in the male's body is caused by age and is some assurance that the piece is not recent. Always check Mergansers closely however, as they are among the most frequently reproduced.

# 2 : DECOYS

THE DECOY, a more or less realistic representation of a bird designed to lure wildfowl within gunshot, is collected primarily within the United States, though European examples will be encountered and Canadian decoys form an important separate classification. While many birds have been imitated as decoys, including crows, owls and doves, the majority of forms fall within two categories — ducks and shorebirds. In each of these enthusiasts distinguish between working decoys, which were actually used or "hunted over", and purely decorative wildfowl carvings. Many well known carvers produced both types. Collectors include duck hunters, folk art enthusiasts and carving buffs.

1
This Bobwhite Quail is a decorative carving made in Illinois during the 1970s. It was designed as a piece of sculpture, not as a working decoy, and such pieces are attractive in their own right. But with faked wear and paint loss they may be passed off as much older than they really are. Always check paint and wood closely for signs of age.

The value of a decoy is primarily dependent upon the reputation of the carver, the rarity of the individual work and, to a lesser extent, aesthetic considerations. The last are of most concern to those who pursue decoys as a form of folk sculpture. Since a connection with a particular maker is so important the faking of either makers' marks or their styles is the customary avenue of fraud.

## The Prevalence of Fakes and Reproductions

Jeff Waingrow, author of *American Wildfowl Decoys* and a leading authority in the field, notes that ". . . generally speaking, faking of famous makers' work is uncommon". This is due to a great extent to the fact that those who seek such pieces are usually extremely knowledgeable sportsmen and carvers, they are very familiar with the styles of the carvers whose work they seek and are thus extremely difficult to fool. Shore birds may bring as much as $50,000 at auction, and a pair of Merganser ducks recently sold for $93,500. With this kind of money at stake the market for the best decoys is small and most trading is done among a limited group of experts.

On the other hand, there are many fakes and reproductions among birds selling for $1,000 or less, especially those retailing for a few hundred dollars, which are often bought by people knowing little or nothing of the field and seeking only a certain "look". The commonest kind of fake is the outright reproduction, in which both body and paint are new. In most cases the paint will be distressed to create an illusion of age and use. The makers of such reproductions tend to focus on the more spectacular and hence more saleable types such as swans, Canada Geese and Mergansers—see *Ill. 6*, p. 19. New heads may be joined to old bodies, lost beaks might be replaced or an older body recarved to add feathering to enhance its appearance. Most such work is relatively crude as the amount to be gained in this price range does not justify fine work.

2
Shorebirds received hard treatment. This charming country example shows chips, cracks and several coats of worn paint. Check such pieces for repairs, particularly the replacement of bills, which were often broken off and lost. Such a repair decreases the value of a bird.

## Points to Watch For

Always be aware of prices and be suspicious of a good looking bird that is well under the normal market value. For example, any decent period swan decoy will bring at least $1,500. If you are offered one for $500 it probably has problems.

Working decoys were repainted each year and should show several coats of paint with worn spots, small chips and cracks from wear and age (*Ill. 2*, left). Shot holes can occasionally be seen, though they are not common as most sportsmen do not shoot birds on the water. Wear is usually simulated with sandpaper or steel wool. Examine worn areas under a magnifying glass. If deep, rough ridges or gouges appear, the wear is artificial. True, old wear produces smooth, spiderweb-like crazing with softened edges.

Few makers marked their birds, though many owners did. Familiarize yourself with the marks of well known carvers. Always compare a mark with an example of the carver's signature in a book or on an authenticated example. Like other parts of the decoy, the mark should show proper wear. It is also important to familiarize yourself with the techniques of carving and painting employed by the makers whose work you seek, since most attribution is based on a particular carver's style. Never buy a bird simply because it is said to "look like a Nathan Cobb", or "resemble a Joe Lincoln goose".

Decoys can be bought in many places, but if you want to buy quality go to a reputable dealer with long experience in the field. Most of these will warrant their attribution of a bird; and, equally important, they will still be in business if you have reason to make a complaint. One of the characteristics of the faker is his rapid disappearance once the sale is made.

**3** *above*
These fine shorebird decoys all date to the early 20th century. The Greater Yellowlegs in the centre is by the famous carver, A. Elmer Crowell. Learn to recognize the style and carving techniques employed by a craftsman like Crowell, as few such makers ever marked their work.

**4** *below*
Tin shorebird decoys were made in factories during the second half of the 19th century. They are popular with collectors but be sure to check the paint to see if it is original. Since the paint is frequently lost and the body rusts, such decoys are liable to have been repainted.

# 3 : AMERICAN FURNITURE

A T THE TOP END OF THE MARKET, fine examples of authentic American antique furniture now command very high prices, reflecting their quality, beauty and authenticity. The danger area for many collectors, unable to afford these first quality items, is the mass of furniture that has perhaps the right form, but lacks both the detail and conviction that any authentic work of art must possess. Such pieces, looking not unlike—in some cases very like—the exemplars are rarely if ever the bargains they purport to be. It is always better to buy a genuine item of a humbler form than to pay for a dubious example of a desirable form.

Would-be collectors must realize that for every piece that has come down to us intact there are many more pieces that have suffered some kind of alteration or restoration over the years. These pieces were not always looked upon as antiques, but as old or used furniture to be put aside or perhaps altered to fit the owner's needs. As interest in collecting American antiques has developed during this century, these wrecks or altered pieces have drifted into the market place to be reprocessed into "original" high-priced forms by unscrupulous people.

In addition to reprocessing there was always the matter of "improving"—making a more valuable form out of a genuine piece. Fully trained restorers must, of necessity, have all the skills required to make any part of a period item, and these skills can be subverted on occasion into "improvement" rather than legitimate restoration.

To make the situation even more confusing, during the Centennial period in America (the last quarter of the 19th century), cabinetmakers were legitimately making copies of 18th-century forms. Although similar in appearance (carving style and proportion excepted), one major difference is that Centennial furniture was constructed with dowels instead of the mortice-and-tenon joints of the 18th century. In addition, machines were used in the Centennial period, and the tell-tale marks of those machines are very much in evidence.

Seven years after the Centennial Celebration in America an article under the title "Faking Antique Furniture in New York—1883" by Ian H. G. Quimby appeared in *The Decorator*

1 *top right*
A block and shell Connecticut secretary as it appeared in an auction flyer for an estate sale held on site and off the beaten track. It is basically original with the exception of the brasses and feet, which were added in the 19th century.

2 *right*
The same secretary as it appeared after "improving". The feet have been replaced with more sophisticated ogee bracket feet which had to be set back from the mouldings to cover the marks left

by the turned feet. The brasses, with the exception of the side handles, are replaced.

The primitive bonnet with original finials was removed and the tops of the doors were re-shaped to accommodate the new, more sophisticated arched bonnet top. The escutcheons on the doors have not been repositioned and are too high and close to the tops of the doors. Finally, the finials and Corinthian capitals from the original piece were later used on another "improved" piece.

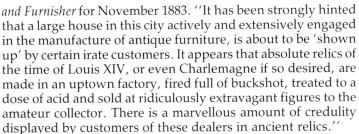

**3** *left*
The characteristic dowel construction of Centennial furniture.

**4** *right*
An exploded view of a Queen Anne chairback showing the mortice-and-tenon construction of a genuine 18th-century piece of American furniture.

*and Furnisher* for November 1883. ''It has been strongly hinted that a large house in this city actively and extensively engaged in the manufacture of antique furniture, is about to be 'shown up' by certain irate customers. It appears that absolute relics of the time of Louis XIV, or even Charlemagne if so desired, are made in an uptown factory, fired full of buckshot, treated to a dose of acid and sold at ridiculously extravagant figures to the amateur collector. There is a marvellous amount of credulity displayed by customers of these dealers in ancient relics.''

During the same period, New York cabinetmakers such as Ernest Hagen were making exact copies of Duncan Phyfe furniture. Even today, pieces made by Hagen are often mistakenly catalogued as originals, since they were made exactly the same way Phyfe and his contemporaries made them. These pieces were not made as fakes but as superb reproductions using the same techniques and materials that the early 19th-century craftsmen would have used, but they can muddy the waters of collecting.

## Boston and Philadelphia Fakes

In the 1920s, when collecting and interest in American antique furniture began in earnest, fakers in Boston were busy making pieces from old parts, creating rare butterfly tables from plain tavern tables (see *Ill. 1*, p. 37), blockfront bureaux from straight front ones, veneering over solid fronts, adding inlaid eagles, fans and bellflowers to plain tables, clocks and chests. They were also recreating fine Federal pieces such as Hepplewhite and Sheraton sewing tables, tambour desks, card tables and veneered bureaux.

In Philadelphia at the same time, dishonest cabinetmakers were making elaborately carved scrolled top highboys and chests-on-chests from plain flat top ones. They carved the pedestals and legs of plain tripod tea tables, added English mahogany trays as tops and made more valuable piecrust tea tables, or they made similar tables by using the bases of fine pole screens and adding birdcage supports and piecrust tops. See pp. 78-9 for ways to identify these illegitimate pieces.

## The Categories of Antique Furniture

To arm himself against these deceptions the collector needs to be aware of what makes an antique genuine, and of the background of restoration. He needs to know what the expert or dealer looks for in an antique, how restoration occurs and how it is graded.

Pieces can be allotted to five categories from perfect original to outright fake. Within these categories there are various degrees of restoration, from minor to major.

**1. The Perfect Piece** The piece with all its structural parts intact and glue, blocks, inlay, surface, edges, finish, etc. in a perfect state of preservation. It retains its original brasses, finials and decorative carving. The genuine antique radiates its own authenticity and shows the following features:

**patina**—the surface quality of the piece, a natural glow that develops after many years of care and shines out to the observer

**erosion of edges**—this natural erosion develops after generations of waxing, polishing and handling

**shrinkage**—wood shrinks across the grain and this causes irregularities where elements are joined: after 200 years mortice pins become compressed and pop out; a chair's splat with its vertical grain shrinks from side to side, while the crest, with its horizontal grain, shrinks from top to bottom, causing a minor break in the flow of design where they meet

**colour of structural elements due to oxidization**—these structural elements were left untreated and therefore oxidized naturally over the centuries, turning various shades of brown; to simulate this natural colour the faker must stain the altered pieces of wood, but this produces an artificial colour that can be spotted easily by the experienced eye.

**contrast of structural colour depending upon exposure**—structural elements that are more exposed to the air will oxidize more and turn a darker brown than protected elements; for instance, the undersides of the bottom drawers of a highboy will be much darker than those of the upper drawers—see *Ill. 2*, opposite.

All of these points reflect the natural ageing of the object over the centuries and can be seen by the naked eye—as long as it is a trained eye.

**2. Minor Restoration** The basically intact genuine piece with a few missing blocks, a possible crack in a bracket foot or a small missing segment, some chewed off edges on a drawer lip, a segment of moulding broken or missing, a chipped toe, finials or pendants restored, some or all brasses replaced, drawer runners replaced, cracks filled in, and so on. These are still fine pieces: they are just showing the normal wear and tear of everyday use for 200 years.

**The Gentle Art**
Over 60 years ago Herbert Cescinsky wrote *The Gentle Art of Faking Furniture*. In it he said: "There is more English antique furniture exported to America in one year than could have been made in the whole 18th century."

American cabinetmakers were no more principled than their English counterparts. In 1845 an article appeared in the Portland, Maine *Transcript*, concerning the faking of Mayflower furniture. The faker describes how he is going to cut down an overly large bed to one that is a more saleable size. "He says we have no idea of the enlightened interest which the ladies take in everything antique, and he feels quite certain that he could sell it [the bed] at a very handsome price, especially if he adds a little carving to one corner and breaks off the top of one of the posts."

**3. Major Restoration (Original Design)** A piece with greatly restored areas of inlay, or with a new foot or feet, a new drawer front, new base, a case piece with new bonnet mouldings or a partially restored bonnet, or a piece restored a generation ago but with a family background that might give it a false promise of complete authenticity.

All these restorations are part of the preservation process and restore a piece to its original form; they may or may not seriously devalue the item. Unfortunately, many of these restorations are poorly done, sometimes by amateurs but often by inexperienced cabinetmakers. In this area the loudest differences of opinion occur and do, to a great degree, depend on the importance and rarity of the piece in question. Defining these restorations requires experience and judgment, and a piece in this category may be misunderstood or go unrecognized by inexperienced collectors and dealers.

An attempt to outline here what would be considered acceptable by people of good will encompasses too many

[1] *above*
A side view of a genuine highboy with drawers from both the upper and lower sections pulled out. The dovetailing to both drawers is a good match—if it were not, one might suspect a marriage. Other points to check are compatibility of timbers and decoration to both parts and compatibility of backboards.

[2] *left*
The underside of an authentic period lowboy with an upper drawer pulled out. Being much better protected from the oxidizing effects of the atmosphere the bottom of the upper drawer has remained much paler than the undersides of the lower drawers, which are, of course, permanently exposed to the air.

1 *above*
An "amputee"—a Chippendale
side chair about to have new feet
spliced on.

2
A similar Chippendale side chair to
that shown in *Ill. 1* above, but
with the legs and feet now
complete. If genuine this chair
would command a top price; the
faker however has to try and sell it
as original but at a bargain price.

variables to be feasible. It is perhaps enough to state that the
general principle of acceptability based on rarity and importance should temper the judgment employed.

**4. Major Restoration (to Create a More Valuable Form)** A
piece that has been altered to increase its price. This is the area
of fraud: value is being created where it did not exist before.
These pieces have been altered to deceive and, no matter how
beautiful, are misrepresentations and false bargains. They
may appear in a private or public sale with a wonderful provenance which may be true to the original form, but the provenance of the altered section is obviously not going to be
revealed in the catalogue. The seasoned expert knows what to
look for because over the years he has accumulated his list of
likely alterations, and he therefore examines a piece with these
things in mind.
Fifteen common alterations are listed here but they are just a
few of the conversions that the expert looks for:

☐ making a butterfly table from a more common tavern table
   by cutting the sides of the top, hinging them, and adding
   butterfly wings for support

☐ adding arms to a side chair (in this case the chair will usually
   be narrower in the seat than a true armchair—see p. 63)

☐ cutting down large pieces (sideboards or sofas) to make
   them smaller and more desirable (see p. 66)

☐ adding feet to the top sections of a highboy or chest-on-
   chest when the two sections have been separated (see p. 50)

☐ adding a top to the lower section of a highboy or chest-on-
   chest to create a lowboy or a chest

☐ marrying highboys, chests-on-chests and secretaries
   (joining the top of one piece to the base of another)

☐ making more desirable round-leaf tables from square-leaf
   tables (see p. 68)

☐ carving a shell or fan on the lid of a desk where one did not
   exist or replacing the plain interior of a desk with one that
   has blocked drawers and fan carving

☐ replacing bonnet or scrolled tops on highboys, secretaries
   and chests-on-chests which had been cut off to fit them into
   low-ceilinged rooms, or adding bonnet or scrolled tops to
   pieces that originally had flat tops.

☐ putting new or recarved legs on chairs, tables, highboys and
   lowboys; adding ball and claw feet or ogee bracket feet to
   pieces with plain bracket feet or whose feet were missing

☐ switching clock works from one case to another

☐ adding a label of a famous maker to an unmarked piece

☐ adding legs to highboys, lowboys, chairs and tables with cut
   legs; these are called "amputees".

**5. The Complete Fake** A piece that has no roots in history but has been created with the intention of deceiving. This, without a doubt, is the most vicious of all the crimes perpetrated upon the collecting public. Important forms are made from scratch, sometimes with the aid of old parts, but more often with new wood, by a skilled craftsman with knowledge of regional motifs, forms and woods. Today, with many pieces of American antique furniture bringing hundreds of thousands of dollars, the incentive to fake is considerable.

Demand decrees what fakers will supply—it has been this way for generations. Even before the great Philadelphia pie-crust tea table was sold in January 1986 for more than $1,000,000, fakers were making and selling this desirable form along with rare corner chairs, bombé bureaux, block and shell Rhode Island bureaux and kneehole desks. Now that the million dollar mark has been reached, the collector can be sure another rash of fakes will appear on the market.

This is where the dealer has a tremendous responsibility. Like a doctor or an attorney, if he hangs out his shingle he should be an expert; but many are not. Of course, if a dealer makes a mistake it won't be fatal, but it can certainly be expensive, and if he continues to make the same mistake or worse, it can and will have a long lasting effect upon his or her reputation and on dealers in general.

Collectors have a responsibility too—a responsibility to exercise self-restraint, to resist temptation, and to use common sense. Why would a rare form be offered at a very advantageous price? Is it the collector's lucky day? Probably not, but it may be the faker's.

3 *above*
A Queen Anne highboy originally made with a flat top but subsequently given a bonnet top to increase its price. The irony is that the alteration succeeded only in reducing the value of the piece.

4 *below*
A "Chippendale" corner chair. It is a total fake, but was accompanied by a history tracing it back to the Revolution. With or without its (fraudulent) provenance it simply does not radiate authenticity.

5 *right*
A genuine Queen Anne corner chair, Philadelphia *c.* 1740-60. Although superficially similar to the fake example illustrated left, this piece has, to the trained eye, what the other lacks—the authentic quality and character of its period.

# 4 : CONTINENTAL FURNITURE

THE ART OF COPYING is as old as time itself, but in terms of European furniture it is practical to discuss only the 17th century through to the present day, quite simply because earlier pieces are rarely seen on the market or outside museums. It is as well, at this point, to bear in mind that the older the piece is, or is purported to be, the more likely that it has sustained alteration or at the very least repair.

It is necessary to distinguish between the fake and the reproduction, the deliberate forgery and the genuine copy, while at the same time bearing in mind allowable restoration or repair. The marriage is another, often unhappy, area of alteration to furniture that bears further examination.

## The Copy

This is possibly the least contentious type of potentially deceptive furniture. Copies are mainly confined to the 19th and 20th centuries because the 17th, 18th and first quarter of the 19th centuries were mainly periods of progression. One style followed on from another, either as a natural evolution, such as the Rococo from the Régence, or as a direct conflict with and reaction against the former style, for example when the sophisticated Transitional style emerged out of the excesses of the Rococo about 1750. It is no accident that both these examples are taken from French or, more correctly, Paris furniture, as Paris was the main disseminator if not the actual source of new material in these periods.

## Copies of French Furniture

The 19th century, in its second quarter, saw a troubled Europe that had just emerged from a long and commercially damaging war. Restoration France experienced a brief and uncertain return to porcelain-mounted furniture, notably by A. L. Bellangé, inspired by the work supplied in the 1780s to Marie-Antoinette by the *ébéniste* Martin Carlin and the *marchands merciers* Poirier and Daguerre. The advent of the Second Empire in 1848 saw a full-blooded return, the seeds of which had been sown in the two previous decades, to the styles of earlier centuries. Unfortunately this was not in any particular order—Gothic, Louis XV and Louis XVI were followed by Baroque and Renaissance.

The products of these revivals can be divided into two types. First, the exact copies of earlier, mainly Louis XV and Louis XVI pieces; and second, the eclectic pieces that either muddled up one or more styles or "improved" upon the golden years of the past.

"Improved" furniture styles were a result of the spirit of their age, which sought constantly to change and innovate, reflecting the massive changes in industrial, manufacturing and social organization since the early years of the Industrial

[1]
A nonsensical piece, dating from the late 19th century but incorporating late 17th-century *pietra dura* panels. The carcase is probably Flemish and the top is reminiscent of late 17th-century table cabinets, but its proportions are altogether improbable.

Revolution. This was the age of the machine, of gas, iron and steam, which not only made more furniture available to more people more cheaply but allowed ideas to travel faster as well. Fashion therefore became more international and was communicated at a speed unknown in earlier years.

To a large extent eclectic or "improved" designs are not relevant to copies, or even to the fake or married piece. However, it is important to keep in mind an image of the pure earlier styles so that any obvious move away from the earlier period can be spotted quickly and identified. A knowledge of the development of styles is therefore useful, if not essential. So many collectors fall into the trap of buying a "Louis XV" piece that is clearly 19th-century in origin and concept, not because of some highly technical constructional details but because it simply does not follow the form of an 18th-century piece. *Ill. 1*, p. 39 is an example of a Louis XV form adapted for 20th-century use: the principles of the design are of the 18th century but the proportions and lines are not.

If the categorization of eclectic or improved pieces is at first daunting, the overall rule is to think of proportion. As the great houses of Europe were built smaller, so the scale of the furniture to go in them was proportionately reduced. Town houses in Paris and other capital cities followed this trend by the 19th century and, with the growth of the population and the emergence of a new middle class, the shortage of space for housing became more acute; families increasingly began to live in apartments rather than houses. The consequent reduced scale of a piece of furniture is an immediate tell-tale sign—sufficient at least to arouse suspicions and initiate a detailed examination of the article.

Proportion is the key, vital to the definition and distinction of a reproduction piece. The word "copy" implies an exact replica in size and detail. A "reproduction" implies a copy, but without necessarily keeping to the exact size and often skimping in detail, normally to keep costs down. The illustrations below are of two commodes, identical in form but very different in finish and quality. The first dates to the

2 *below, left*
This commode is a popular model, copied from an early Louis XVI original *c.* 1775. The panel is based on one for the duc de Penthièvre's commode, now in the Musée Condé at Chantilly. It dates from 1860-80 and is 36.6 in. (93cm) high by 68 in. (173cm) wide.

3 *below*
This commode was made in 1920. It is the same height as that in *Ill. 1* but only 53.9 in. (137 cm) wide, a much more convenient width. The earlier copy is superior in every way: it has a more elaborate and pronounced breakfront, covered in a flowerhead and geometric trellis; the mounts too are finer and more elaborate. This later copy is however of good quality—it is only in direct comparison that the differences become apparent. Both marble tops are thick but not as thick as an 18th-century top—as marble became more expensive to quarry and as power saws became more available, slabs were cut thinner. Note that the "better" commode has a moulded edge to its top.

1860-80 period, is larger and of far better quality. The second dates to *c.* 1920. The presumption that the smaller the piece and the less attention to quality the later is the date of manufacture, is a dangerous rule but a useful reminder.

The eclectic piece is often found repugnant, especially if it can be readily dismissed as ''19th-century'': the purist is quick to recognize all the faults inherent in 19th-century revivals—at least he is if he has recognized the piece as being ''late''. Copies can sometimes be dismissed equally swiftly, often simply because their condition is superior to that of their models. It is surprising how the most sophisticated period royal commode can become vulgar to modern taste when it is fully restored and cleaned. This vulgarity is often even more evident in the exact copy.

The exact copy however is often a superior work of art in its own right and in recent years is at last being recognized as such. The 19th-century craftsman was proud to copy what were considered the best of 18th-century pieces. Quite often these were royal items, but not always. It was comparatively rare, however, to copy pieces made prior to the 18th century: these were left to the ''improvers''. The usual reason is that earlier designs were quite simply too large for modern living.

There were approximately 2,000 *ébénistes*, *bronziers*, *sculpteurs*, *modeleurs*, *menuisiers* and *doreurs* in Paris by the 1880s working for the makers of the superior *meubles de luxe*. A large proportion of these fine quality pieces were copies of either Louis XV or XVI examples. There were approximately 50 retail outlets for quality furniture at this time, underlining the popularity of the style that had worldwide and often royal patronage. The whole of Europe, including Great Britain, both North and South America, Imperial Russia, India, and Egypt were customers of the Paris trade and the quantity that was produced is constantly seen, in ever decreasing amounts as its popularity rises, in the world antique market today.

One of the greatest of these copies must surely be that of the roll-top desk known as the ''Bureau du Roi''. The original was

1 2
An original Louis XVI commode (left) and a copy from over a hundred years later (right). The copy from the Jones Collection at the Victoria and Albert Museum, London, would not have been deemed a fake at the time of making. It is exactly the same size and follows faithfully the features of the original. Only the marble top is different: the copy has the more popular *brêche violette* marble, whereas the period example has the fine, pure white Carrara marble that was so fashionable in the latter part of the 18th century.

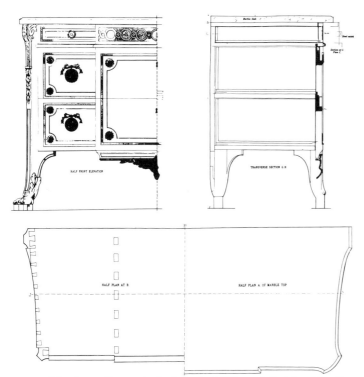

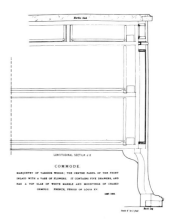

HALF FRONT ELEVATION

TRANSVERSE SECTION G R

LONGITUDINAL SECTION J K

COMMODE.

MARQUETRY OF VARIOUS WOODS; THE CENTRE PANEL OF THE FRONT
INLAID WITH A VASE OF FLOWERS. IT CONTAINS FIVE DRAWERS, AND
HAS A TOP SLAB OF WHITE MARBLE AND MOUNTINGS OF CHASED
ORMOLU.   FRENCH, PERIOD OF LOUIS XV.

HALF PLAN AT B.

HALF PLAN A OF MARBLE TOP

**3** a, b, c, d *above and left*
These four scale drawings show
exact details of the construction and
proportions of the Louis XVI
commode on the facing page (*Ill. 1*).
They are taken from *Drawings of
French Furniture*, printed in 1899 and
drawn by W. G. Paulson
Townsend; they are clearly
intended for use.

Certain significant details can be
made out. For example, the drawer
tops are rounded off and the drawer
bottoms have chamfered edges.
Also, a small square block can be
seen under the chamfering and
attached to the bottom of the
drawer—it is the drawer runner,
suggesting that this has been
replaced, as the side would
normally be of a piece. The
replacement is due to wear—the
commode was over a hundred years
old when the drawings were
executed in 1899. Would the faker
think to put on replacement drawer
runners as a double bluff? The
answer is most emphatically "Yes".
The copy (*Ill. 2*, opposite) did not
have such a refinement, although it
was almost certainly inspired by
these drawings.

The top, on the left with the
marble removed, shows a flat
surface (they are more commonly
panelled); dovetail joints hold the
side to the top and mortice and
tenon joints hold the drawer
dividers. It is here that most 18th-
century commodes are signed,
under the marble so that the
customer could not see the
obligatory *ébéniste*'s signature and
circumvent the retailer by going
directly to the maker.

started by Jean-François Oeben in 1760 and finished by Jean-
Henri Riesner in 1769. Copies of this desk are recorded by
several of the great 19th-century makers, who by no means
restricted themselves to pure copies. Examples are recorded
by A.-L. Beurdeley, François Linke (who made one for the
1878 Paris Exhibition when he was only 33), Zweiner and
Henri Dasson. Dasson's example is the most accessible. It is
today in the Wallace Collection in London and was commissioned by Lord Hertford at a cost of 90,000 francs. This
figure represents approximately £200,000 to £250,000
($300-375,000) converted to today's values, a staggering sum
even when taking into consideration the far higher disposable
income available to the rich of the time.

Permission to copy the piece from the original, which is now
in the Louvre but at the time was in the *cabinet intérieur* of the
Empress Eugénie at Saint-Cloud, was not difficult to obtain as
Lord Hertford was well known to the Emperor Napoleon III.
However (and incredibly), the stipulation was that no
squeezes or moulds were to be taken from the original. Consequently all the bronzes, which are extremely elaborate, had
to be measured and then sculpted in wood to match the originals. In sculpting the bronzes an allowance had to be made for
the inevitable shrinkage during the casting process. Carving a
piece of wood to the exact proportion of the required bronze
was common practice at the time. However, to model it
accurately from existing work required craftsmanship of
extraordinary quality. This surely establishes that the 19th-
century craftsman, forgetting for the moment the idio-
syncrasies of design, was at least as accomplished as his forebears—see *Ill. 1* and 2, p. 39.

The exact dates that such items were copied is often
uncertain. Certainly the Empress Eugénie had a love of Louis

This steel lock dates to the Louis XIV period *c.* 1700. The steel has rusted and the edges of the lock show traces of hand filing. Note that the upper screw holes are considerably larger than the lower ones—this does not help with the dating but no copyist ever makes them like that and few fakers would think of it. The tongue is half out, the next notch can just be seen—a typical French double-throw lock.

2

A straightforward lock of the type used in France from the second quarter of the 19th century to the early 20th century. It still has a double throw (here fully extended) but is made of brass and is much smaller than its predecessors.

XVI classical furniture as early as 1850. The Board of Trade in London held an exhibition called "Specimens of Cabinet Work" at Gore House in 1853, showing 18th-century and earlier French masterpieces; a further important exhibition was held at the Manchester Art Gallery in 1857. The Marquess of Hertford was well into his career as a collector by the 1850s, commissioning John Webb, for example, to copy the Elector of Bavaria's desk made by André-Charles Boulle. Two copies were in fact made between 1855 and 1857.

The Musée Retrospectif exhibition, Paris, 1865, must have been a further impetus. Many items were lent by Lord Hertford, notably the Gaudreau commode made for Louis XV in 1739, with mounts by Caffieri; this model was certainly copied several times in the 19th century (it is a little too lavish and complicated for the 20th-century copyist) and it would be logical to conclude that the copies were made after, possibly inspired by, the 1865 exhibition. Few if any of the copies of this model are signed and some could well be of English origin. There is documentary evidence to show that Lord Hertford sometimes commissioned more than one copy of an original piece already in his possession, as well as pieces he was unable to buy.

These exhibitions, together with important sales of great collections in England gave rise to copies being made by both French and English craftsmen up to the Great War of 1914-18 and, to a lesser extent, during the inter-war years. It can be very difficult to tell the difference between English and French cabinet work of this period. London was certainly a great centre and its political stability was an incentive to many French craftsmen to settle in England in the mid-19th century.

There is constructive evidence to support the theory that French firms supplied mounts for English carcase work and there was a considerable to and fro of trade, especially from Paris to London. There is a further theory, rapidly gaining credence, that Paris firms not only exported copies to New York but that they also exported "spare parts" and marquetry.

The psychology of buying or commissioning copies in the 19th century was altogether different—snobbery did not enter into it. Indeed, Francis Watson in the Wallace Collection catalogue points out that Lord Hertford was paying far more for a commissioned copy than he was for many of the original pieces he purchased for his collection. He paid £2,500 between 1853 and 1855 to John Webb for a jewel cabinet, now at Windsor; the cabinet had been lent to the Gore House exhibition of 1853 by Queen Victoria. This is a prime example of these early exhibitions inspiring fine copies, and the sum paid for the copy would now be roughly equivalent to £200,000 ($300,000). Webb appears to have been used to make copies of French furniture made in London and Henri Dasson for pieces in Paris. This is an interesting point in that it appears to confirm the theory that English craftsmen of the period were equal to the French and that it was simply a question of expediency as to who made the copy.

The practice of commissioning fine copies had been a

popular one throughout the 18th century, especially with paintings, so that the copy could be admired and discussed at home as the original had been admired on the Grand Tour. This trend continued well into the 19th century and the pieces were seen as complimentary to existing collections. The copies were in no respect intended to deceive—indeed Francis Watson (ibid.) states that ''Each of Lord Hertford's copies varies slightly from the original. . . . Possibly Lord Hertford did this to prevent the perpetrations of frauds, should his copies ever fall into the hands of dealers.''

It is difficult to obtain a clear picture of the quantity of 18th-century furniture that was copied exactly in the 19th. However the proportion of chair frames made as exact copies of Louis XV and Louis XVI models is high compared with that of cabinet work. As an approximate guide, possibly as many as one in five pieces available on the market today would fall into this category.

The main discussion inevitably centres on French copies and their English counterparts. Other European countries however were quite capable of making copies but rarely on such a grand scale as the French. There were fewer royal items of an international flavour and access to royal pieces was possibly restricted. What had started out in France as copying the finest pieces of the Louis era with a sincere desire to emulate their sophisticated forms became in other countries a race to produce copies of sometimes quite ordinary items. As the rapid development of the 19th century progressed, each country chose to copy the very best that it had produced, whatever the period. Whereas the French had only to go back to the monarchies of the 18th century, the Dutch, for example, looked back to the 17th.

3
A very small lock only about 20 years old. It is a determined effort at faking but is far too small to be of the 1730-50 period it tries to simulate. The steel has the robustness of a tin can compared to that of the lock in *Ill. 1*. The tongue has only a single throw—an elementary mistake.

4 *below*
This table top by the *marqueteur* Joseph Cremer is not a copy but a mid-19th century recreation of the Louis XV period. It should not be mistaken for an original 18th-century table as the form and shape did not exist in the period. The inspiration is Rococo but the inlay is too profuse, too busy for the 18th century.

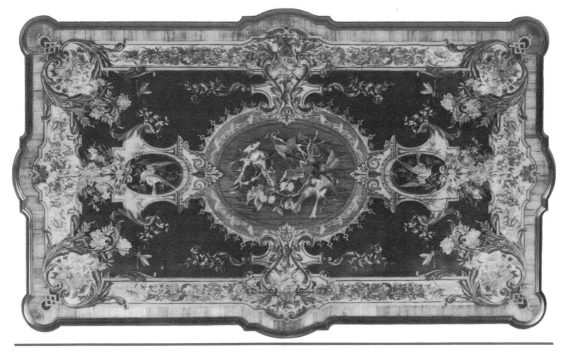

## Copies of Dutch and Spanish Furniture

The period of the greatest flower paintings of the Dutch masters, the floral marquetry work of Amsterdam and the Hague and the incredible work of Jan van Merkeren was recaptured from the middle of the 19th century, either in a purely 18th-century form but with 17th-century-style marquetry, or by simply taking one of the many plain and unadorned 18th-century walnut or mahogany pieces and inlaying it. The Flemish draw-leaf table, one of the earliest types of extending dining table, is a common subject for reproduction; the copies, mainly dating to the early part of the 20th century, realize about half the value of 17th-century pieces.

Spain, too, recaptured its golden era—this time the 16th century. The early 16th-century Mudéjar style of Moorish geometric ivory and coloured woods became popular, especially as French and, to a lesser extent, English taste turned towards the Middle East and Araby for exotic inspiration.

Spanish craftsmen seem to have been able to produce copies of earlier work easily. They were looking back 300 years, but neither the standard of work nor the materials had changed much. This can make it most difficult to distinguish copy from original or fake from copy. Only with experience and very careful study can you tell a late 18th-century drawer lining from an earlier one. Nineteenth-century examples inconveniently seem to slip back to the earliest period: possibly these really were intended to deceive.

**1** *below, upper left*
A mid-18th century Dutch mahogany bureau of typical form. This would have been a plain mahogany piece when made; the inlay was added approximately a hundred years later, when the Dutch successfully revived 17th-century style marquetry.

**2** *below, upper right*
A typical Napoleon III side cabinet, made in a similar style in several countries. It has, however, had original 17th-century panels added to the doors, probably taken from a large Dutch *armoire* that was too big for 19th-century taste. The remainder of the marquetry is all mid-19th century.

**3** *below, lower left*
A Spanish cabinet-on-stand, heavily influenced by Moorish work and popular in the late 16th century. This is a late 19th-century copy but, as with many of these pieces, it is very difficult indeed to tell the age from a photograph. Here there is no reduction in scale, which would normally be a giveaway. Its good condition may make one suspicious but it is a very dangerous premise to think that something has to be a copy just because it is in a very good state. Stands however have rarely survived with period *papeleiras* or chests, and this one is poor. The carving is flat, uninspired and similar to the mass of late 19th-century carved furniture from Holland.

**4** *far right*
A Louis XV kingwood and tulipwood small *armoire* that has been altered to suit 19th-century taste. The most common alteration is that done here—the top panels of the doors were removed and glass panels inserted. This effectively turned a cupboard into a more saleable display cabinet. Also, all the gilt-bronze mounts were added in the 19th century. The piece shows that no amount of work, however elaborate, was too much for the 19th-century dealer; and remember that the 18th-century original would have cost very little to buy at this time—certainly less than the cost of a copy.

The top of a small table once in the collection of Lord Roseberry and included in the Mentmore Towers sale of 1977. The wood and metalwork are all 19th century, probably *c.* 1840-50, but the plaque is an 18th-century Sèvres original. This enhances the value of the table considerably, provided the plaque is not damaged. Although condition is a dangerous factor in determining age, this table is very fresh and does not ring true as an 18th-century piece.

## Collectors and Collections

It is important at this stage to understand the strength of the English furniture industry of the 19th century in relation to copies of earlier pieces. The whole of Europe saw a vogue for the Romantic and England was no exception—indeed England was responsible for a huge production of furniture in 18th-century styles, especially those of the Louis. Alongside this manufacture many of the Bond Street dealers, such as Edward Holmes Baldock, were buying antique pieces direct from France; many of these items, some branded with Baldock's initials, were "improved" and additions were made to cater for contemporary taste.

The great 19th-century collectors such as Lord Hertford, the Duke of Hamilton, the Rothschilds and John Jones bought such pieces. Their taste was reflected in the shops selling both contemporary and antique furniture and, when their collections were eventually dispersed, they in turn renewed the enthusiasm for the Louis styles. Many pieces were copied, for example after the Hamilton Palace sale of 1882, likewise on the bequest of the Jones Collection to the Victoria and Albert Museum in the same year.

The great 19th-century collections consisted therefore in part of authentic antique furniture in its original state, in part of antique furniture re-dressed to contemporary taste and in part of copies. More and more interest is being focused on these copies. They are to be seen at most of the better museums in Europe. (American museums have had to concentrate more on period or contemporary innovative design. They have not had large quantities of excess furniture at their disposal and have therefore spent their resources on "purer" examples.) Though there is a tendency today to dislike or even scorn the copy, this will pass as they and the background that fostered their manufacture become better understood.

When the catalogue of the Jones Collection was first published in 1922 this small *secrétaire* was thought to be a fine example of the Louis XV period. In fact the porcelain mounts are 18th-century Sèvres but the carcase is *c.* 1840.

1

At first glance this is a typical German walnut bureau cabinet from the middle of the 18th century. The chest of drawers is fairly common but the addition of an upper part, with a bureau writing flap and a section of short drawers, makes it far more desirable. The inclusion of a marquetry parrot is guaranteed to make it an easy seller.

In fact, the top and the bottom do not belong: they sit uncomfortably together, there is little or no synergy between them—the middle part does not even seem to fit. The sides are both crossbanded but the banding to the base is far larger and cruder than to the top, which also has boxwood stringing. There is no similarity at all between the crossbanding of the upper, short drawers and that on the long drawers at the bottom.

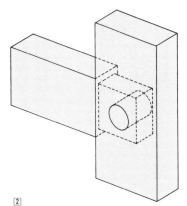

2

An exploded view showing a simple French mortice and tenon joint with a pin (goujon) inserted for added strength. After a few years as the surrounding wood shrinks the pin will stick out by one or two millimetres, cracking the decoration.

## The Marriage

A huge amount of two-part Continental furniture has been "married": a piece has been borrowed from one period source to be allied with another.

This is easy to imagine in the example of an 18th-century bureau that has had a bookcase added to it at a later date. The bookcase could either be contemporary, taken from another piece of furniture, or made up for the purpose. The bookcase has little value in its own right and the bureau has its value, or at least its practicality, enhanced by the addition. A quick look at the back of the whole piece should decide whether the panelling matches as it should if both parts are contemporary. A look at the sides will show whether the decoration, if any, or veneer is compatible. Lift the top part away from the bureau— is the top of the bureau veneered or decorated? does it have good quality wood hidden away? Few cabinet makers would spend money or time on materials that were never to be seen. The faker certainly would not.

Few stands survive with their cabinets today. This is because they were often itinerant pieces that travelled from house to house in the 16th and 17th centuries. Larger, static cabinets have also lost their stands, some of which make very nice pier tables. It is unusual these days to find an original stand so be very suspicious; aim to prove the stand belongs, or at least that it is of the period.

Alongside marriages of independent or quasi-independent pieces, a great many items of furniture were made up to re-use fine old parts—panels in particular. *Ill. 1*, p. 41 is an example of the type of cabinet that was made up, seemingly in great numbers, during the second quarter of the 19th century. The inspiration for these pieces was the contemporary love of antiquity, which frequently manifested itself in gothic and medieval artifacts. The demand produced many married pieces and possibly some of the earliest fakes. A powerful source for the romantic vision in France was Alexandre du Sommerard. He owned the Hôtel de Cluny, which with its medieval and Renaissance contents was presented to the nation on the owner's death. The collection was not conscientiously catalogued until the 1920s and many of du Sommerard's pieces of furniture were then judged to be fakes, or at least made up from old carving and panelling.

The cabinet (*Ill. 1*, p. 41) from the Soulages Collection is another victim of 19th-century lack of expertise. The acquisition of the collection from France was, at the time, a great coup for Henry Cole, supported by Prince Albert. The collection went on display in the Victoria and Albert Museum in the 1860s. Many other pieces in this collection were more than dubious and most of it now lies unseen in the museum's stores. But the display of both the Cluny and the Soulages collections led to copying and this may explain the wealth of eclectic pieces that came onto the market from the 1870s onwards, when the Renaissance style gathered commercial momentum. *continued on page 41*

1 *left*
A fake butterfly table. The entire piece has been stained to cover up the fact that the top and bottom did not always go together. Butterfly tables were among the earliest categories of American furniture to be faked, with many examples being made from plain tavern tables.

2 *above*
A detail of the arm of a fake chair. The craftsman has simulated the popping out of the mortice pin by leaving it long, but has had to stain the head. The match with the surrounding wood is unconvincing—compare *Ill. 3*.

3 *right*
A detail of a genuine 18th-century chair showing how an original mortice pin stands proud as the surrounding wood shrinks. Note that the colour of the head of the pin is almost identical with that of the leg and stretcher; compare *Ill. 2*.

**1** *right*
The understructure of a fake lowboy. The drawer bottoms have been stained a muddy colour and an attempt has been made to disguise the recarving of the skirt with black stain.

**2** *below*
The understructure of a genuine lowboy showing original unstained drawer bottoms. The colour is a natural golden-brown except where the drawer bottoms have rubbed against the frame.

**4** *below*
The underside of a genuine Hepplewhite card table, *c.* 1790-1810.

The overall colour is a natural golden-brown, the patch behind the gate being lighter because for much of the table's life the gate was closed, slowing up oxidization. Compare *Ill. 3.*

**3** *right*
The underside of a fake Hepplewhite card table. The structure has been stained and muddied up to simulate the effects of age, but the perpetrator got it wrong.

The part of the frame onto which the swing leg closed would have been protected from the air, would therefore have oxidized less and consequently would be paler in colour than the rest of the underside. In the unlikely event that the swing leg had been open for the whole of the table's purported life, this part of the frame would have been the same colour as the rest. Under no natural circumstances could it have become darker, as here. Compare *Ill. 4.*

**1** *left*
A fine quality commode by one of the best cabinetmakers in late 19th-century Paris, François Linke. It follows the basic form of a Louis XV commode of *c.* 1750, but the proportions are incorrect and the mounts are too thin and too profuse—none of them could really be 18th century. The asymmetry of the mounts on an 18th-century piece tended also to be better balanced and the mixture of veneer and Vernis Martin was unheard of in the period though common practice in the second half of the 19th century.

**2** *below*
The interior of the commode shown in *Ill. 1.* It is too highly polished to be an original 18th-century example. The dovetails are of a quality that would have made them exceptional on a 1750s piece and the drawer linings would have been of indigenous woods in the 18th century and not of kingwood as here. A serious student should not mistake this for an original piece of Louis XV furniture, but of its actual period it is one of the best.

1 *right*

An honest copy, made in the third quarter of the 19th century, of a small *table à écrire* from the Louis XV/XVI Transitional Period of the 1770s. A purist might argue that the top is modelled on work by Oeben and the base is in the style of Lacroix, but otherwise there is little to suggest it is not a period piece, except possibly that the finish, like the condition, is very good. However, the market now requires that 18th-century examples be restored to ''as new'' condition, so this suspicion is double edged.

2 *below*

The interior of the table in *Ill. 1*. The inside of the drawer under the writing flap is highly polished—a typical 19th-century feature—and the marquetry trellis interior of the deep drawer is unlikely, though not impossible, on an 18th-century original.

*continued from page 36*
## Alterations

A popular alteration was to reduce the size of a piece to accommodate it to contemporary apartments. Taller pieces were especially vulnerable. In a commode a drawer can be removed easily and neatly, though a loss of proportion may give the game away. Look at the drawers—is the graduation even? Are the drawers numbered on the back by an earlier repairer and if so, are the numbers now consecutive? Reducing in width or depth is both far more complicated and easier to tell.

Certain items were altered in the 19th century to a specific usage and are now being converted back to their original state. The Louis XV and Louis XVI *petite commode* or *table en chiffonière*

1 *right*
A large walnut cabinet of architectural form purporting to be from the Henri II period in France, *c.* 1560. It forms a part of the Soulages Collection bought by the Victoria and Albert Museum in the 1860s and bears all the allegorical hallmarks so popular in the 16th century (and revived in the 19th). The centre panel of David and Goliath is flanked by Justice and Fortitude, Judith and Holofernes.

At the time of acquisition the carving was attributed to Bachelier of Toulouse. The main panels may well be by him, but they are the only parts that date to the 16th century. This is an early example of 19th-century romantic makers devising pieces in an imaginative Renaissance style, using important old panels. In recent years it has become common practice for dealers to buy the whole piece at auction simply for the early panels and to leave the carcase behind.

It is open to question whether this piece should be described as a fake, a marriage or a romantic copy.

2 *far left*
A print taken from a book of designs *c.* 1560 by Jacques Androuet du Cerceau (*c.* 1510—*c.* 1585), reprinted in Paris by E. Baldus *c.* 1880. It shows the typical balance of 16th-century furniture, which was not observed in the eclectic piece shown above (*Ill. 2*). Quite clearly the maker of the cabinet, probably from the Toulouse area, had seen the du Cerceau prints and took one of the winged squatting female griffins directly from the 16th-century source.

3 *left*
A design from *Drawings of French Furniture*, 1899, showing the authentic construction of cabinets similar to that in *Ill. 2*, as made in France throughout the 16th century. Reference is made to the wooden pins (*goujons*) that were used at the time (see *Ill. 2*, p.36) and the sophisticated chamfering can clearly be seen to the back, front (carved) panels and the middle and lower shelves. The front ball feet and the rear block feet are later additions or replacements but are stylistically in keeping.

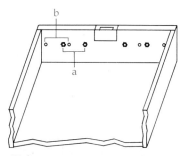

**1** *above*
Tell-tale signs of the reduction of an 18th-century drawer. When it is reduced in width, the original handles (in position *b*) will be too close to the sides. They have to be moved in to position *a*—if indeed the original handles are being used again, rather than updates. Then check the face of the drawer: if there are no filled holes to correspond the drawer has either been re-veneered or later veneered.

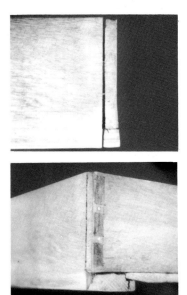

**2** a, b
A drawer that has been reduced in depth. The dovetails have been cut through and the joint has been remade, crudely, with modern nails. On an 18th-century chest such as this the alteration stands out a mile, but only if the drawer is taken right out.

is a very popular item in today's small apartments. In the 19th century these were commonly altered into what were delicately known as "night tables". The three small drawers were taken out to make a cupboard for a chamber pot. Today they are very popular, either as bedside tables or as drawing room furniture and so the drawer linings are put back. Do not therefore be puzzled by an old looking carcase with new drawer linings.

Another common alteration was to remove the end cupboards from French commodes and make them into corner cupboards; this however is rarely satisfactory to the eye. The remaining chest of drawers can be veneered at the sides—though again the proportions would be unsatisfactory. Fine 18th-century commodes have also been altered to accommodate wash basins. No one would even consider making such a drastic alteration to an expensive piece today but similar alterations, on a lesser scale, must be being made to pieces that are considered of little value in today's market.

## The Fake

"Fake" (a word shunned by most experts) when applied to furniture means an item made in an earlier style with intent to deceive. The dictionary definition also includes: "to rob or attack . . . to doctor . . . or counterfeit". In the context of furniture "to doctor" includes the arrangement of marriages and "to rob" is certainly a result of successfully passing off a fake as a genuine article. "To counterfeit" underlines the intention to deceive but is further defined, *inter alia*, as "to copy without authority". This can be seriously misleading. No authority is needed to copy an old piece of furniture, save for permission of access. To take the example of the Marquis of Hertford, it was his friendship with the Emperor Napoleon III that procured access for Mr Webb of Bond Street to take measurements in order to make a copy. Nobody today thinks of Webb's work as a fake—there was no intent to deceive.

The fact that no permission is necessary means that any competent cabinetmaker can set himself up to fake furniture (I do not intend to be chauvinist, but there is little or no reason to believe that there were ever female cabinet fakers).

There is little evidence to suggest that furniture faking was ever done much before the latter years of the 19th century. Major museum collections contain fakes of works of art from earlier dates, but little or no faked furniture. Is it that furniture was too difficult to fake? Is the reverse true—that it was so easy to counterfeit that modern expertise has not yet advanced enough to detect untold pieces of fake furniture in the galleries of the world? Is it not profitable enough? Is there insufficient demand for fine furniture? The answer to all of these questions must be a resounding no. Furniture is certainly difficult to fake but by no means impossible. Modern expertise has advanced a long way and is so analytical that fakes can surely, by now, be identified. Even given the high costs of labour today it is always possible to make the more sought after pieces at a cost

## Woods, Inlays and Surface Treatments

One of the easiest ways to tell that something is wrong with a piece is to recognize that it incorporates a material that had not been introduced in the period from which it purports to come. Once a material had been introduced, it could, of course, be revived at any time, but fashion kept quite a tight hold on the standard items of furniture and there is reason to double check if a piece of expected form includes an unexpected wood or type of decoration. The chart is necessarily only approximate, but is designed to show which materials you would expect to see used period by period in the main Continental furniture-producing countries.

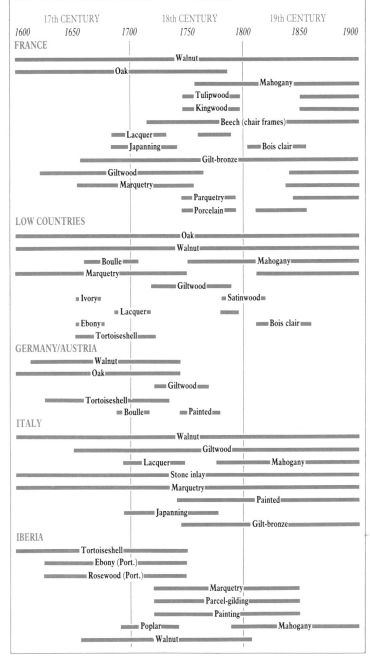

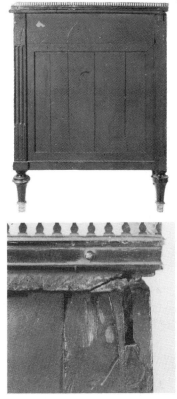

3 *above, with detail*
The back view of one of a pair of corner cabinets whose proportions make one suspicious at first glance—they do not fit the corner of a room as a normal corner cupboard would. They have in fact been taken from the ends of a very expensive Louis XVI commode—a practice that would be uneconomic today but would have been possible in the second and third quarters of the 19th century when 18th-century French furniture was still relatively cheap.

The cupboard has a very convincing appearance of age and is typical of the carcase work of the 1770s and 80s. The inner frame is nicely made with mitred joins and the back panel has split as is quite common; but the added gallery and its seating board look very out of keeping. And why has the maker gone to all the trouble of carving a stop-fluted column that will never be seen? Before the alterations this part must, rather inexplicably, have been on view. The right-hand leg is odd too—it has clearly been added, or at least the construction has been adapted. And why is the tenon showing in the detail—was it cut through when the piece was altered?

sufficiently below the market price to enable the perpetrator to make his profit. And the demand for furniture over the last hundred years has always been high enough to stimulate the art of the faker.

It is this last point that needs the closest examination—there are unlikely to be fakes until the market demand is strong enough for the originals. Then the faker can step in, often as not trading not only on his skills as a craftsman but on the greed and covetousness of the buyer, be he the end user—the collector—or the intermediary—the dealer. Certainly one point must ring clear: a fake is only good if the judgement that approves it is poor. A copy may be good, very good, but for example the sophisticated French reproductions made in the second half of the 19th century were not intended to deceive—above all, many were signed by their makers. The frightening thought to conjure with is: what if a craftsman of this standard were to become a rogue maker?

**The Skills Required** Demand for French furniture rose in the early part of the 20th century. England wanted good 18th-century furniture as much as it wanted Queen Anne in the pre- and inter-war periods; America had the same requirements. French taste, always somewhat patriotic, meant an even greater demand for the Louis styles. Other European countries, without an international following for their domestic styles, produced fakes of their own earlier work.

It may be a dangerous assumption but it is probably fair to say that any good fake would have to be made a) in the country from which the piece to be faked originates, and b) with only slightly less conviction, that the faker should be a native of that country. The craftsman must feel the very bones of the piece he is to copy.

A piece of furniture has many components and several skills are needed to create it. For example, to make a "Louis XV" commode one would need to:

1 a, b
Dovetails on an original 18th-century pine-lined drawer, front and rear. The work is not very sophisticated, but the dovetails are even and neat. The scribing line is clearly visible in both.

1. find wood of sufficient age;

2. cut it to the required thickness of veneer—approximately 1.1mm;

3. ensure the thickness is not too even;

4. make the carcase—worth several points in its own right, especially when it comes to the dowels;

5. make the drawers correctly—one of the most obvious areas, but one that consistently lets down the fake;

6. cast the bronzes and handles;

7. gild or lacquer the bronzes and handles;

8. cut and colour the marquetry and/or stringing;

9. apply the veneer and let in the marquetry;

10. decide how much age or patination to apply.

If the faker has not selected his timbers carefully then the wood itself will give the game away. If the wood is from another piece of the period he is imitating then there will always be the possibility that there will be old joint marks or holes, albeit carefully covered up. This applies especially where drawer handles are concerned.

One of the easiest ways to tell the difference between a piece of 18th- and a piece of 19th-century furniture is to look at the drawers, not necessarily at the dovetails, but at the standard of finish. The drawers of many 18th-century commodes are poorly finished—they were not intended to be seen by contemporary owners. The interior of most 19th-century pieces by contrast is well finished—often veneered and frequently polished (see *Ill. 2*, p. 39).

Then look at the dovetails. Handmade dovetails have a narrower tail attached to the drawer facing than the receiving joint at the side of the drawer. Machine dovetails have an even-sized positive and negative tail or fan. If the joints are machine-made then the piece has to be after the 1880s and was more probably made in the 1920s.

A further check is that sides of 18th-century French drawer linings very commonly had rounded tops. Copyists often omit this detail (except M. Millet of Paris in the second half of the 19th century) and so do fakers. However, do not be led into the trap that every piece that lacks this detail is a fake—the guideline is not a rule.

Patination often makes or breaks the fake. Too much dirt is easily spotted, too little becomes immediately suspicious. Dirt applied in the wrong place(s) is a certain giveaway, so is wear in places that would not normally be subject to use. This is especially so with chair and stretcher rails of the Régence period—chair legs are often quite wrongly distressed on the inside. In the same manner veneer is aged and distressed in places that would never normally be affected by everyday wear (though very occasionally this is a result of restoration with old veneer).

Examine the dirt. On a piece of dubious parentage it may be no more than old sawdust and glue—both in plentiful supply in a cabinet workshop. Nibble away at the dirt with a small blade: if it breaks sharply away it may well be mainly glue. Also be on the lookout for long runs of fresh glue—they may indicate that the piece is not very old, though of course they may simply indicate that it has been freshly repaired. However, the clever faker may even build in "repairs" to his work as a double bluff.

The colour of the timbers used must be even all the way through if it is old wood, traditionally seasoned for seven years. Kiln-dried wood will have no depth of colour. The faker makes up for this by applying colour liberally to the show wood, but there is a sharpness, freshness and lack of depth to fake colour.

Modern taste however has done the faker a great favour. In many European countries, France and Germany especially, the vogue is for everything to look brand new. This view is not

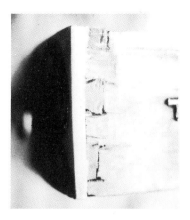

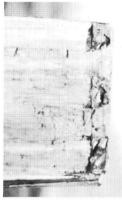

**2** a, b
Dovetails from an out-and-out fake commode made in the 1970s, front and rear. This drawer is pine lined, but the sides are not smooth enough and the dovetails are appalling, filled up with dust and glue. Compare the authentic 18th-century drawer in *Ill.1* opposite, where the workmanship is by no means fine but is nevertheless vastly superior to this.

shared by the English collector, who admires patination more than most and abhors re-polishing. American collectors share both attitudes: some re-polish, some don't. But in a large part of the market it is as if the faker himself had dictated fashion to suit his own ends.

**Signatures and Stamps** Signatures are a constant problem on European furniture, especially on French pieces. A would-be cabinetmaker in Paris in the 18th century had to spend a total of nine years in training before he was allowed to call himself *maître*, and from 1741 onwards every master was obliged to stamp his work with his name. This practice continued until it was abolished by the Revolutionary Council in 1791. With the Restoration in 1815 some of the better makers stamped their furniture again, although this was not a requirement. The practice spread until it was comparatively common by the third quarter of the century. However, it was not until 1882 that there was any publicized study of the use of the stamp in 18th-century France. In that year another exhibition devoted to the glories of the previous century was mounted by the Union Centrale des Arts Décoratifs, at which the use and advantages

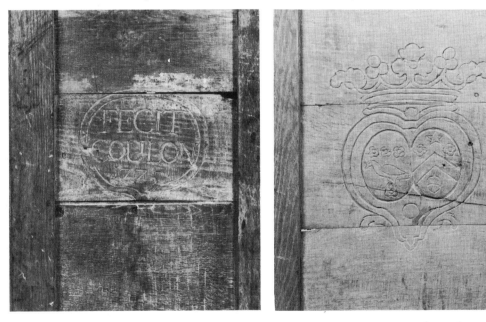

[1] *below*
A faked maker's stamp. There were three cabinetmakers of this name working in Paris in the second and third quarters of the 18th century, but the letters here are unusually large and are carved into the wood, not stamped. There is no reason why there should not be a date, as here, but it was not common practice in the 18th century. Dates were often added to makers' marks in the third quarter of the 19th century, however—perhaps this indicates the date of this stamp.

[2] *above, right*
A faked château inventory stamp. Its heraldry does not ring true and it is carved, not stamped.

of the marks was aired. This corresponds to the period from which fakes of 18th-century furniture began to arise.

It is fairly common to find false stamps on French furniture. Sometimes the piece is a perfectly genuine 18th-century example that was for some reason unsigned originally; or the signature of a lesser known cabinetmaker may have been replaced by that of someone more saleable. Pieces with replaced signatures are quite often "improved" — embellished with *bronze doré* mounts, either taken from another piece of the period or cast at the time the work was carried out. Mounts are very often difficult to date but at least they give the appraiser a sporting chance — added 18th-century mounts often look stylistically wrong, for example. Also it is always important with French veneered furniture to look for evidence that old mounts have been removed. Often the small pin holes can be seen, carefully filled in with dirt and glue, and if the faker has not done his job too thoroughly there may be slight variations of colour around the replaced mounts. Unfortunately, it was common practice in the 18th century to have mounts re-gilded or re-lacquered, and therefore they may have been taken off. If they have been returned to exactly the correct places then suspicion is not aroused, but if there are different pin holes alarms may sound for the wrong reasons.

Stamps may also be removed. Certain dealers in the postwar period are known to have taken the signatures off English 19th-century pieces in the Louis styles. Today an item in the French style with an English maker's stamp — for example, that of Edwards & Roberts — would be just as saleable as a French piece or even more so. Thirty years ago it would have been to the detriment of an item not to have been French, so the stamps were removed.

Château marks are also falsely applied. A perfectly genuine piece by a good maker will be easier to sell and will fetch more with a good provenance. If the "improver" knows his business he will use the mark of a château to which the existing maker is known to have supplied furniture. Both makers' and château marks are well documented, but it is surprising how often the faker will apply stamps that are implausible.

## 20th-Century Fakes

There is a tendency for people to write off automatically any piece that reproduces an 18th-century or earlier style as "19th century". Undoubtedly fraudulent imitations and replicas were produced in the late 19th century, but the greatest period of deception has been since 1918.

With the dramatic increase in the value of furniture of all nations in recent years, there are many more dubious pieces on the market. Workshops in the backstreets of many capital cities are still being asked to alter furniture to suit market trends and requirements. However, it is difficult to believe that today there are many people actually producing fakes. "Improvements", yes—constantly; but actually faking furniture is usually too difficult. Continental workshops are, however, making very sophisticated modern copies that reproduce older pieces with uncanny accuracy, even down to poor quality drawer linings. These would not begin to deceive an expert and the amateur must learn to look beyond the sales talk and examine the very soul of his purchase. The deception is more likely to be in the description than in the piece.

Nevertheless, informed opinion is well aware that there is considerably more Continental furniture on the market today than can possibly have been made for the 18th-century market. Care, thought and specialist advice should be taken with every step, every purchase.

**3** *above*
Metal, especially gilt-bronze, furniture is very difficult to date accurately and many fake pieces, which feel instinctively not quite right are termed simply "19th century" as a letout. Even so, the faker will obtain a good price for his wares as 19th-century metal furniture is also popular.
This table is modern, made in Paris within the last 10 to 20 years. Careful inspection will show very poor details to the faces of the female terms and the marble is very fresh, with no damage or signs of patination.

**4**
A table top made in the mid-1970s in Italy, painted in the manner of 17th-century scagliola or poor man's marble. These are being produced in great numbers. Though they are not fakes, they are very convincing, with a degree of distressing and an element of the naïveté one expects in 17th-century work. After a hundred years this will be very difficult to date.

# 5: ENGLISH FURNITURE

T HERE ARE BEYOND ANY DOUBT numerous pieces of deceptive English furniture on the market among the mass of good honest pieces. But provided you are aware of exactly what a piece is, can use it, will enjoy it and can afford it, there is no reason not to buy. Problems arise only when a piece that is not genuine is passed off as the authentic article — and at the price of the authentic article.

A great many pieces that are not quite genuine took on their present form with no trace of fraud and no motive of greed. Cutting down a large piece of furniture to make it fit in a room smaller than it was designed for is a perfect example. The ignorant repair of a badly damaged piece of furniture with wrong materials is another.

Fashion, too, is of the utmost significance. We may scorn the ignorance of our forebears who chose to update old fashioned furniture by reshaping or redecorating it, but we change our styles too.

Furniture, however stylish, always has a practical purpose. If that purpose becomes redundant — as with the thousands of washstands that were made before modern plumbing — do we simply throw away a mountain of furniture? Or should we adapt it?

Thus if we combine the triple motives of economy, fashion and practicality it is not difficult to see the reasons why so many antique pieces exist that are not quite what they seem or are not quite as they were made.

For complex reasons, attitudes to furniture were changing by the 1830s. Throughout the 18th century one new style had followed another, but by the end of the Regency, the taste for older things which the dilettanti of the late 18th century had fostered in élitist seclusion was becoming the public taste. The prices of Queen Anne, Georgian and earlier items started their erratic rise, the cost of manufacture fell with mechanization and a margin appeared in which the faker, reproducer and pasticheur could operate.

## Fakes

There are few examples of the out-and-out fake, if by that we understand a piece of furniture made entirely from scratch and purporting in every detail to be an example of an earlier period.

Faking can be undertaken only by those workshops with access to materials of the right sort—old and seasoned timber, hand-cut veneers, hand-made steel locks and screws, clout nails and hand-forged hinges, handles and even castors. Such furniture was made by men of considerable skill, and pride in their craft rarely allowed them to resist leaving some trace, almost like a signature, that would give away the identity and true provenance of the piece to a trained eye. However, in the

[1]

A fine quality modern reproduction of a William and Mary ladies' writing bureau. A wholly honest item, its overall design is true to the period but certain details—the cockbeading to the drawers, for example—reveal its origins.

This has been a popular model since the turn of the century, prone to faking as well as legitimate reproduction. Some high quality examples are still to be found dating from the 1920s; deceptive when they were made, they can be even more so after 60 years' wear. Check for oxidization of exposed timbers and thickness of veneer.

**"Old Gothic Style"**
The burgeoning interest in antiques of the latter part of the 18th century is well illustrated by this entry from the diary of Sophie la Roche for 15 September 1786: "We visited Messrs Jeffries' silver store . . . antique, well-preserved pieces, so Mr Jeffries said, often find a purchaser more readily than the modern. This is because the English are fond of constructing and decorating whole portions of their country houses, or at least one apartment, in old Gothic style, and are glad to purchase any accessories dating from the same or a similar period . . ."

1920s and 1930s when walnut furniture was extremely fashionable, several highly skilled makers were constructing furniture that was true in almost all its details to its William and Mary or Queen Anne models. Whether or not they intended to deceive is a moot point. They re-used old drawer linings for example, but gave themselves away by using thin machine-cut veneers.

Classics of these makers are more often in the William and Mary and Queen Anne styles, with the small fall-front bureau on open stand with turned legs and joined stretchers being particularly popular; so too were demi-lune card tables and glazed-door china cabinets. Any such piece on the market should therefore be looked at with considerable care, as they can still deceive. For example, the mouldings on the originals were applied in small sections with the grain running across the moulding rather than along its length. The timber has naturally shrunk across the grain, opening up gaps between the sections. These 20th-century makers applied their cross-grain moulding in exact replica, spaced the sections to simulate contraction and even made the edges curl slightly away from the carcase — a refined touch.

Signs of wear as well as thin veneers can often betray these pieces. The distressing applied to them is often not wholly compatible with real use — the surface bruising round keyholes, the wear of shoes on stretchers, scuffs to legs and feet are all quite difficult to simulate credibly in just the right places.

[2] *above, left*
Hand-cut and machine-cut veneers. Underneath is a piece of thick 18th-century veneer, on top an example of machine-cut veneer, much thinner.

[3] *above, right*
The same two pieces of veneer seen from above. The hand-cut version (*left*) shows its saw marks, whereas the machine cut veneer presents an altogether smoother surface.

## Pastiches

A pastiche can be more difficult to identify than an outright fake. It is a piece that started life as one kind of furniture and was altered to quite another. It will retain a substantial proportion of its original bodywork or carcase — perhaps 25 or 30% — and so old timbers will be visible and proportions are likely to be convincing. A cursory inspection may well indicate that the item is genuine — it is only if you know that such items have been prone to alteration that you are likely to make a more thorough examination.

The chest of drawers of modest merit turned into the highly desirable kneehole desk or dressing table is a typical example of the profitable and deceptive pastiche. Another is the lower

1 *right*
A fine walnut chest-on-stand of the George II period. It is most unlikely that anyone would now divide it, given the high price it would fetch as it stands, but at various times since it was made its constituent parts, suitably amended, would have fetched more than the whole.

2 *above, far right*
It is a relatively simple matter to lift off the top of a tallboy, add bracket feet and be left with a chest of drawers. These are usually readily identifiable: they are unusually tall, they have three drawers rather than the customary two in the top tier and the cornice is much too substantial for an authentic piece.

3 *far right*
When the chest part is removed, one is left with a highly desirable writing table.

4
A fine early George I period walnut side or dining chair with shaped hoop back, solid centre splat, curved seat frame, drop-in seat and cabriole legs, carved at the knee and terminating in claw and ball feet. The points to look for are: the deep seat frame; the cabriole leg, given elegance by the carved shell running from the seat rail across the joint and onto the knee of the leg; the heavily pronounced inward curve of the bracket, both to the front and the side of the knee; the well formed claw and ball; and, of course, the whole chair is of highly figured walnut—the legs are cut from the solid, the seat rail and back splat are veneered. Compare *Ill. 5.*

part of an 18th-century tallboy with open base turned into a fashionable writing table. Or the scrambled set of chairs, in which perhaps six original chairs have been disassembled, some new parts made and eight chairs made up, all of which consist of a majority of antique parts.

## Reproductions

The reproduction, a copy of an earlier style, is by no means new; nor is it necessarily disrespectable.

During the 18th and 19th centuries, when large estates were split up and the contents of grand houses dispersed, it was by no means uncommon for sets of furniture to be divided. The recipient of, say, 12 from a set of 24 chairs might wish to recreate the original set and would commission a chairmaker to produce a dozen duplicates. These would be honest copies, not pastiches, but inevitably the materials would be slightly different from those of the originals and the workmanship would be of a different quality.

The period from which the best "out of period" pieces come is approximately 1830–60. They are therefore antiques in their own right and can be expected to show considerable signs of ageing. Several factors conspired to make this period the best for reproduction, especially of George II and George III fine mahogany furniture. First, the tradition of craftsmanship at the highest level was by no means dead. Second, the advent of mechanization meant that some pieces could be produced relatively cheaply in multiples. And third, "antique" furniture was beginning to be appreciated in its own right.

During the latter part of the 19th century, and particularly in the Edwardian period at the beginning of the 20th, a different kind of reproduction became commonplace. There was a great revival of most of the later 18th-century styles — Chippendale, Adam, Hepplewhite and Sheraton. The resulting furniture was not so much reproduction as pieces made "in the style of", and neither proportions, materials or methods of manufacture were wholly true to their models. Reproductions of this period are rarely deceptive and should usually be taken at face value.

## Alterations

The honest alteration is a most intriguing phenomenon that accounts for many dubious pieces on the market. There are two principal types: the structural adaptation of a piece, for which the reasons can be either honestly practical or dishonestly commercial, and the later decoration of pieces to make them more acceptable to fashionable tastes; again, the motive varied from the pure to the profitable.

**Structural Alterations** Imagine a farmer requiring extra cupboard or drawer space in his bedroom. He travels to a country house sale, and acquires one or perhaps two magnificent tallboys which he takes home. But even if they will go up the stairs they are too tall, when put back together, to stand up in his low-ceilinged room. What more natural than to have the local carpenter fill in the open top of the bottom part to make a chest of drawers, and put some new bracket feet on the top part for another chest? Pieces in this altered form, particularly those that date from the walnut period (c. 1700–1735), can be very valuable and sometimes make the money of original chests of drawers.

5

A fine example of an out of period piece—compare *Ill. 4*, opposite. This mahogany side or dining chair in the early George I style is handsome and well proportioned. Because it was made approximately 100 years ago, it is well patinated and shows signs of wear. However, the seat rail is too shallow for the period, especially given that it is moulded. The curve of the legs is too pronounced, and the feet are a little too shallow. Finally, the material is not compatible with the shape and style of the chair; by the time mahogany was in general use for fine furniture, this style of chair had gone out of fashion. This has to be a 19th-century reproduction.

6

An honest alteration. The left-hand part of this 17th-century draw-leaf table had been cut off to make a side table. The work was roughly done and finished with an extraneous backboard and a pair of homely feet.

Take as another example the table on the previous page. Originally this was a mid-17th century oak and walnut extending dining table of what we would now consider an attractive small size. But at some time in its life it was thought too large — its then owner required only a third of it. One of the three leaves forming the top was used and the others placed in a shed. The frame was cut quite roughly, crudely fixed with pegs, the top was attached and a small side table had come into being. The rest of the frame, fortunately, was stored alongside the redundant leaves. Careful restoration was needed to bring the table top and the two parts of the frame back together. The marks of the saw-cuts through the rails and stretchers, which will always show, might lead one to suspect that something far more sinister had happened to the table: it might, for example, have been reduced in length to increase its value. But the alteration was wholly honest and made for reasons of practicality.

In the mid-19th century a minor industry established itself in the structural alteration of Tudor and Elizabethan furniture. The public taste for this kind of furniture followed a sentimental view of Elizabethan England as a place of honest good cheer (Sir John Falstaff), chivalry (Sir Walter Raleigh) and bold initiative (Sir Francis Drake); unfortunately, few citizens had houses of knightly dimensions. As the population had grown (980,000 Londoners in 1800; 2,000,000 in 1840) more and more people found themselves living in terraced houses of increasingly modest size. Original Elizabethan furniture simply did not suit. Shops accordingly sprang up in the major cities to supply dismembered parts of carved room panelling, ponderous tables, tester beds and throne-like chairs. These parts were then reassembled on a smaller scale with frame members newly made for the purpose.

**Marriages** Just as two-part pieces of furniture such as bureaux, cabinets and bookcases were split up during the 18th and 19th centuries, so it became inevitable that there would one day be a demand for their reunion. Unfortunately it was a rare occurrence when the original partners found each other again. More often such a union was of items that had never seen a partner before — writing bureaux, for example, were made more desirable by having a bookcase added. The secretaire chest with drawers or cupboards underneath was accorded the same treatment, as were plain low cupboards and chests of drawers.

It should be an unvarying rule to look closely at all two-part pieces, however handsome, to see if they have been married off. Provided both parts are of the same period and as long as they are sold today as a marriage no harm is done. The price difference however between such a piece and an original is considerable.

Proportion, colour, quality and the similarity of timber used are all general things to look for, and if all seems right there are three specific points at which to check the initial impression. First, when a cabinet was designed to sit upon a cupboard or

1 *below*
A two-part chest-on-chest or tallboy of the mid-18th century, of a type that has so often been divided. The upper part would have bracket feet added and the space behind the cornice would be filled in. It would never look right however.

The top of the lower part would have to be filled in to make it an independent piece. The size of the rebated moulding should arouse suspicion, but is not in itself conclusive. The presence of three deep drawers (rather than four graduated) should also cause second thoughts, though authentic three-drawer chests do exist. The two features taken together are likely to mean that the chest was once the base part of a tallboy.

2

An oak sideboard typical of the Warwick School style, *c.* 1865. The carving owes something to the example of Grinling Gibbons and something to Neoclassical taste, finished with a generous sprinkling of sporting motifs.

desk base, it was made narrower and shallower than the base in order that it might fit within a retaining moulding. The retaining moulding is nearly always fixed to the base rather than to the bookcase or cabinet top. Second, and more important, is veneering to the top surface of the base part. When the upper part is moved the top surface of the base should show carcase timber. Veneering was always expensive and the cost was unjustified if the surface was not to be seen in ordinary use. The presence of veneer does not necessarily mean that the two parts have been married, but the absence of veneer is always a good sign.

The backboards are the third place to look. Whatever their quality—very best panelled or rough hewn planks — ideally they should be the same on both parts. If both backs have been treated similarly it is still no guarantee of original association, but if they are different it is not a good sign and more detailed examination of the piece is called for.

## Decorative Alterations

**Carving** Nineteenth-century enthusiasm for Tudor, Elizabethan and generally "Gothic" furniture did not stop at re-using old carved parts in new settings. Carving was a minor rage — and not just for humble artisans, but as a pastime for the genteel. During the 1850s Warwick became a centre for carving of the most elaborate kind. The ornamentation ranged from fruit and clusters of flowers through to warriors in Tarzan-like fur drapes brandishing anything from a trident to a club; hunting trophies, hunting scenes and musical instruments were meat and drink to the carver, whose imagination was the only factor limiting what might appear on

**Hidden Carving**
From time to time a hidden part — the back of a side table or the lining of a drawer — is found partly or fully carved. The explanation is that carving was done by the batch for application to rooms that were being panelled. Surplus pieces were taken by the joiners and used, rather than waste the timber, in places where they would not show. The value of the piece of furniture is neither augmented nor diminished by the presence of hidden carving, but its interest is enhanced.

**1** *left*
A fine mid-18th century mahogany side chair with the unusual feature of cabriole legs to the back as well as the front—a sign of high quality. It is unusual to find a piece as good as this that was not decorated with carving. Even if it was not carved when made, this was perfect material for late 19th- or early 20th-century carvers.

**2** *left*
The leg of a George II walnut dining chair, showing how clearly original carving stands proud of the lines of the member.

**3** *above, right*
The back of a George II period dining chair. The quality of the carving to the crest rail is high and

it stands well proud of the outline, suggesting originality, but more interesting are the curls terminating the splat and those ornamenting its sides. They are neither perfectly identical nor perfectly symmetrical, indicating that they were hand carved. No 19th-century machine would have tolerated this imperfection.

one of these extraordinary pieces of furniture. While its popularity meant the style was much copied elsewhere, the finest examples are still referred to as being of the Warwick School.

Unfortunately, when requiring something upon which to practise, many an untalented amateur was let loose upon a plain piece of 16th- or early 17th-century furniture. It is for this reason that so many panelled or boarded blanket chests of that period should be viewed with some caution when they are elaborately carved. The finest would have received lavish attention when made, but the majority, being modest domestic items, were left undecorated save for a chipped carved edge or moulded border.

The reassembly and recarving of oak furniture from the 16th and 17th centuries, done largely during the 1850s and 60s, was perpetrated in the main for innocent reasons. This of course does not make any difference to commercial values today: the article in question is not genuine; it is not as it started life. However somehow this kind of alteration does not seem quite as bad as an alteration done solely to increase value. Such, unfortunately is so often the case where mahogany furniture of the 18th century has been recarved.

Eighteenth-century furniture was rarely attacked by the vicar's carving class following the Warwick School, but in furniture workshops. Good mid-18th century mahogany furniture in the curvilinear style, elegant and full of shape but perfectly plain, went in one end of the workshop to come out carved with the most elaborate Rococo and Baroque designs at the other. And of course the value of a carved piece of 18th-century furniture, created as a work of art, is vastly higher than that of the plain middle class item.

Much of this later carving was done in the early 1900s, following the passion for furniture in the manner of the 18th-century high style Rococo and Baroque designers such as William Kent, Thomas and Batty Langley and, of course, Thomas Chippendale. The work is now some 60-80 years old; decades of wax, dirt and handling have all added depth of colour to the new carving.

So how do you tell? There is one guiding rule. When a piece of furniture was to be carved, the maker allowed sufficient timber for the carver to create his designs in high relief. When the job was finished the carving appeared encrusted, as if the scrolls, shells or whatever motifs had been applied. When the piece of furniture was to be plain, no such extra timber was required or allowed, so that any carving that was added subsequently would have to be incised below the outline of the existing surface. Flat carving of this type can easily be seen when viewed obliquely.

Carving is unfortunately only one kind of potentially deceptive surface decoration. Whereas stripping, repolishing and the attempted application of distressing or signs of wear (see page 60) are really quite easy to discern, by far the most taxing deception is later veneering.

Later Veneering The commonest example of later veneering is when a piece of early 18th-century oak furniture — say a chest of drawers or a small bureau — is taken into the workshop and its surface decorated with walnut veneer.

The piece, because of its thoroughly genuine carcase, will have pleasing proportions, and when you turn it up to view the underside, all the proper signs of age and wear will be visible. It appears to be genuine. But pull out a drawer. An 18th-century drawer made for an oak piece will necessarily have its front made of oak; if the drawer was made to fit in a walnut-veneered piece the situation is different. The drawer lining may be made of oak, but the drawer front will not be — or not entirely. The face of the drawer front was to be veneered, so it was a waste of money to use more expensive oak when cheaper pine would do as well. Yet when the drawer was opened one did not want to see a bare pine surface at the top of the front and veneer applied to it would not have withstood wear. The solution was to place a slip of oak along the top of the drawer front. The depth of this slip varied enormously, but below the oak some pine or other cheaper wood will show if the piece was made to be veneered. Solid oak on the inside therefore almost certainly betokens a piece

## The Signs of Later Veneering

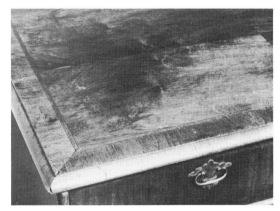

1 *above*
The top is quartered in the correct manner, but the plainness of the timber is very apparent; similar pieces from the early 18th century were usually decorated with highly figured veneers.

1 *above*
A walnut chest of drawers with straight front and the usual arrangement of two short drawers over three long, on straight bracket feet. At first glance it dates from about 1720, but all is not quite as it should be.

First, the bracket feet are slightly late in period to go with the type of moulding dividing the drawer fronts—either an overhanging drawer front or a cockbead would be expected. The chest may however be of provincial make.

Second, the grain of the veneer is straight and uninteresting, although the drawer fronts do have diagonally cross-banded borders. On a 1720 piece it would be normal to have herringbone (double diagonal) borders.

3 *left*
One of the back corners of the chest. The cracks in the veneer show that it is thin—too thin to be 18th-century. The likelihood is that the chest was reveneered in the 19th century or later. The drawers should yield further clues.

4 *right*
One of the top drawers: it is made of pine, not of oak as one would expect on a quality piece of the period. However, country pieces were sometimes made with pine drawer linings.

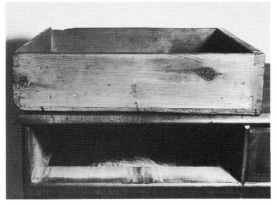

**5** *above*
A side of the same drawer. The single dovetail joint (on the right) is not stopped. This is fairly primitive construction and consistent with an early date.

Another point that shows clearly is wear at the centre of the drawer's supporting rail. This is where a secret spring lock has been allowed to rub as the runners have worn down—the drawer has been supported on its front rail rather than on its runners. We should now look for the spring.

**6** *above, right*
The underside of the same drawer, showing the remains of the secret spring. This was a locking device much used during the 17th century. A piece of hardwood, usually oak, approximately a quarter of an inch thick and two-and-a-half to three inches long, was fastened to the underside of the drawer at a slight angle, so as to protrude like a tongue. As the drawer slid home

this tongue clicked down behind the front rail, preventing the drawer from being opened until the spring or tongue was pushed up from the underside. This was possible only when the drawer below, which was fitted with a conventional lock, was opened. Thus three drawers could be secured with only one relatively expensive steel lock. This, then, is a good sign of age, as are the signs of wear from the drawer runners.

**7** *above*
The interior of the drawer front. It shows, as one might expect on a chest of this period, that several sets of handles have been applied. The first would have been the split-pin type, the marks of which can be seen towards the sides. The next handle was evidently a Victorian turned wood knob, the fixing of which required a large hole to be drilled right in the centre. The plug

for this hole is clearly visible. Finally, two split-pin fixings for a swing or drop handle can be seen just above and to either side of the plug.

**8** *above, right*
The face of the same drawer, however, shows no holes through the veneer corresponding with the marks inside. The veneer is therefore later than the drawer.

This then is a late 17th/early 18th-century pine chest of drawers of provincial manufacture, probably intended as a bedroom piece. Originally it would have been waxed or possibly painted and it stood on simple turned bun feet. It is not a reveneered chest but later veneered, and is the work of an improver of mediocre skill, probably done in about 1920.

that was not intended by its maker to be veneered, or one of foreign provenance.

More evidence of later veneering can be found on drawer fronts. It was quite common practice to update chests of drawers from time to time by changing their handles (and it is perfectly acceptable — even desirable — to change them back to handles of the original pattern though of later manufacture). The handles were secured by drilling through the drawer front and fastening them at the back, the earliest with split pins and later with bolts. In the 19th century, when turned wooden knobs were fashionable, quite large holes had to be bored, often with a screw thread.

If a piece has had its handles changed at some time, there will almost certainly be two sets of holes visible on the inside of the drawer front — more if there has been more than one change. Yet the perpetrator of later veneering is trying to produce a handsome article, and he will hardly drill through his new veneer to create matching holes. It may be necessary to remove a handle to make sure, because perfectly genuine holes might be hidden under the handle's backplate, but if the holes on the face do not correspond with those on the inside you can be sure that the veneer is not original. But do note that what you are looking at might be the result of re-veneering in the course of restoration. Check the other drawers in the same way. If there are none, the next test — the thickness of the veneers — may prove conclusive.

Eighteenth- and early 19th-century veneers were all cut by hand, the sawyers often using multi-bladed saws. It is

*1 below*
A collection of 19th-century panels of inlay in the manner of the late 18th century. These were used in great quantity for the revival of Sheraton-style furniture in the last quarter of the 19th century and on into the 20th. Made by specialist inlay cutters, they were supplied to cabinetmakers ready for use. Note the poor quality of the figure in the central panel and the pattern number written on the back of the piece lower left.

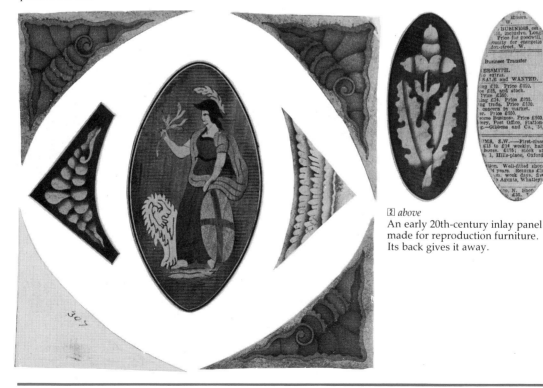

*2 above*
An early 20th-century inlay panel made for reproduction furniture. Its back gives it away.

impossible to cut by hand a veneer noticeably thinner than 1/16 in., but the machines that took over veneer-cutting from the early 19th century could cut it almost paper thin. The manufacturer could derive at least twice as much veneer from a given plank as before, though it was more fragile and therefore less serviceable. If then you can find an edge or a chip in the veneer of any piece purporting to be 18th-century you can quickly tell from the thickness whether that piece of veneer is compatible with the date of the carcase. Even allowing for wear at the edges, a uniform thinness will be apparent if it is of the machine age.

Also, a veneer "bubble", more common on highly figured timbers, can be a guide. If the raised area is thin enough to be depressed easily the veneer is machine cut or the surface has been sanded down to remove damage.

**Marquetry** English marquetry appears in three main periods: the late 17th–early 18th centuries; the late 18th–early 19th centuries and the late 19th–early 20th centuries.

Seventeenth-century marquetry showed a definite influence from the Continent and was fashioned in two main styles: arabesque or seaweed, and floral. Arabesque marquetry was made with two timbers only — boxwood or holly and walnut — and the style was precisely what one would expect from the name: fine, intertwining scrolls of the most complicated patterns. The best examples are so fine as to suggest movement. Floral marquetry used holly, boxwood, most fruitwoods, walnut, ebony and any woods that would

successfully take a dye. The colours of floral marquetry when new were astounding in their brilliance and range — greens, blues, reds, yellows, black and white — but over the last 300 years they have faded to a palette of mellow browns.

Details on 17th-century marquetry, such as the veins of leaves and petals, were cut through, which is the most laborious way of producing the effect. In marquetry of the Classical period however, from 1775 through to the end of the 18th century, such details were etched on once the marquetry had been cut and laid. Late 18th-century marquetry that shows

3 *above, left*
A late 17th-century piece of English marquetry, showing appropriate signs of age.

4 *above, right*
A detail, showing the raised grain effect where glue has squeezed through and solidified—a good test of the panel's authenticity.

**Walnut veneers laid on oak**
Exceptions to the guide that walnut veneer laid on solid oak indicates later veneering include the doors of long case clocks. Because the inside of a door was seen every time it was opened it had to be of quality timber, and therefore it is standard to find solid oak doors on walnut veneered clock cases.

fine detail created with a saw rather than by engraving will not be English but Continental. If it is found on a piece of furniture purporting to be English there is every reason to be suspicous. Marquetry from the late 19th and early 20th centuries, when so much of the work was done by machine stamping, will also show engraved, not saw-cut detail.

Given the appreciating values of good quality late 18th-century furniture in the early 20th century, it was inevitable that some plain pieces would be fitted with marquetry panels to lift them into a higher price bracket. However, it is difficult to set in panels of marquetry and leave the surface as flat and perfect as it would have been in the original. The way it is done is to set the new work to stand proud and then polish it down flush. However, over the ensuing three or four years the glue contracts and the let-in piece sinks — a fault easy to spot when the surface is viewed obliquely against the light. You can also feel the dip if you stroke the surface lightly.

On a genuine article there will be raised grain or glue ridges. These arise where tiny crevices in the grain were first oiled or waxed, causing them to swell. When the wood shrank, it squeezed out excessive oil, brickdust and polish from the pores. Over the years this debris has caught minute particles of dust and solidified to create a ridged effect. The lines created by the saw cuts in a marquetry pattern cause a similar result as they have allowed the glue to squeeze gently through to the top surface. The patterns therefore can not only be seen, they can be felt. This is something the faker of marquetry has not yet managed to achieve.

## Distressing

A considerable amount of bunkum is talked about distressing; some of it is highly imaginative — for example thrashing a table top with chains — some of it is downright ridiculous — such as firing a shotgun at a chair frame to create the appearance of woodworm.

If a piece is distressed to deceive, the activity is plainly reprehensible, but if it is done to tone in a legitimate restoration, it is arguably perfectly respectable — if a chair has to be restored with a new leg, or part of a top needs repair on a chest of drawers or a table, the new part can spoil the look of the whole unless it is harmonized. A skilful polisher can simulate virtually any surface, colour and condition. Simple

1a
The William and Mary bun foot of the late 17th century varied considerably in detail: this is the archetypal shape, much revived in the 19th century.

1b
One of the popular variants on the bun foot shape. Bun feet could be ornamented with rings and some of the finest were carved with foliate motifs.

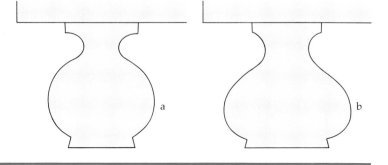

staining will tone in restored pieces, but large surfaces — the top of a period chest, for example — may sometimes by given the mellowness of age by bruising with a clinker, staining and polishing.

No genuinely old piece will be evenly worn, but the faker has often proved himself incapable of self-restraint, and instead of simulating wear only on those parts that should be worn with use, he has also treated surfaces that would, if the piece were genuine, be in near pristine condition. Wear in improbable places is a very bad sign. For this reason it is always worth looking at how you naturally handle a piece you are appraising. You will put your hands where countless others have put theirs, each time leaving a minute trace of oil from the skin. Over the course of a century or two, this will result in darker patches; if you do not see them you should be very wary.

Note that polished surfaces present far less of a problem to the faker than unpolished surfaces. Polished surfaces can be doctored, but plain wood is much more difficult to treat. The interiors of drawers, for example, should never appear stained or greasy; it is extremely unlikely that anything could have happened to them to create such an effect legitimately. On finer pieces of furniture the interiors of small drawers (for example, those in bureaux) will look almost brand new, as they will have had little or no exposure to circulating air.

## Bureau-bookcases

Slant-front writing desks with drawers below were made to stand on their own as well as to form bases for bureau-bookcases and can be found dating from the late 17th century. An early example of the two-part form has for some time been so desirable that it is both tempting and profitable to arrange a marriage.

A bureau made to stand alone will differ slightly in shape from one that was intended to support a bookcase — it will have a shallow top and a gentle slope. The bureau made to receive a cupboard over will have a deeper top and therefore a steeper fall. It is also unlikely that the top of the bureau will be veneered if it is then to be hidden by a cupboard, though this is not an absolute rule. It is preferable to find the retaining moulding where the two pieces join fixed to the bureau rather than to the underside of the cupboard, since that is the logical

**Dwarf library bookcases**
The demand for low waisted library bookcases at various times has been in part satisfied by removing the secretaire drawer from a less saleable secretaire bookcase. The result is likely to show a lack of proportion, and the side effect of course is that each time this is done there is a spare secretaire drawer for re-use somewhere else . . .

1 c
The plain bracket foot, used on middle quality furniture from about 1720 to about 1780.

1 d
The typical shape of an ogee bracket foot as used on fine quality chest and cabinet furniture from 1740 to 1775.

1 e
The splay or French foot, which appears on fashionable chest and cabinet furniture from c. 1780 to c. 1810. In its severest form there is only a modest kick-out at the toe; the most exaggerated examples start their sweep at the junction of the foot to the carcase. In general, the more generous the sweep, the more luxurious the piece.

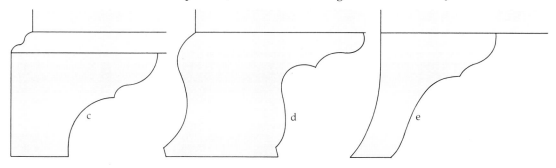

c                 d               e

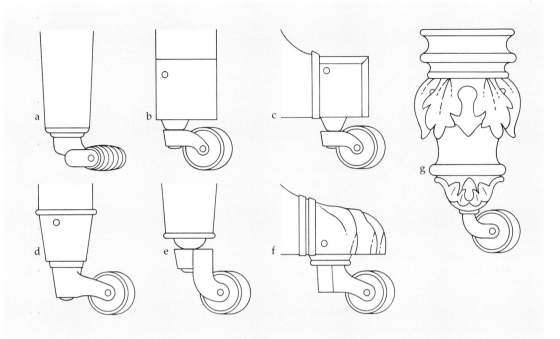

**1a**
The type of castor, with the wheel made of leather discs, used about 1740-60 concealed beneath claw and ball feet or to terminate square, untapered legs.

**1b**
The square cup castor, c. 1760-75; by now the wheel is likely to be of brass.

**1c**
Plain toe castor used on 18th-century splay-leg furniture; if it tapers it is likely to be post-1790.

**1d**
The tapered cup castor: from about 1785.

**1e**
The simple brass castor used on small pieces of furniture in the last quarter of the 18th century.

**1f**
The lion's paw castor, used on splay-leg furniture 1800-1820 and on much reproduction furniture since.

**1g**
Cast gilt-metal castor of the late Regency—after 1825. The decoration of the castor now reflects the ornamented foot.

place to put it if it is to be more than mere ornament.

Another useful clue to a mismatch is that many cabinets made to sit on bureaux and secretaire chests were fitted with a row of small drawers at the bottom. These will properly be of the same quality of construction and of the same timber as the small drawers in the fitted part of the bureau or in the secretaire drawer. As with all two-part furniture, check overall for compatibility of quality, timber and back boards.

## Chairs

In the 18th century, the average upper middle class household would probably have had a set of 24 chairs — certainly a minimum of 12. Over the years, these sets have been divided by inheritance and it is now rare to find a set of 12 or even 10 dining chairs from the late 18th or early 19th centuries. In the 1950s and 60s long sets were not in demand — sixes were what the market wanted, made up of six singles, five singles with one carver or four singles with two carvers. At that time carvers, highly valued today, bore only a small premium over singles, and all were relatively cheap.

But demand has changed in the last ten years. As large pedestal dining tables have come back into fashion, longer sets of chairs are required to accompany them, and eights or tens are much sought after.

Scrambled Sets The simplest solution would be to copy up to the number required, but this is relatively expensive in materials and labour and the result is not as authentic-looking as the alternative — to scramble the set.

[2] *left*

Two from a set of fruitwood dining chairs, *c.* 1800. Notice the difference in seat width: the carver to any set of late 18th- or early 19th-century dining chairs will always have a wider seat than the single.

There is a tremendous demand for sets of six or eight chairs that include at least one if not a pair of carvers. As there were only one or two to original sets of 12 or more chairs there has been an obvious temptation to add arms to singles to meet demand. Therefore put a carver face to face with a single, compare seat widths and you will see immediately if this deception has been practised.

The easiest sets to scramble are those with stuff-over seats and a minimum of carving. Drop-in seats of course leave all the seat rails exposed, and remaking them is more expensive in materials and finishing. Carving too is expensive. But the overstuffed seat is upholstered onto beech rails, which have often become weakened through several re-upholsterings and, quite possibly, through woodworm as well. They therefore need replacing, and to do this you must take the chair to pieces. At this stage the opportunity presents itself to increase the size of the set.

[3] *above*
The kind of Regency mahogany dining chair with stuffed over seat that is a favourite candidate for scrambling.

If a couple of copies are taken of each component you have enough parts to make two reproduction chairs. But if when the chairs are reassembled one or two copied parts are introduced into each chair you get two extra chairs identical with the others — all of them are in the main made from original, authentic parts. None of the chairs is wholly authentic, none is a copy, all are identical and if the job is well done it is extremely difficult to discover.

To recognize a scrambled set you have to look for the incongruities. If, on a given chair, one leg is original and one newly made, check for a plausible match of the scuff marks at the bottom. Remember that although differences in timber would have been well concealed when the set left the workshop, a very few years' use may reveal new stain and polish.

The scrambled set of chairs is a good example of the opening comments to this chapter: providing you are made aware of any alterations, and the chairs are priced accordingly, there is no reason not to buy.

## Chests of Drawers

Apart from the later veneered chests of drawers whose oak is dressed up as walnut, which are dealt with under "Later Veneering" on page 55, the most characteristic chests that are not quite genuine are those that result from dividing a tallboy Honest alterations that they almost always are, they betray

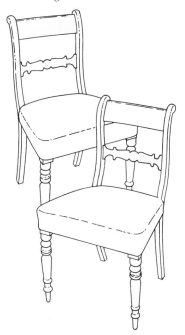

[4]
The effect of scrambling a set of chairs: only one or two parts need to be new on each chair, thus the majority of each remains original.

**1**

A fine, mid 18th-century tallboy.
Despite its having only three
drawers, the base could do duty as
a separate chest of drawers more
convincingly than the lower parts of
most tallboys once its top was filled
in. However the rebate, modest
when it is part of a chest-on-chest,
would be over-emphatic on a chest
of drawers. Compare *Ill. 2.*

**2**

A mid 18th-century chest of
drawers with original rebated top
(compare the base part of *Ill. 1*). The
size of the rebate is not nearly
sufficient to have accommodated a
top part. It would also be unusual
to find a four-drawer base to a two-
part chest.

their origins quite easily by their improbable proportions.

The proportions of a chest made by dividing a tallboy will
never be as fine as those of a chest made as such. Eighteenth-
century furniture makers had an incredible ability to build
furniture of even the humblest sort with the correct
dimensions, and so any disproportion may be a warning sign.
If you take the top part from a tallboy it leaves the bottom with
drawers too deep and cumbersome to sit beneath a filled-in top
— or at least, to do so with conviction.

An 18th-century chest of drawers will have an overhanging
top or, more rarely, one which bears what is called a caddy
moulding to the edge (a quarter-round moulding setting the
top back no more than half an inch). The bottom half of a
tallboy however has a deep retaining moulding in which the
top part sits. Merely filling in the top results in a stepped-back
effect too pronounced for it to be original, and it is also most
unusual to find one where the top has been filled in with the
correct timber.

Because of its height the top part of a tallboy is allowed a
wide, deeply moulded cornice, often further decorated with a
dentil moulding or even blind fretwork in the Chinese or
Gothic manner. Such a heavy moulding was never applied to
something below eye level — while it looks fine seen from
below it is ponderous and bizarre when you look down on it.
Also it was fairly common, particularly in the walnut period, to
put three short drawers along the top row surmounting three
long drawers of graduating depth. Three drawers along the
top of a chest of drawers are an indication that the piece is the
upper part of a tallboy, particularly if there is a wide overhanging moulding as well. A close look at the feet will then
almost certainly show whether or not all is as it should be.

The exception to this is the tall chest of five long drawers
below two or three short ones — a type that was produced in
the North of England after the mid-18th century, usually in
oak. Its intermediate height — 5-6ft (150-180cm) — obviates
the possibility of its being converted from anything else.

## Cupboards

It is usually possible to tell by looking at the doors when a large
cupboard has been reduced in height. Glazed doors, provided
that the panes are rectangular, can be reduced by removing
one tier of panes; blind doors can be cut down at will. But in
either case an unconvincing proportion may result, and unless
the doors are trimmed both top and bottom the keyhole will be
out of place (it should be about central or a little below if the
piece is really tall). A further guide is that the tenons of the
cross members should pass right through the door stiles.

## Kneehole Desks

One of the classic alterations to enhance value is the
transformation of a chest of drawers into a kneehole desk.
Examples of this particular deception are more likely to date

4 *above*
When the cupboard doors are opened, spiral turned columns can be seen in the corners.

3 *above*
Alterations are usually executed for aggrandizement, but by no means always. The heavy glazing bars of this cabinet, forming plain rectangular panels, suggest an early date, though the style of the lower cupboard doors is more that of the mid-18th century. The disparity could well be the result of provincial manufacture, particularly if the piece was made on a large estate where so often the rules of construction were confounded by the restrictions placed on the maker by the materials to hand.

5 *above*
Conclusive evidence—the underside reveals a stretcher that bears no relationship to the cupboard.

6 *above*
As it was meant to be: an attractive oak cabinet-on-stand of provincial manufacture dating from between 1700 and 1710. We must assume that the cupboard had been added for utilitarian reasons.

7 *below*
What needs to be done to a relatively commonplace 18th-century chest of drawers to make it into a much more expensive four-footed kneehole desk.

from early in the 20th century — good quality chests of drawers have become expensive now in their own right and the craftsmanship required to do this job well is of a high and therefore expensive order.

Kneehole desks (also known as dressing tables) appear only in the better qualities of 18th-century furniture. The best type, dating from the mid-century up to the 1780s, have six bracket feet, but large numbers were made with four feet only, one at each corner, leaving the kneehole apparently without visible means of support.

It is the four-footed type that is easier to make out of a chest for it saves having to effect two old bracket feet in the centre. Even then, it is no mean task. When the drawers are cut to accommodate the knee-space, old drawer linings are required to make the extra inner sides. The dovetails at both front and back of the new drawer sides have to match the original joints.

Be aware of, but not overly concerned by, the common practice of wiping the joints and edges of drawers with a "rubber" or quick brush of stain, as though attempting to disguise inadequate joinery. It may well be something sinister but it could indicate nothing more serious than a replaced cockbead.

A surer sign will be the effects of wear on the inside of the carcase where the drawers slide — generally around the drawer opening and more especially on the bottom. Marks of wear should always be compatible with any moving parts.

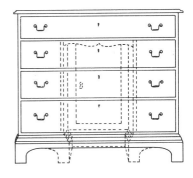

8
The most rewarding result of the kind of work undertaken in *Ill. 7*, above—a six-footed desk.

1

The interior of a sideboard carcase with a drawer removed. In the foreground is the front rail, to the right the backboard and to the left is the panel that divides this drawer cavity from the next. At the base of this panel is the drawer runner fixed with hand-made nails.

The details all suggest authenticity. The dividing panel has remained light in colour where it has been protected by the drawer, but has darkened at the back beyond the point where the drawer was stopped from closing fully onto the backboard. The wear to the runner is exactly compatible—dipping towards the back, then rising again where the darkening of the divider occurs and where the drawer never ran. If the runner does not rise again at the back, and if the back half-inch of the dividing panel is not darkened, the piece has probably been reduced in depth.

2 *below*

A fine example of a Hepplewhite period mahogany sideboard *c.* 1775, decorated with carving and inlay, all original except for the handles.

At the point where legs and carcase meet there is an applied strip of astragal moulding. Check that this does not conceal a join where turned legs have been cut off and replaced with square tapering ones. Remove one of the lower drawers, look into the corner and ensure that the stile continuing into the leg is one piece of timber.

## Sideboards

Eighteenth- and 19th-century sideboards were practical, working pieces of furniture as well as being objects upon which to lavish ornamentation according to the wealth of the owners. They had to be large enough to hold food and drink, plates and glasses as well as give room to serve. Elegant as proper period sideboards are, they have proved rather large for modern homes and for some periods of 20th-century taste.

It is by no means uncommon therefore to come across unnaturally shallow sideboards with altogether authentic fronts and timbers and an otherwise convincing appearance. There are two easy ways to tell if a sideboard has been reduced

3 *above*

An early turned leg sideboard in mahogany, dating from about 1805-1810. In its time it was the equivalent in quality and standing of the Hepplewhite piece (*left*) and therefore too good to have been "improved"; it is however not quite as saleable, therefore less likely to be faked.

in depth. Remove a drawer and look at the runners. You should see some wear and particularly a dip towards the back (see *Ill. 1*, left). The last half inch should show no signs of wear at all, as the drawer would not run that far, being stopped so that it would not hit the backboard and stress its joints. If the runner is still dipping when it meets the backboard you probably have a reduced piece: the back has been brought nearer the front.

If the runners have been replaced — as they all must be, sooner or later — there is another test. Look at the back corners, beyond where the drawers reach. You should see a darker area — the result of oxidization and the accumulation of dirt. Again, if the sideboard has been reduced in depth this part will have been cut off and you will see only clean wood right to the back.

One of the more serious alterations to sideboards is replacing good, honest, turned legs by those of the square tapered variety. This is because the square tapering leg is of an earlier period, and therefore, up to the present anyway, more valuable than the turned leg. The first turned legs were plain

*4 below left*
The next stage, now with the centre space filled in, slightly heavier and dating from 1810-1815. This is material for the improver, who would replace the legs with square tapering ones and disguise the joint with an applied moulding. The lower central drawer is also removed, arched brackets fitted and the item may be reduced in depth for good measure.

and elegant and continued the spirit of their predecessors. The main part of the column was tapering and terminated in a spade or flared foot. Gradually, the turner added more and more ring decoration to the legs, making it possible to date turned leg furniture of the Regency period quite accurately by the complexity of the patterns of rings as well as by increasing heaviness as the period progressed.

A sideboard's leg is the extended stile of the carcase — it is not added on. If the leg is cut off at the bottom of the carcase and another one joined to it, there must be a means of disguising the join. This was done by applying a band of stringing or line inlay, or by attaching a thin astragal moulding. The stringing could comprise any combination of popular veneers such as satinwood, kingwood, rosewood, boxwood or, particularly after 1800, an inlay of ebony or ebonized timber. One would expect to find this black line inlay rather more on turned leg sideboards, when it was also quite common to find some of the ring turnings of the legs ebonized. If therefore you find a line of stringing or a line of cross

*5 above*
This is the commonest type of early 19th-century sideboard. The multiple ring turnings to the legs indicate an 1810-1820 date. It is on this type, because it is so common, that the improver has found his easiest work. However, the black line inlay to the drawer fronts is a giveaway—it indicates a post-1800 date and is therefore quite incompatible with any amount of alteration that creates the appearance of a sideboard of the Hepplewhite period.

▣ *above*

A late 18th-century oval breakfast table, the top crossbanded and line inlaid, the edge reeded, on a finely turned column and four splay legs. These tables became fashionable during the 1950s, and in response to the demand a number of rogues appeared on the market.

▣ *above*

The underside of the same breakfast table (*Ill. 1*), showing both the high quality fitments and the lack of oxidation where the supporting block fitted the top closely. Neither of these signs of authenticity is conclusive, but it is wise to be wary if either is missing.

▣

A detail of the underside of the same table. It shows signs of handling in the darkening at the edge and it also shows the marks where in the past ladies clamped their needlework to the table's edge. This is the sort of detail that "improvers" rarely bother with.

banding on a sideboard with square tapering legs at the point where leg and carcase meet, check that the grain of the wood is consistent above the inlay and below it.

An original square-legged sideboard is more likely to have applied astragal moulding at the top of the leg rather than inlay, but such a moulding was nearly always applied to other parts of the sideboard as well — typically to the drawer fronts and the panels on the upper parts of the legs. Line inlay superseded applied decoration but followed the same patterns.

An even more drastic way of "improving" the legs of a sideboard, done in the 1920s, was to dismantle the carcase entirely, fit square legs from top to toe, rebuild and disguise the newness of the joints.

## Breakfast Tables

Just as the huge dining tables of the 18th century were cut down and remodelled earlier this century, many breakfast tables were similarly adapted. Often the alteration was simply to improve their appearance but, more frequently, the larger breakfast tables were reduced in seating capacity at the same time as sets of six or at the most eight chairs were in vogue.

The most desirable breakfast tables are still those of the late 18th century in the Sheraton style. Oval versions are more highly prized than rectangular. The key features are a top without a frieze and a fine four-splay base, each leg sweeping down and out in an unbroken curve from a "gun barrel" centre stem.

Breakfast tables of the early 19th century tended to become heavier, with the addition of a frieze to the top and a more cumbersome column. These tables were sometimes made with the top divided and extendable: a single leaf could be dropped in to allow two more place settings or two small leaves could be added to the outer edges, supported on lopers. The lopers passed through holes cut in the frieze and the leaves were attached with brass U-shaped clips.

There was of course no point in adapting 18th-century examples, except when they were huge. It is generally the 19th-century versions that have been tampered with. Ten-seaters have been reduced to a more manageable six-seater size, rectangles have been cut to ovals or rounds, friezes have been removed to simulate the delicate appearance of Sheraton models and columns and legs have been trimmed to a graceful George III sweep. The result is that early 19th-century tables seating eight or ten are now scarce, but there is an abundance of not-quite genuine smaller tables of deceptive elegance.

Cutting a rectangular table into an oval is not as easy as it sounds: it is surprisingly difficult to draw an oval that is thoroughly pleasing. If a table has been cut down either to an oval or to a round, it is usually not too difficult to tell, however. The original, in normal use, will show signs of darkening round the underside edges where it has been handled, and these signs will be approximately uniform. A table that does not show this patina of handling at all has either not been used (rare indeed) or has been cut out of a distinctly larger one. If it shows darkening in some places — especially at its widest points — but not in others, the chances are that it has been cut down but has retained one or more of its maximum dimensions. The adapter will rarely have bothered to simulate handmarks on his new edges, and even if he has tried, the result is rarely convincing.

Another useful check for cutting down is the presence of a series of small dents to the edge of the underside. These are the marks left by the small wooden clamps that ladies used to hold needlework, painting frames and so on, for breakfast tables were likely to be used throughout the day and not just for meals. Again, it is unlikely that an improver will have bothered to add these marks, for they are not a requirement of the form but merely an attractive confirmation of an otherwise wholly authentic table.

The presence of reeding on a table's edge is no guide at all to authenticity, since when it was cut down it was standard practice to reed the edge to finish it off. Table edges are however rather vulnerable, and a reeded edge that is largely free of cuts, dents and scratches — or one that is uniformly distressed — should be viewed with caution.

The removal of the frieze to a breakfast table usually leaves traces, unless it is done in conjunction with substantial cutting down. Whereas the rest of the underside (except for the part covered by the block) will have been exposed to the air and will have darkened accordingly, the thick line near the edge where the apron was screwed to the top will be of unexposed and therefore lighter wood. The screw holes can be filled and the marks polished over, but it is almost impossible to disguise the alteration completely; the unexposed timber is and will remain slightly different, and there will be an abrupt end to the haphazard ring of handmarks. The only way to avoid this problem is to cut the table within the line of the apron — but then it will not show handmarks at all.

A tilting top to a breakfast table is no guarantee of originality. Some pedestal-base or two- or three-part dining tables had this tilting feature to each main segment. Look for signs of any previous attachments on the underside of the edges and check that the reeding or moulding to the lip does not conceal places where the small rectangular tongues protruded or fitted into the leaves of a dining table.

**Altering The Legs** As the 19th century progressed the legs of pedestal tables became more ponderous. The simple downward sweep of the Sheraton style was more and more interrupted by a knee. Earlier in the 20th century this was an unfashionable feature and it sat ill with an "improved" top. It therefore became standard practice to shave off the knees until the legs showed the sweeping form of the finest exemplars. The legs could then be reeded to add conviction. This is a difficult alteration to distinguish, and perhaps the best guide is proportion. A good 18th-century pedestal table always has a very substantial support — it will be gracefully executed but there will be plenty of it. If the legs look delicate and short rather than handsome, they may have been redrawn.

The column too might be reworked. The block and legs would be taken off, the column put on a lathe and turned to a gun barrel stem. Only the freshness of its appearance and the marks of the chisel (which should not appear on an original piece) will reveal this refinement.

If a breakfast table shows no signs of these alterations it should still be checked for the compatibility of its parts. The block should have left a precisely matching pale area where it fits the underside for example, and the catch or catches should not have been moved. Bear in mind too that breakfast tables of quality have always been expensive and therefore the catch, castors and any clips should be of the finest manufacture.

## Dining Tables

Early 18th-century dining tables were formed as though a row of drop leaf tables had been attached to each other. By the 1770s two D-shaped ends were added. These were free standing, each being supported on four legs matching those of the centre drop-leaf. A frieze rail set back slightly from the edge secured the legs to the top. Additional leaves could be inserted between the centre table and the D-ends and a further refinement was to make the leaves of the centre part detachable, so that the whole table could be reduced to seat six people comfortably.

Its versatile nature has meant that this type of table has been prone to separation and alteration: the centre drop-leaf, useful but unfashionable in its original rectangular form, can be cut to create a more desirable oval, and the two D-ends could be used as side tables or joined with an odd leaf to make a small dining table.

The dining table of a wealthy man in the late 18th century would have been up to six feet wide, supported on as many as six pedestals and with extra leaves. A more ordinary household would have a table with three pedestals, the centre one probably having four splay legs, the two ends having three such legs and the top with a minimum of two extra leaves. Large dining tables were made through much of the 19th century, but as great houses were demolished and families split up leaves and tables were dispersed.

In the early 20th century, large multi-pedestal tables were virtually unsaleable and even the smaller sizes — two or three pedestals with a three- or four-part top — were cut up for timber. Alternatively, many a pedestal table had its top removed, which was then given a frieze and set on 18th-century style legs to augment the supply of 14-leg tables, which remained in demand. Regency tables of this type were built with turned legs, often being decorated to match the chairs of the same period. It is this model that went out of fashion earlier in the 20th century to create another reversal. Turned leg tables 12 feet long make a fraction of the price of

1

The underside of a D-end dining table. It is made from good 18th-century timber and the frieze is correctly constructed in sections, the grain of each piece running in the opposite direction from its neighbour to prevent warping. But the "V" shape notches made to receive the fixing screws are 19th century—the 18th-century notch for a fixing screw was of semi-circular form. There are also redundant screw holes, symmetrically arranged and consistent with the fixings of a frame of the kind that supported a pedestal table. This then is an earlier top re-used.

their fellows supported on pedestals. Inevitably, there are a number of pedestal tables on the market that have recently been amalgamated from several old tables to meet this demand.

Guides to spotting the made-up dining table are similar to those for checking breakfast tables. The undersides of the tops and leaves will inevitably show where earlier fixings have been removed; look for paler strips and disguised screw holes from previous runners or lopers; make sure the fixings for leaf clips are all compatible, and that the small rectangular tongues, or, later, the round pegs that secured leaf to leaf are matching and original.

To see if a fine oval drop-leaf table has actually been reduced from a rectangle check that when the leaves are up the supporting legs are not too close to the outer edge. There should always be a good proportionate overhang; it depends on the size of the table, but generally speaking less than 2 in. (5 cm) is not enough.

## Kettle Stands

Many of the finest quality kettle stands were made with a turned spindle or fretted gallery round the top. In the 18th century fretted galleries were made of three-ply mahogany, but this detail was normally neglected in the profusion of early 20th-century copies. If the fret was cut in the 19th century it will probably be coarser as the machine saw bands tended to be thicker. Also, if there is a fault in the machining of one of the sections in the gallery it will be repeated identically in the other sections — this is particularly evident on octagonal or hexagonal kettle stands.

The natural way to pick up a kettle stand is as you would lift a tray, and therefore an authentic 18th-century example should show a darkening all round the rim of the underside from repeated handling, but the wood should be paler towards the centre where the hands do not naturally reach. The block that fixes the column to the top may well be of oak, with the grain running counter to that of the top.

[1] *above*
A Regency period rosewood pole screen, the banner showing an early example of Berlin needlework. Many of these screens have been adapted into occasional tables by removing the pole and using the banner, which was often glazed, as the table top. Such tables sold much better than the pole screens from which they were made.

Look for signs of abrasion on the back of the banner where it rubbed against the pole, and for screw holes where the retaining clips were fixed. Good quality screens had applied cresting rails, as here, and there may be traces of their fixings.

If a kettle stand has been made up with a period tray adapted to make the top there will be tell-tale signs. A tray that has seen any wear worth the name will show signs of its use on the underside — the sort of wear that comes from setting it down on a stone sink or standing it on edge against a wall. This kind of wear is completely inappropriate for the underside of a table, which should show signs of handling but not of any other kind of damage.

If you find a kettle stand that appears to have a former tray for its top, it is quite likely that it is one of the legion of kettle stands/wine tables whose bases are adapted from pole screens. Pole screens were commonplace in Georgian and Regency drawing rooms, but had fallen out of favour by the end of the 19th century. As the kettle stand soared in popularity and price it was a relatively easy matter to cut down a pole screen on proper tripod base to provide the column, add a slight turned extension to it, conceal the joint with a turned ring and fit a tray top. Well done, these adapted pole screen column supports are very difficult to discover. Look for compatibility of grain throughout the column.

Somewhat easier to notice are conversions of pole screens into wine tables but using the screen as the table top. In the Regency and Victorian periods, pole screen banners became smaller. They were often panels of needlework and beadwork, glazed and fitted in a rosewood or walnut frame carved in the Rococo Revival manner. Many of them were removed from their poles, the poles were taken away from their bases and the tops were fixed back to the bases to make small drinks tables. But banners and screen panels were made to slide up and down their poles by means of two hoops screwed to the back of the panel. If the pole screen has been adapted into a table signs of these fixings will probably be visible. There are also likely to be signs of abrasion at the outer edges of the screen where the pole would have rubbed against the frame.

## Sofa Tables

[2]
A perfectly genuine early 19th-century sofa table. These have long been much in demand and therefore prone to faking. See p. 77.

Sofa tables dating from the late 18th century are perennial favourites. Of rectangular form and with two small hinged leaves, early designs were supported on standard ends so that they could be pulled over sofas or daybeds. This was essentially a weak structure and it was not long before a stretcher was introduced. Some stretchers were of rectangular section, some were turned and tapering or even scrolled in the heavy Regency form, but whichever the decoration, a stretcher precluded the table's use for its original purpose. They were however delicate and attractive pieces of furniture, and so they remained in production.

During the Regency period the centre column support on a platform base with legs or bun feet became fashionable and remained so for much of the 19th century, until the standard-end variety, with its more elegant, swept legs and a high or medium placed stretcher, returned to favour.

**3** a, b *above*

Corner reinforcing blocks on seat furniture can be highly informative. The pictures show both ends of the underside of a mahogany and beech window seat in the French Hepplewhite style, *c.* 1775.

The correct 18th-century method of strengthening an overstuffed upholstered seat frame was as shown in *3a* (top). Before upholstering the rail was cut to receive a strut dropped in from the top at an angle of 45° across the joint.

If signs of these joints can be seen at one end or on one side of a piece but not at the other, it is likely that at the very least rails have been replaced, and at worst that the piece is made up.

The shaped angle blocks shown in *3b* are typically 19th century, used consistently from the 1850s onward. They have the advantage that it was not necessary to strip off the upholstery to fit them, as they were screwed on from underneath. But at no time in the 18th century were such blocks used on English seat furniture. If found on a piece of apparently 18th-century make they should indicate innocent 19th-century restoration (as here) but the piece ought to be checked carefully to make sure it is not of Victorian manufacture.

The strengthening of corners on drop-in seat furniture was quite different. Corner struts were not used so instead makers applied corner blocks of quadrant form made up of two pieces of wood. These blocks were extremely effective and should be still in place.

**1** *above*

A George II mahogany library armchair, *c.* 1750, on four cabriole legs. The carving can be seen to stand proud of the outline of each leg and arm support and the generous proportions of the chair embody the qualities of mid-18th century English furniture at its finest. This chair is one of a set of 12; compare *Ill. 2.*

**2** *right*

A George II mahogany library armchair, *c.* 1750. Not only does it resemble very closely *Ill. 1,* but documentary evidence shows that it is from the same set, which originally comprised 24 chairs. A dozen were gilded in the 19th century to aggrandize them.

**1** *above*
An authentic George II period mahogany fold-over top card table of considerable style—and exactly the kind of piece that was ''improved'' in the early 1900s to enhance its value. Tables such as this were carved at the knee, given shells and scrolls at the feet, ornamented with a pierced frieze and their tops were finished with ribbon or Chinese motifs round the edges.

**2** *right*
A deception in reverse. Whereas all walnut furniture should be examined closely for signs of later veneering or even of 20th-century manufacture, this piece demands inspection because of its lines. It is in fact a perfectly genuine George I walnut lowboy, but the curve of the legs is understated to a significant degree (compare *Ill. 3*, below). At first sight one might well suspect that this was a later piece of slightly inferior design subsequently dressed up.

**3**
An elegant oak George II side table of just the kind that ''improvers'' seized upon in the first two decades of this century to veneer with walnut. Its style and workmanship are above reproach, but the fact that it was made in oak suggests that it was probably a provincial piece.

Had this table been later veneered, the drawer front—if not the veneers—would have given it away, as part at least of the front would have been made of softwood if the piece was intended to be covered with veneer.

**4** *opposite*
A fine mid-18th century mahogany kettle stand on tripod base with baluster stem and dished top. The demand for small tripod tables has led inevitably to the adaptation of tripod pole screen bases into tables by adding tray tops. During the first 20 or 30 years of this century it was possible to find 18th-century drinks trays quite easily. They were made in mahogany as well as cheaper wood, and could be any size from 8 in. (20 cm) up to 30 in. (76 cm) in diameter. But the bottoms of such trays always show signs of wear and use, and it is therefore advisable to inspect the undersides of tripod tables of this sort.

**5** *below*
The underside of the stand in *Ill. 4*, showing where the pillar or column is joined to the top with a separate turned disc. In this case the disc is made of oak, which implies good quality manufacture, as do the fine turning of the column and the proportions of the piece in general.

Some junction discs are made of ash, beech or other less important timbers and are prone to woodworm and warping. They may therefore have been legitimately replaced, but a new block could also indicate a marriage.

The undersurface of the top shows a fine all-over patina, carried on to the block where countless hands have picked up the table. There are no scratches, dents or bruises, such as would have been caused if the top had once been used as a tray. The top, then, is authentic. The tripod should be checked, however—see *Ill. 6* opposite.

**8** *above*

A mahogany tripod base, tray top table, *c.* 1765. This attractive piece of furniture is constructed from a period tripod base and a contemporary drinks tray. It is a little too low for its width: a table of these dimensions would have stood at normal table height, that is, approximately 29 in. (74 cm).

**7** a, b *above and below*

A kettle stand in the classic style with hexagonal top, the edge of which has a raised beading. The surface is lightly distressed, and gives a most pleasing appearance, but the distressing is very even in nature—a hint to exercise caution.

Examining the underside of the tripod (*7b*, below) gives the answer right away. The broad striations are the marks of a band saw, made even more prominent by the application of polish. This is therefore a machine-made piece and cannot predate the early-middle of the 19th century, despite its 18th-century style.

There is no point in polishing the underside unless to simulate patina: this makes it probable that the stand is a recent reproduction. The underside of the top shows no handling marks, confirming this view.

**9**

The carved tripod base of an 18th-century mahogany tea table.

The fact that the edge of the top, the column, the knees and the feet are all carved suggests that this is a table of particularly fine quality. However, if you look closely at the profile of the carving you will see that it is confined within the lines of the parts—it does not stand proud. This table therefore started life plain and has been carved later.

**6**

The underside of the tripod to the stand shown above and left. The patina here too is general, the colour rich and deep. The iron strengthening bracket appears to be of the right date and may therefore be considered original.

Every detail of this stand points towards authenticity. Though none of them on its own would be conclusive, taking all the points together we may safely assume that this is an original piece.

1 *above*
A walnut chest of drawers of the 1710–1720 period, the drawer fronts and top decorated with panels of marquetry. This is apparently a quality item and should be checked carefully.

2 *left*
The bracket feet are the only parts of this chest that are obviously wrong — they are too late for the carcase, which should, if it is authentic 1710–20, originally have been fitted with bun feet. The plugged hole revealed by removing the bottom drawer is typical of such feet having been fitted and then removed, either because they were damaged or to update the chest.

3 *above*
A drawer front from the same chest. In amongst the marquetry it is possible to see old holes that have been camouflaged adjacent to the handles (upper right, for example). These then are not the first or original handles. This is by no means sinister — much worse to find evidence of such handles on the inside of the drawer but not on the outside. Restoration of this sort on a fine piece of this period is in general reassuring.

4 *right*
The drawers, too, support the general impression. In this one the lining paper covers up the evidence of several sets of handles, but just enough is torn away to reveal an oak slip above an otherwise pine drawer front — exactly as one would expect. Had the front been of solid oak then the chest would have been either Continental in origin or later veneered.

In short, this is a sound piece not entirely in its original condition but fully restorable. Its faults (replaced handles and feet) are so typical of its age that they are in themselves reassuring.

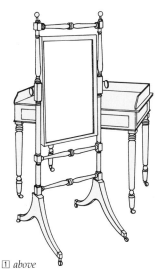

**Adapted Dressing Tables** Earlier in the 20th century demand led to the adaptation of much later pieces of furniture into apparently earlier sofa tables. The classic case is the alteration of a Victorian dressing table and its union with a late 18th-century, but until recently unsaleable, cheval mirror. Tables of the type shown in *Ill. 1* were generally made in pairs. One, the washstand, had holes cut in the top to receive the various fitments, such as the jug, basin and soap dish. The other was made with a solid top as the companion dressing table.

The thumb moulding from the edges of three sides of the top of such a dressing table was removed and the edge was either crossbanded or reeded. The leaves were taken from a small Pembroke table of the correct period (until the 1960s these were cheap and plentiful). The standard ends of a cheval mirror were then cut down to table height and joined by means of tenons (the correct method) into the underframe of the top. If the table was wider than the cheval mirror the original turned stretcher of the mirror could be extended by inserting a section, turned and perhaps ebonized, to fit. Alternatively, the standard ends would have the stretcher removed and the holes it left disguised with turned paterae, thus reproducing the first type of sofa table.

Where the legs on the wash stand were cut off the end grain of the timber would arouse no suspicion, as this is how the corner blocks of such a table frame were constructed. So apart from polishing and checking that all the screws and hinges used were old, little more needed to be done.

This kind of alteration would hardly be a worthwhile commercial proposition now that Pembroke tables and cheval mirrors command respectable prices. But sofa tables contrived some 20 years ago exist, often with the benefit of waxing, polishing and two decades of loving care. It can be difficult then to tell one of these fraudulent pieces, even if you know what to look for.

However, after a quarter of a century there will probably be signs of staining and stained polish being used in certain places; when it was applied it blended in, but now it may stand out plainly. If signs of tampering or restoration appear at places where an alteration might have occurred — such as the junction of the legs to the frame or the edge of the top — or if the leaves do not match in quality (which may be visible under strong light or sunlight) and if the rule joints between top and leaves look unnaturally raw or unnaturally dirty, then the piece could well be a modern contrivance, and should be priced accordingly.

A complication arises from a design fault in this type of table. If the grain runs across the top the veneer may have shrunk and cracked. To repair this the restorer would loosen and refix the top having closed up the split. Unfortunately this makes the top too short to allow the leaves to hang vertically. Easing the position of the hinges is one remedy, but the problem may be so bad that extra fillets of wood have to be inserted to the top. This is a necessary repair and does not of itself indicate any lack of authenticity.

1 *above*
A Victorian dressing table of the type that has been remade into a much more saleable sofa table, together with a cheval mirror, which provides the legs and stretcher. The back, sides and legs of the table were discarded, leaving the top, to which flaps were added from a Pembroke table. The ends of the mirror need to be cut down and the stretcher may need lengthening.

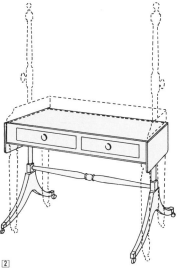

2
How a dressing table (with flaps added) and a cheval glass fit together to make a sofa table.

## Tripod Tea Tables

One of the most altered pieces of furniture is the tripod-base tea table. These were made in enormous numbers and in every range of quality from the 1740s onwards. The finest had dished or tray tops, the edges of which, during the period 1755–70, were carved and shaped in "piecrust" fashion. Alternatively they had a simple raised lip to form a tray top, the upper edge of which might be inlaid with a stringing of contrasting timber or even a brass line. The main surface of the top was sometimes brass inlaid but this is rare — the commonest form was plain and solid.

The tops were supported on single columns, the best of which were carved in classical or architectural forms with Rococo, leaf-capped and scrolling motifs. The legs would be carved at the knee, and the most desirable have claw and ball feet. All the carving will appear to stand proud of the outline and the claw and ball foot (representing the Sacred Pearl of Wisdom being held by the dragon's claw) should always appear as a good round ball seized by life-like claws.

Slightly lower down the social scale a finely carved base would support a perfectly plain, flat top. This would be fairly thick, approximately an inch at the centre, but chamfered on the underside of the outer edge to give the appearance of thinness. On tables of lesser quality there is less carving or none at all, but there is nothing wrong with a finely drawn plain table of this type, and good examples should not be undervalued.

*1 below*

An attractive mahogany tripod tea table with baluster turned stem, surmounted by a birdcage fixture and plain circular top. This is a most desirable type of table, much prone to "improvement" in its grander forms. But improvement is not the only point to watch for. In use, some bases and tops have been damaged beyond repair, and the surviving parts have sometimes been married off with alterations as necessary.

The top of this table does not sit perfectly on its centre—a bad sign—and it is unnaturally thin for a table of this proportion. It may be that the top has been reduced in thickness. To check for reduction, ascertain the lines of the two runners underneath, look obliquely along the table top and discover whether or not there are any dips or rises that fall on the line of one or other runner. See *Ill. 2,* opposite.

Nevertheless a plain top table will make only a fraction of the price accorded to a dished top, and it soon became evident to furniture makers and dealers that the old plain tops were sufficiently thick to give room for "improvement". Fortunately there are some very clear guides to indicate when such a table has been upgraded.

Nearly always, tripod tables were made to tip. This was done by pivoting the top on one side of the square supporting block that was fixed to the top of the column. Two runners were fixed to the underside of the top, precisely parallel and fitting close against the block. Two rounded sections like thick dowels were carved from the block to extend into two holes in the runners cut to receive them, forming the hinge. The top was fastened with a metal latch.

A sophisticated variation was the birdcage, which enables the top to turn as well as tip. This was made of two blocks of exactly the same size, approximately four inches apart and joined by (usually) four turned columns. The lower block had a large hole cut in its centre and the upper block a much smaller hole, again in the centre. The top of the column was turned to form a large spindle, which passed through the lower block. The top of the spindle was turned to a much smaller diameter to pass through the smaller hole in the top block, forming a column around which the two blocks would swivel without wobbling. To fasten the block or birdcage to the column, a wooden wedge was slipped through a hole cut in the column.

All these features can point towards — or away from — authenticity. First the runners are fixed to the underside of the table top with screws (originally, of course, hand-filed screws). An original tray top was made thick enough for these screws to be turned home without coming through the upper side. But when an "improver" dishes the top he has to take out a sufficient depth over most of the surface to leave a pronounced rim, and he must go as close as he dares to the ends of the screws to achieve this. Even if the original screws are removed and cut short, the holes stopped and the screws replaced, the holes themselves will still show or there will be small bumps in the new tray's surface. So to ensure that a tray top is original look carefully across the top along lines corresponding to the runners below and see if there are any regular marks. They may be disguised by distressing, scratches or stains, but once you know where to look, they are easy to spot.

Dishing a top is done on a lathe. The result, therefore, will be perfectly circular, but an 18th-century top will never be perfectly circular, for the wood will have shrunk across the grain and there may be as much as half an inch difference between the diameter measured along the grain and the same dimension across the grain.

Some piecrust borders have been added to table tops by simply gluing on sections of wood and then carving them into the correct patterns. The joints, however well disguised with carving and hard wax, can usually be discovered, and a strong light will reveal the grain of the timber not running in perfect accord with the rest of the top; tray tops and piecrust edges were not made like this in the 18th century. It might just be an innocent repair, but beware.

Wood's behaviour gives us another guide. Turn the table up to make sure the top does in fact belong to the bottom. When wood is exposed to the air it darkens gradually; and if a top has been in place upon its block for some considerable time this area will have been less exposed and will be lighter than the rest of the underside. If all is exactly as it should be, the area of light timber will match precisely the block which has protected it. While signs of more than one latch are acceptable as latches do break, all should have been fixed approximately in the same place; old holes and associated marks should be around the central position, not to one side.

Birdcages provide excellent guides to authenticity. Not only should there be a pale patch corresponding with the block, but period blocks will by now have shrunk. The columns however will not have shrunk in height (only in diameter) and so should protrude very slightly above the top of the upper block, where over the years they will have left perceptible bruises in exactly corresponding positions. These bruises along with the patch of paler wood are things the faker rarely achieves.

[2]
An examination of the underside shows that numerous screws have been used to fix runners. This is not necessarily a bad sign—it may only indicate that certain restorations have taken place. The catch, which may be a replacement, is not fitted in the original position, as the filled screw holes show. There is also a redundant hole to the right of the right-hand runner. Neither of these is a good sign.

There are bruises made by the slightly protruding columns of the birdcage—a good sign—but there are too many of them—a conclusively bad sign. This top has not only been reduced in thickness but was previously fitted to another table. Signs of wear suggest that the union or marriage occurred some considerable time ago, and it was probably done for reasons of utility rather than with intent to deceive. Nevertheless, this table is worth less than half its value had it been wholly original.

# 6:GLASS

DESPITE THE FACT that it is only a relatively small amount of glass that fetches high prices — prices comparable with works of art in other fields — there is quite a substantial amount of glass on the market that could deceive collectors. Some of it is undoubtedly made or altered to deceive buyers and enhance prices; much more is the result of honest reproduction. While it is only sensible to assess all antique glassware with careful knowledge, a blanket of suspicion should not be cast over old glass in general.

Whether a piece of glassware could be deceptive depends to a considerable extent on the seller. The maker of an entirely legitimate reproduction cannot be accused of deception, but the subsequent seller, by ignorance or design, may misdescribe a piece and so render it spurious. It would be unjust to refer to the factories making reproductions of 18th-century English glass in the 1930s as fakers, but it would be kind indeed to describe as anything less than fraudulent people who know their provenance yet try to sell them as authentic articles.

Knowledge is the key, and the purpose of this chapter is to record the kinds of glassware that have been reproduced or faked and to give some indications of how to tell them. Book-learning however, can never be the sole guide. The metal varies in appearance and feel, and it is only by handling and looking as well as reading that a fairly reliable sense of the genuine can be built up.

Museums provide many examples to look at and learn from: collectors' societies offer opportunities to look, handle, discuss and acquire knowledge. A great deal can also be learned from good dealers who, incidentally, by supplying a proper descriptive receipt bind themselves to their honest opinion and will make amends if they should be proved wrong.

**[1]**
On the left, a Roman head flask, 1st-4th century in style, possibly a European copy of the last ten years—height 6.7 in. (17 cm). On the right an imitation Roman jug rolled in sand—height 7 in. (17.8 cm). These are in current production.

## Ancient Glass

Forgeries of Egyptian glass sculptures began to appear early in the 20th century. In 1912 the British Museum purchased four glass canopic jars now shown to be fakes, probably made in Egypt; other items include Shawabti figures, statuettes and small animal sculptures. Common features were the purple-blue colour, the occasional remains of mould marks, and hollow moulding — originals were always cast in the solid. The maker cast the forgeries from moulds taken from ancient pieces; detection therefore relies on technical examination and methods of construction. Almost all the forgeries have been deliberately broken and repaired, with some portions missing to add the appearance of age.

The most notable glass products of the Roman Empire were the cameo glass vases of the 1st century A.D. In 1878 the Venice & Murano Co. showed imitations at the Paris Exhibition; Pauly et Cie, another Venetian firm, made similar versions. The glass used for Venetian cameo was a soda lime glass which resulted in softly modelled outlines giving an

**[2]**
The Corning Museum of Glass owned an Islamic ewer which showed signs of restoration. The Museum suffered a flood and the ewer was soaked. The water dissolved the glue and the piece was shown to have been made up from fragments.

impression of age. A pitted surface, common to all Venetian cameos, helps the illusion. Two vases which have deceived until recently are a ''1st century A.D. Roman vase'' in the Toledo Museum in Ohio, which was published in the first guidebook to the glass collections, and a tall vase in the Moore Collection at Yale University Art Gallery, described in 1927 as ''Hellenistic first century B.C.''.

The Mainz firm of Ludwig Fellmer was a major producer of Roman shapes. A page from their pattern book, published by Spiegl in *Glas Des Historismus*, shows simple flasks and bottles and more complex jugs and vases with trailed and pincered decoration, as well as mould-blown vases in barrel shape reminiscent of the genuine ''Frontinus'' marked pieces of the 1st century A.D.

Modern sources for ancient glass forgeries are the Israeli, Turkish and Egyptian glassmakers; they work in primitive conditions, using clay moulds taken from original glasses. The wares they make are determined, as always, by market prices: the most popular fakes are small mould blown bottles or altar cruets decorated with Christian symbols. Artificial ageing can include acid etching, putting a covering of sand onto the surface of the hot glass, and the application of chemicals while the glass is hot. Occasionally the forger will glue genuine flakes of iridescence onto the surface of the copy. Modern chemicals sprayed onto the glass can induce a deceptive flaking effect. Weathering is an important part of ancient faked glass as it very conveniently disguises joins, as well as possible discrepancies in colour matching.

The Corning Museum of Glass in upstate New York has identified some ancient glasses as ''marriages'' of genuine broken fragments. The identified conglomerate vessels show ingenuity in combining quite disparate elements, such as sticking together two genuine and complete objects to form a hitherto unrecorded shape.

**German Historical Reproductions** In the last half of the 19th century, archaeological excavations, the development of museums, exhibitions of famous glass collections, publications such as Ruskin's *Stones of Venice* and pattern books crammed with eclectic designs created a fashion for historical reproductions which swept Europe.

In Germany, the style known as ''Historismus'' covers all copies from Frankish claw beakers to 18th-century enamelled Humpen. The Rheinische Glashütten-Aktien-Gesellschaft — the glassworks of the Joint-Stock Company in Köln-Ehrenfeld in the Rhineland — was the most important factory for this work. Founded in 1864, it made table-glass and bottles but from 1879-90, under the directorship of Oskar Rauter, it concentrated on revivals of Roman, Venetian and Old German styles. Designs used blown glass techniques with a little cutting and engraving but no painting or gilding. Subdued colours included the characteristic ''antique-green''. The flawless quality of Köln-Ehrenfeld glass means that it is impossible to mistake it for anything but Historismus.

3
Two ''Historismus'' vases. On the left, clear glass with applied prunts painted green and with engraved scroll-work. Possibly from the Köln-Ehrenfeld factory in the 1880s— height 6.3 in. (16 cm). On the right, a four-handled green vase with slight iridescence. It bears a very faint circular mark ''SAALBURG'', and was made by Loetz Witwe, Austria, for Tschernich & Co., Haifa—height 7.3 in. (18.5 cm).

4 *below*
Designs drawn from the 1886 pattern book of the Rheinische Glashütten.

Page from a pattern book and price list of Carl H. Muller, Hamburg, reproduced from *Glas des Historismus* by Walter Spiegl, 1980.

In 1865 Carl Heinrich Muller moved from Thuringia to Hamburg where he established a glassblowing workshop. His copies of 16th- or 17th-century Venetian goblets were made by lampwork and sold as authentic pieces by dealers in the Netherlands. From 1876-7 Muller combined his stylistic and technical innovations to create many dragon-stem goblets and covers which, almost without exception, were classified as 16th- or 17th-century. Increased awareness and research into

19th-century glass records has helped to identify these fakes.

At Petersdorf in Bohemia, Fritz Heckert operated a glass decorating works from 1866 and added glassmaking facilities in 1889. His pattern books illustrate an astonishing variety of deliberate imitations of Humpen, decanters and beakers enamelled with figures, coats-of-arms, inscriptions and dates. Genuine glasses in museum collections would provide inspiration but Heckert's enamelling is flat and without modelling.

## The Venetian Revival

The fashion for historicism coincided with the revival of the Venetian glass industry in the 1840s. In 1861 the Museum of Murano was opened with the express intention of stimulating this revival by offering antiquarian models, including Roman glass and Venetian glasses from the classic periods of the 16th and 17th centuries. This achieved the desired result and for the next 40 years Venetian glassmakers dealt almost exclusively with copies and variations based on their glorious past.

The most famous company was that set up by Antonio Salviati in 1859 with English patronage, but there were numerous others, often specializing in certain aspects of antique reproductions. One example was Francesco Borella, who made objects with gold leaf decoration based on Roman examples discovered in the catacombs. Rosa Barovier Mentasti provides a detailed account of the entire period in her book *Il Vetro Veneziano*.

The obsession with the past has never totally left Venice. The houses of Scalabrin and Daltin and Valle Valerio make enamelled and gilt versions of 16th-century marriage goblets and processional bowls; Antico Forno, Paolo Rossi and Piero Ragazzi specialize in reproductions of archaeological finds and mosaic glass, while Vetraria Alt make imitations of 19th-century paperweights and ornaments.

Following the exhibitions of Venetian glass in Paris and London in the 1860s and 70s, European and American glass-makers joined the rush to create exact 16th-century copies. English glassmakers were able to examine the originals in the collection formed by Felix Slade which was displayed as early as 1850; it was donated to the British Museum in 1868 and published in 1871. Jenkinson in Glasgow, Northwood in Stourbridge and Lutz in America created serpent-stem goblets and latticino vases and bowls with a high precision worthy of the originals.

## 18th-Century English Glass

Collectors of 18th-century English glass have a number of pitfalls to contend with. They are in three main categories. First, there are the deliberate fakes, of good quality and proportions with all the right combinations of feet, bowl and stems, but the quality of the metal is suspect. Next are the glasses in designs that never existed in the original repertoire

2
A beaker of soda glass with air bubbles, figures on either side of the coat-of-arms, the name IONES TAMATZ and the date 1624. Another "Tamatz" beaker in the Corning Museum is dated 1610. Both were made by Fritz Heckert, who based them on an original in the Kunstgewerbemuseum, Berlin; height 4.7 in. (12 cm).

3
A Venetian cameo glass vase, dating probably from the 1870s. The decoration was copied from a terracotta plaque of the 2nd century B.C. Venetian cameo glass of this period can be deceptive. The metal used was a soft soda lime glass, which was inclined to pitting. This, combined with the softness of the relief cutting, can give a misleading impression of great age. English cameo glassware of the same period shows much crisper, sharper carving in the harder metal.

This glass has the very flared bowl often associated with Dutch glasses of the 18th century but the foot is solid and much too flat. It would seem to be 19th century, if not later. There is little wear on the base and under ultraviolet light it shows a complete soda content.

**Slag**
A generic name given to pressed glass of the late 19th century with marbled colouring of purples, greens, blacks, blues and whites. It is said to derive from the addition of the waste by-product from steel furnaces. Some technologists doubt whether that material would constitute a compatible mixture with glass. Modern copies from the original moulds have been made at the Davidson factory.

and where the material is quite obviously wrong. The third category — and perhaps the most difficult to spot for the beginner — are the glasses of 18th-century date produced in Europe and Scandinavia in imitation of *"verre d'Angleterre"*, the fashion for which swept Europe after the discovery of lead glass by Ravenscroft in the 1670s and the subsequent development of an English national style.

Continental glassmakers undertook visits to English glasshouses in an effort to discover their secrets while English glassmakers were enticed abroad to work in developing glass industries. A notable example was James Keith, a master glassblower from Newcastle who emigrated to the Nostetangen factory in Norway in 1755. The impact of the English style on Norwegian glass is evident until 1830 and is echoed in Finnish, Swedish and Dutch glass. The Peter F. Heering collection of Danish glass contains many examples often thought of as English. The whole question of Scandinavian imitations needs to be more widely publicized. Even now it is possible to come across glass described in saleroom catalogues as English and dated to the early 18th-century, when in fact it is Scandinavian and 50 years later.

Eighteenth-century glass began to be reproduced during the 19th century by glassmakers eager to compare their own skills with those of their predecessors. The appearance of deliberate fakes in the early 20th century coincided with the beginnings of research into the history of English glass and the increased numbers of sales in the auction rooms. In 1897 Albert Hartshorne published *Old English Glasses*, the first complete survey of the subject; the next 30 years saw publication of the classic works by Francis Buckley, Grant Francis, H. J. Powell, W. A. Thorpe and Dudley Westropp, among many others.

With the revival of the Adam style in the Edwardian period the glass firms churned out imitations of 18th-century glasses to match the reproductions of period furniture. A glance through company pattern books, especially in the Stourbridge area, for the appropriate dates reveals page upon page of lookalikes. Silesian and baluster stems do not occur very often; the outright favourites were air and opaque twists with some facet cut stems and the occasional drawn trumpet stem. The large firms of Stevens and Williams, Thos Webb & Sons, H. G. Richardson and Walsh of Birmingham were the chief producers and may have supplied the Birmingham retailers Hill-Ouston. The catalogue issued by that company in 1934 offered a bewildering assortment of cut, blown and engraved glass with some emphasis on reproduction and "antique" services and individual items. Special attention was given to wineglasses, which are the most accurate of the antique copies and the most frightening for collectors.

Pattern books, catalogues and photographs of fake glasses are obviously of great help when it comes to identifying forgeries, but there is no substitute for constant handling. Only in this way can both knowledge and a sixth sense be acquired. Each period of glassmaking used certain techniques peculiar to its own time which, when recognized, can give

② *right*
Part of a page from the pattern book
of H. G. Richardson and Sons,
Wordsley, 1910–1916. Many of the
glasses were bought in from other
makers including F. & C. Osler of
Birmingham to be cut and
engraved, often by freelance
decorators. The facet-cut stem wine
at the top could be bought with
matching tumbler, jug, finger bowl
and monteith (although the last two
items both meant a double lipped
wine cooler). Matching services
often consisted of glass bought from
different firms. In 1918 Richardsons
made red and white twist glasses
mentioned in the pattern book as
''foreign reproductions made on
gadget''—see p. 87.

③ a, b, c *below*
A selection of reproduction 18th-
and 19th-century drinking glasses
from the 1934 Hill-Ouston
catalogue. The Hill-Ouston
Company was based at the
Alexandra Works, Macdonald
Street, Birmingham; the address of
the London showroom was 50 Frith
Street, London W1. This catalogue
was the ninth issued by the firm.
The goblets are often seen at
antique fairs masquerading as
genuine 19th-century examples.

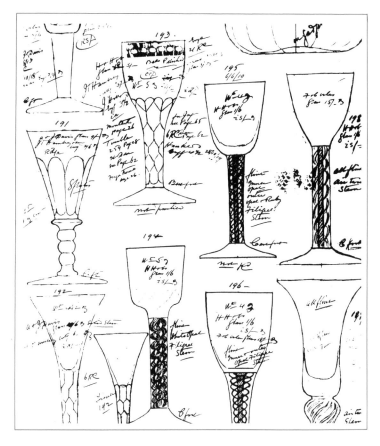

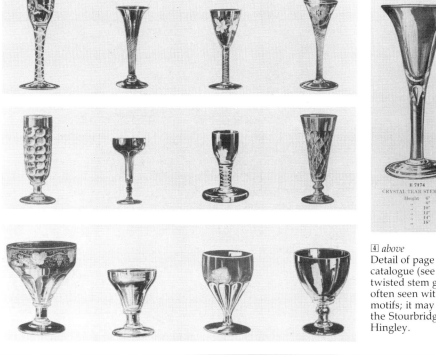

E 7174
CRYSTAL TEAR STEM VASE
Height 6"
    8"
    10"
    12"
    14"
    18"

E 7261
TWISTED STEM VASE
Height 11"

④ *above*
Detail of page 36 of the Hill-Ouston
catalogue (see *Ill. 3*, left). The
twisted stem glass on the right is
often seen with engraved Jacobite
motifs; it may have been made at
the Stourbridge works of L. & S.
Hingley.

① *below*
Lead glass and balusters. *left*: A wineglass imitating "façon de Venise" glasses of the late 17th and early 18th centuries. The collars at the base of the bowl are correct as is the winged stem. Although shape and proportions are accurate the metal, which is soda, is too clear and bright, even though it shows the very fine air bubbles of the originals. A genuine glass would certainly have had a thinly blown folded foot (the foot of any glass generally tells one far more than any other single element). Late 19th or early 20th century, height 4.9 in. (12.5 cm).
*centre*: A copy of a short ale glass of the mid-18th century. Apart from the metal, which has the brightness of brand new glass, the foot has no pontil mark and is not folded. On closer examination the ribs on the bowl have not been twisted by hand but show the uniformity of a mould blown glass. Probably of Continental origin within the last ten years, height 5.9 in. (15 cm).
*right:* A wine or dram glass, 4.7 in. (12 cm) high, attempting to look like a 1710 baluster but made in a variety of sizes at the Edinburgh and Leith Glass Works *c.* 1920. The same factory was making large baluster goblets with folded feet just after the Second World War which were very good copies with a reasonably accurate greyish tinge. The designer of this glass had obviously looked very closely at classic early English balusters, including the folded foot (a leftover from the Venetian influence but a practical idea that added strength and reduced the risk of chipping).

clues to date and place. An awareness of these methods will allow the collector to spot the types of fake that appear in the Hill-Ouston catalogue. Out of all the techniques the most contentious and misunderstood feature is the pontil mark.

## The Pontil Mark

The pontil mark is simply the scar left when the finished glass is broken off from the pontil iron. During the 18th and 19th centuries most tablewares were transferred to the pontil rod in order to allow excess glass to be sheared away, to shape the pouring lip and to add the handles on jugs. The practice continues to this day for certain items such as jugs and large bowls. Virtually all hand-made glass, whether it is contemporary or antique, will carry signs of a pontil mark. It is not a guarantee of age.

The appearance of the pontil ("punty" or "puntee") on 18th-century glassware was a feature that was not lost on the makers of reproduction glasses. One Stourbridge firm that specialized in this trade was H. G. Richardson and Sons. From the 1840s until the 1880s the company pioneered many new techniques, but by the early 20th century they were concentrating a noticeable part of their output on reproductions. The drawings of "old glass" in their pattern books often bear the additional note "pontil not ground" or the equivalent: "not puntied".

There are genuine 18th-century glasses that do have ground pontils. Facet-cut wineglasses are one example where it was simple enough to grind the pontil as part of the cutting process. The cutting wheel leaves a more or less circular area of polished glass in various diameters, some as small as the original pontil, others go across the entire foot. More expensive pieces would also have the scar removed, including cruet bottles and containers fitted into silver or plated stands. The flat base helped the glass to stand firmly and avoided damage to the stand or to table tops.

A variation on the classic pontil mark is a type sometimes called a waffle. It worked on the same principle, but the molten glass on the end of the pontil iron was impressed with a criss-cross pattern, using the glassmaker's pincers. The result was that only four small points were stuck onto the glass, making it easier to remove the iron. It is seen most often on European glass, including Venetian. In the 20th century some of the ''Monart'' vases made by John Moncrieff of Perth have a raised circular pontil, usually matt, which may occasionally still bear the factory paper label. Studio glassmakers sometimes use an oxy-acetylene torch to re-heat the pontil, thereby softening the sharp edges and eliminating the need to grind it away. Other studio glass firms will impress their trade mark into the pontil while it is hot.

The collector will come across glass without any visible sign of a pontil. The classic example is the majority of Roman blown glass, although there are odd exceptions to this rule. Some glass which is hand made is stuck onto a large flat disc of glass on the end of the pontil and any unsightly marks on the edges of feet or bases may be ground away. In such instances other factors need to be looked at to give a clue to age. Glass that has been pressed in metal moulds will not have the pontil mark; examples include 19th-century items and mass produced moulded 20th-century glass such as Crystal d'Arques.

## Other 18th-Century Fakes

Engraved Jacobite and Williamite glasses have been produced continuously since the originals were made and therefore accurate dating becomes a priority. In the case of Williamite glass, one needs to look at shape, style and colour as the engraving tends to follow an established tradition of William III on horseback surrounded by various mottoes and inscriptions, including many references to the Battle of the Boyne on 1st July 1690. With Jacobite glass suspicion is usually aroused if the glass carries too many explicit references to the Young

[3]
A wineglass dated about 1870 held in the gadget as it would have appeared during manufacture.

During the 19th century in England the gadget was introduced as a speedier alternative to the pontil rod. It consists of a hollow steel tube about 54in. (135cm) long containing a spring-loaded rod. The working end of the gadget consists of two jaws which open when the plunger is operated. The foot of the hot wineglass is slid into the jaws, which are clamped back to hold it while the bowl is opened out and the rim is sheared. The action and pressure of the jaws leave a ghost image on the top surface of the foot. The mark left on the underside is a characteristic ''T'' or ''Y''. When the glass has been completed the plunger is pushed to open the jaws again and release the glass.

The period for the introduction of the gadget has been given as c.1760–1800. This seems too early however, as no glasses of that date carry the ghost image of the jaws. The majority of glasses with the mark date from the 1860s onwards and it is likely that the gadget did not come into use until about this time.

[2] left
Airtwists and facet cut stems. *left*: The form of a 1785 wineglass complete with hollow diamond cuts on the stem and a cut and polished border to the bowl. To an unsuspecting customer the stem and bowl of this glass may give little cause for doubt, except for the clearness of the glass itself; the foot however once again gives away an early 20th century date—it is very uniform and has a flat shallow pontil that more often than not would have been polished in the original. Compare this glass with the design in *Ill. 2*, p. 85—the height of 5.1 in. (13 cm) matches the pattern exactly. In 1912 the price for this glass was 17s. ($1.25 or 85p). *centre*: A copy of a 1750 glass with nearly all the hallmarks of the

genuine item, such as the honeycomb moulded round funnel bowl, shoulder knopped multi-spiral air twist stem, conical foot, a pontil and a marvellous ring when struck. Unfortunately the foot is too perfect and lacks any tool marks. Date *c*. 1920, height 5.9 in. (15 cm). *right*: A cordial glass with square bucket bowl echoing a 1750 glass; the originals are frequently engraved with privateer ships and inscriptions. The slightly flared rim causes suspicion, the mercury twist is uneven, the foot is much too thick and has a shear mark on the edge suggesting the foot was applied as a complete disc and cut down to more acceptable proportions. Possibly early 20th century, height 5.5 in. (14 cm).

[1]
Jacobite glasses of the 20th century. On the left, a glass with a lemon squeezer foot suggesting an 1800 date, but the engraving contains an oak leaf, a thistle, a star, a rose with the customary closed and half-open buds and the word "Fiat"—too many features to be probable. The yellowing tinge of this glass suggests a Bohemian origin, perhaps 1930s—height 3.9 in. (10 cm). The wineglass on the right with an incised twist stem is one of a group of wineglasses which have appeared regularly. It has the same combination of motifs but without the word "Fiat" and the foot is much too flat. 20th century—height 6.3 in. (16 cm).

[2]
A tumbler enamelled after a Beilby goblet in the Victoria and Albert Museum. Made at Cumbria Crystal in the 1970s, signed in diamond point "L.M.S."—height 3.5 in. (9 cm).

Pretender such as roses, oak leaves, stars and Latin phrases and dates — the originals supported the Stuart cause with more subtle allusions. Some "Jacobite" engraving — including the diamond-point "Amen" subject matter — has been added onto genuine period wine glasses.

There is a very real difficulty in judging whether any engraving is contemporary with the glass; 18th-century engraving was of medium quality and is easily imitated. Some historians have attempted to decipher certain hands by looking closely at the details of Jacobite glass but there is still no hard and fast rule that can be applied.

It may be of some slight consolation to collectors to know that certain glasses have not been faked. Among these are "Lynn" glasses with horizontal ribs which have only risen in price in the last few years, and ratafia glasses which for some reason have also escaped the attentions of the forger.

## Decanters

Decanters from the late 18th century have been copied profusely, whereas the earlier cruciform shapes have been left alone. Replicas of club-shaped decanters in blue and green with gilded imitation wine labels were imported from Czechoslovakia in the 1930s but are too shiny and glossy and their gilding is of poor quality. Another group of fakes which appeared a few years ago were white opaline mallet-shaped decanters with painted medallions. They may have been made in Portugal and were good copies but their extra thickness and the fact that too many appeared at once gave them away.

Irish decanters impressed with the names of the glasshouses such as Waterloo, County Cork; B. Edwards, Belfast; and Waterford Penrose and Cork Glass Co. have been favourite targets. The Cork fakes appear most often. Signs to look for are the bright quality of the metal, clearly readable lettering (sometimes with only the word "Cork") and a noticeable degree of overblow over the edge of the base mould. Period pieces show a fire polished finish on the peg of the stopper. Fake stoppers were blown into a badly fitting mould and one half is slightly staggered, resulting in a bad fit. It is also rare to find a very clear, original Waterford mark.

## Cut Glass

The correct identification of cut glass must be one of the most difficult areas of all glass authentication. In England the same methods of roughing the initial design followed by smoothing and final polishing remained unchanged from the early 19th century until the 1950s. By 1900 the technique of acid polishing was gradually being introduced, which gives some help to collectors. Polishing on a brush wheel with putty powder retained the crispness and grain marks of the stone wheels but acid polishing removes all these signs and tends to round off the edges of the cuts. However, by the early 20th century some accurate reproductions were still finished by brush polishing

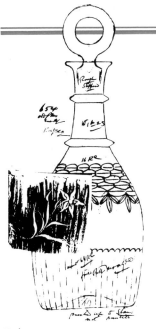

**3** *above*
1916 dated pattern of
H.G. Richardson & Sons showing a
replica of a 1790 decanter, together
with a pattern for decoration. The
notes mention "rough stoppered",
"fine rib moulded", and "pushed
up to stand not puntied".

**4** *below*
Three marked Cork Glass Co.
decanters, but only the centre one is
genuine. On some fakes the name
of the factory is too close to the
pontil mark.

**6** *right*
To make a three-part glass: the
blowing iron is dipped into the pot
of molten glass for the gather (*a*)
which is rolled on the marver and
blown out (*b*). Gradually the bowl is
shaped either by hand or by
blowing into a mould (*c*). A small
gather of glass is applied to the base
of the bowl (*d*) and formed into the
stem (*e*). The foot is then added
either as a blown foot, consisting of
another bubble attached to the stem
and opened out (*f*) or alternatively
another gather, fixed to the stem, is
squeezed into shape by the
footboard. Once the foot is made (*g*)
the glass is transferred from the
blowing iron onto the pontil rod (*h*)
so that any final shaping can be
done. A small bit of hot glass is
gathered on the tip of the pontil rod
and stuck on the exact centre of the
underneath of the foot. The blowing
iron is cracked off (*i*), the glass is
reheated, the bowl is opened out
and the rim is sheared (*j*). Excess
glass on the rim was always sheared
off on 18th-century glasses, leaving
a characteristic nick or bump in the
rim. Finally, the glass is broken off
the pontil rod and taken to the
annealing lehr . The whole
operation is performed by a chair—a
team of four glassmakers, each one
assisting with part of the process.

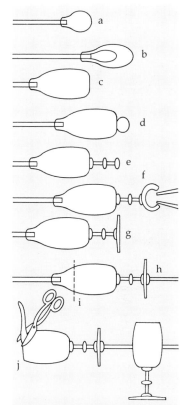

**5** *right*
Opaque and mixed twists. *left*: This
glass has the wrong proportions;
the excessively flared rim does not
leave enough room for the stunted
engraving of hops and barley and
the stem is too thin and spindly.
The stem sits on top of the foot
whereas in the 18th century the
twist would have gone slightly into
the foot. It may be a genuine mid to
late 19th-century attempt at
reproduction, height 5.9 in. (15 cm).
*centre*: Handling this glass gives an
immediate shock because of its
extreme lightness. The entire glass
has been made by lampwork: the
bowl is very thin but has a thick rim
and the granular bubbly texture of
the opaque twist is typical of

modern fakes. Both the air and
opaque twists are jumbled together
and not separate as on genuine
18th-century examples. A very
recent fake, height 7.7 in. (19.5 cm).
*right*: A slightly heavier piece and a
much closer attempt at an 18th-
century glass but it still has signs of
lampwork. The bowl rim is too thick
and is much too irregular. The stem

shows the same grainy effect as the
central glass. It has the major error
that the folded foot turns upwards
rather than underneath (in
lampwork the folded foot turns
upwards automatically while the
glass is being shaped). Very
recently made; height 6.6 in.
(16.7 cm).

[1] *above*
A deceptive cut glass bowl after an Irish pattern, one of a group of similar items often found at antique fairs.

[2] *above*
H.G. Richardson reproductions of "George III" cut glass designs: early 20th century.

[3]
"Demi-Crystal Reproduction Antique Designs" of early 19th-century glass from the Hill-Ouston catalogue, 1934.

to achieve the authentic texture of much older examples.

By the late 19th century the quality of the glass had improved considerably, tending towards "whiter" clarity without the slight greyish tinge of old glass. This comparison becomes obvious if the collector can place a modern cut glass next to a known 18th-century glass. A recognition of this brightness combined with a knowledge of the preferred 19th-century shapes of jugs and other items gives at least two clues to help unravel this puzzle.

**Irish Cut Glass** Many of the firms who specialized in reproduction 18th-century wines also turned out some very good copies of "old Waterford glass". After 1918 old glass, especially Irish, began to make high premiums and it began to be faked. Further confusion was added by Hartshorne and in 1916 by J.H. Yoxall, who perpetrated the myth of the blue tint in Waterford glass. As early as 1920 Dudley Westropp, the first sensible authority on Irish glass, discounted the theory quite adamantly: "I would wish now, once for all, to state that the glass made in Waterford has not the decided blue or dark tint always ascribed to it." Even after such a categorical statement the legend continues.

The nonsensical comments made by Yoxall were reiterated by Mrs Graydon-Stannus who apparently inherited a glass factory in Ireland and became fascinated with Irish glass. From 1926 to 1936 she operated the "Gray-Stan" factory in London which introduced mottled and bubbled glass in the current art glass fashions. It is generally accepted throughout the antiques trade and by glass historians that she was responsible for confusing the history of Anglo-Irish glass and originating Irish reproductions to substantiate her theories. Some genuine glasses, including drawn trumpet wines, were "enhanced" with new areas of flat cutting. In 1920 she published a small book, *Old Irish Glass*, and followed it a year later with a larger revised edition. The text of the book is full of inaccuracies and many glasses are misrepresented — including the candelabra, candlesticks and chandeliers which often feature 20th-century drops and arms, marble "Bossi" pedestals and metal fittings.

## Chandeliers and Candelabra

The difficulties in identifying genuine cut glass objects are multiplied when it comes to chandeliers and candelabra. An invaluable source of information can be the 18th-century trade cards of London glass dealers, but at the end of the 18th century it was already customary for chandeliers to be dismantled and re-formed to the latest fashion. That tradition means that one can never be absolutely certain how much alteration has taken place. The huge market for lighting fixtures in the 19th century has furnished the restoration trade with a readily available supply of components which can be reassembled at will.

Drops for chandeliers were pressed in a mould before being given a final cut to sharpen the edges; a similar idea appeared in 19th-century holloware when cutting shops used pressed blanks. The benefits included a saving on the expense of the rougher plus the cut design being already impressed into the article. It can be difficult to recognize this type of cutting, especially if it is well done. Some Continental glass, currently sold at markets and discount warehouses, is advertised as hand-cut, but a close examination of the surface will reveal the flow marks of pressed glass.

## Identification by Technique

A bewildering variety of techniques and machinery to improve glass production and give novel methods of decoration was patented in the 19th century. The dates of their introduction can be an invaluable help for identification.

**Venetian Diamond Pattern** Apsley Pellatt and Benjamin Richardson introduced this pattern during the late 1840s, using compressed air to blow glass into metal moulds. The finished effect was of a close diamond quilting with the criss-cross ribs in fairly high relief. Other firms such as Powells later took up this form of decoration. But because the idea of moulded glass is normally thought to be a process of the later 19th or 20th century, the pieces are often wrongly dated.

Acid Etching The utility of hydrofluoric acid as a decorating medium was first realized in Sweden in the 1770s, but it was only in the mid-19th century that its full potential was exploited with the opening of acid decorating workshops. The process was two-part: first, the outline was etched and then a second dip in the acid gave the shading effects. Because the acid acts in a uniform way the shading has a matt, satin-like frosted finish with no appreciable grain or pitting.

A variation of the technique became popular from the 1890s and is seen often on glassware made for hotels and shipping lines. Instead of the two-stage process a copper plate was carved with the required design. A fluoride etching paste was filled into the design and transferred onto the glass using tissue paper. The paste etched the glass very lightly, giving a clear if somewhat faint design without the deep linear outline of the first process. Top quality 19th-century acid etching has not been faked as it is almost impossible to achieve the same quality of result—plus the fact that any modern attempt would cost far more than the genuine article.

In the 1870s engineering firms began to market geometric etching machines which led to the mass production of glasses decorated with linear patterns including circles and the Greek key. Since then many countries have capitalized on this quick form of decoration; much of it has come from Belgium. It can be difficult to date these glasses because there is little difference in quality in the actual etching. In the 1970s a great deal of Portuguese acid etched ware of very good quality appeared. The Stourbridge glass firms abandoned etching in the 1970s, preferring sandblasting as a decorative technique.

**Flint Glass**
Lead glass is given a variety of terms which can cause an absolute muddle for the collector. "Flint" is recognized by glassmakers to mean clear, transparent glass and nothing else. It no longer refers to the ingredients of the glass metal. The tradition behind the term goes back to George Ravenscroft, who followed Italian practice and believed he had to use flints or pebbles for the basic raw ingredient. Flints were calcined and ground to give the silica that is now much more easily provided in the form of sand. Even after sand was used, the term "flint" continued in general use and takes us back 300 years in an unbroken line.

The other term that confuses many is the word crystal—cut crystal or crystal glass—presumably intending to suggest both clarity and the sparkle of cutting. Glass itself does not have a crystalline structure as minerals do; in scientific terms it is a supercooled liquid.

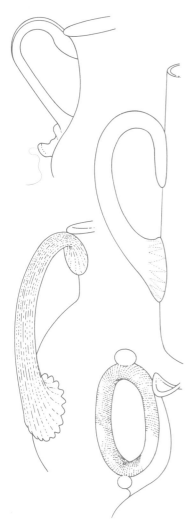

**Sandblasting** In 1870 the American Benjamin C. Tilghman patented a sandblast machine which was exhibited three years later in the Vienna Exhibition. The patent specified "a stream of sand or other abrasive powder, usually dry, but sometimes mixed with water, projected with more or less force and velocity to strike and pulverize the surfaces of glass, stone, metal and other materials upon which it is directed".

First use of the sandblast was on window and plate glass, then it was employed to mark glasses with the government weights and measures mark. From the 1880s it was used on cheap pressed tumblers with commemorative inscriptions. Even at low pressures the sandblast gives a very granular texture to the designs that is quite different in appearance and touch from wheel engraving or acid etching. Letters and numbers will show gaps where the ties in the paper stencil held the central portions of the characters. It is advisable to distinguish this technique as it is commonly referred to as "engraved" in an attempt to give it an upmarket image.

**Intaglio** Intaglio is another term that causes confusion. In general use it means any decoration that is incised into the surface of the object but in 1891 John Northwood I at the Stevens and Williams factory developed a new form of engraving which he also christened intaglio. The new process was a halfway stage between copper wheel engraving and cutting—it did not have the finesse and drawing-like qualities of wheel engraving nor was it restricted to the geometric patterns of cutting. Decoration was still by means of revolving wheels but of small diameter, from 1" to 4", and made of stone. Since it was introduced it has gradually overtaken other forms of decoration so that now it forms the main decorative process in most large glass factories.

The characteristic patterns consist of flowers and leaves, the curving C-shape scroll possible with the intaglio or "tag" wheel being especially useful for the latter. The profile of an intaglio cut reveals one very sharp edge that dips in at right angles into the glass while the other edge is much broader and flatter and shades away back to the surface of the glass.

**The Design of Handles** During the 1860s various methods of applying handles to jugs and vases superseded the traditional method in which a hot strip of glass was attached at the top of a jug, near the lip, pulled downward and attached at a point lower on the body. About the mid-1860s the method was reversed, providing a stronger join at the base of the handle. Handles were now given more attention, resulting in many adaptations—see the examples, left. *continued on page 97*

1a *top left*
The "pump" handle was used throughout the 18th century. It continued in use sporadically even after 1860.

1b *top right*
The "dab" handle, pulled up from the base to give a thinner join at the top.

1c *lower left*
The "shell" handle, introduced in the late 1860s, moulded and then applied onto the glass. The shell was also used for feet and as a purely decorative feature.

1d *lower right*
"Rope twist"—seen in a number of variations, often wrapped around the neck of a jug. The technique is similar to that used to make the incised twist stems of 18th-century wines.

1 *above*
Four mould-blown flasks made to
deceive and acquired in the Middle
East within the last ten years. On
the left is a square section flask with
two panels of the Menorah
candlestick and two with a stylized
plant; purchased in Damascus in
1979, height 4.9 in. (12.5 cm). The
hexagonal flask, centre left, has
very faint images of the Menorah
and other figures. The white stain
on the neck and shoulder is too
obvious an attempt at weathering. It
is a product of a small workshop in
Damascus which specializes in
glasses with Christian and Jewish
symbols; height 3.3 in. (8.3 cm).

The blue flask with an erotic
scene, centre right, was purchased
in Pergamon in 1976 but may be
from the same Damascus factory,
height 3.7 in. (9.5 cm). The amber
flask on the right with interlocking
circles is based on 3rd century A.D.
originals. A flange of glass remains
on the neck where the mould was
badly fitted. It was bought in
Damascus in 1979, height 3.9 in.
(10 cm).

2
The small vase on the left with three
handles is from the same Damascus
workshop referred to under *Ill. 1*
and has been dipped in acid to give
a false patination; height
2.6 in. (6.5 cm). The jug with blue
stripes is probably 1920 or 1930s
Venetian, a very good copy that is
almost successfully ''genuine'',
height 4.3 in. (11 cm). The glass of
the fish fragment may be original
but it has been re-cut; length 2 in.
(5 cm). The core-formed flask is
another Damascus fake; length 3 in.
(7.5 cm).

1 *left*
A selection from the display by Hoffman of Vienna and Prague shown at the 1862 London Exhibition. The styles continued in Northern Bohemia into the 1880s but are often dated 40 or 50 years earlier, especially the decanter with the applied snake, the central vase and the handled jug on the right. It would come as no surprise to find these pieces described as either French or English *c.* 1840-50 but the decoration is generally too ornate and fussy for that period. The Humpen is also much too slick and brash to be mistaken for a 17th- or 18th-century original. Some early 19th-century fake Humpen were made by Johann Georg Bühler who worked in Munich.

The ruby cased vase engraved with figures may have been made by F. Zach who worked during the third quarter of the 19th century, possibly for a time in England. A covered cup by Zach, now in the Metropolitan Museum of Art in New York, was featured in the 1910 catalogue of the J. Pierpoint Morgan collection where the author tried to prove it was made by a 17th-century engraver, even suggesting that he had been a wood carver who worked sporadically on glass. It was not until 1964, when an article entitled ''The Glass Engraver F. Zach: 17th or 19th Century'' by Robert Morgan appeared in *Apollo*, that the oft-repeated 17th-century attribution was finally disproved.

2
This bowl and vase demonstrate the extremes of Venetian reproduction—very careful accuracy contrasts with freer interpretation. The bowl is one of a group of millefiori and mosaic bowls made by the Venice and Murano Glass and Mosaic Co., founded in 1859 by Salviati; 6.5 in. (16.4 cm). They are the best examples of the historicizing attitude inspired by the museum in Murano. In 1878 the Paris Exhibition catalogue referred to ''Reproduction of Roman Murrhine, including Roman Paterae or bowls of various colours.'' Some bowls have a cane with the letters ''VM''—possibly for the maker Vincenzo Moretti, but more likely to be the trademark of the company. Like the originals, the bowl is fused in a two-part mould and ground on both sides. They were made in small numbers due to cost—a 12 in. (30.5 cm) bowl cost 5,000 francs.

The vase with trailed decoration is suggestive of Egyptian core-formed vessels but it is blown and is far too large to be genuine. Made by Fratelli Toso about 1910 and called ''Fenicio'', it is 6.4 in. (16.2 cm) tall.

③ *right*
English colour twist wine glasses, especially with rare colour combinations, fetch high prices, while 18th-century Dutch examples are still relatively cheap and underrated. The red and white twist glass is such a Continental example: under ultraviolet light it fluoresces green/yellow confirming the soda content. The blue and white twist glass shows a very good quality stem but the clarity, the lack of marks on the bowl and the very flat, disc-like foot suggest either a late 19th- or early 20th-century date, made in England with a high lead content (confirmed by inspection under ultraviolet light).

④ *below, right*
These coloured 18th-century decanters illustrate the varying degrees of certainty which the collector can expect to encounter. The Hollands decanter on the left is genuine 18th-century with correct outline, colour and gilding and with the original stopper initialled ''H'' to match the Hollands label.

On the blue decanter in the centre the grain of the stone or iron cutting wheel has left pronounced striations which are a feature of 18th- and 19th-century cut glass. The hollow facets on the body are typical of the 18th century. The stopper, which seems original on first inspection, shows a different composition to the body under ultraviolet light suggesting two possibilities—that it is a contemporary stopper but from a different factory or that it is a very good later copy. Stoppers can easily be ground to fit decanters which have lost their originals. One helpful tip in spotting replacements is that occasionally both stopper and decanter will carry matching marks scratched on at the factory to ensure that they were not split up.

The third decanter has all the characteristics of 18th-century examples but odd details raise some doubts. The stopper has been acid polished and has not been ground into the neck as with the green decanter, the cutting of the Brandy label is crude and ungainly and the glass itself seems too thick overall. But there may be valid reasons behind these queries. The stopper may have been re-cut to remove chips and over-polished, the label may be a later addition or simply poor quality 18th-century work, while the thickness may be a genuine rarity.

The piece is a good example of doubts which often cannot be proved conclusively either way until fresh evidence appears.

[1]
Cased glass has been exported from Czechoslovakia for over 150 years following its introduction in Bohemia. The technique spread quickly throughout Europe and America in the 19th century and is still popular with glassmakers and collectors. Such a vast output creates enormous difficulties in attribution and dating.

This English punch bowl and stand is relatively easy to date because the bowl was a popular Edwardian shape continuing in production into the 1920s. The idea of bowls on separate stands first appears in the late 19th century but some cased and cut glass, which can be proven to be from the 1840s, could be mistaken for modern glass because of its clean and bright appearance. Perhaps the most difficult items to date precisely are the ubiquitous hock glasses with coloured bowls on tall, clear stems.

[2]
These three 20th-century "bubbly" glasses raise a number of questions about date and country of origin when viewed out of context.

The candlestick is a 1985 replica from the Jamestown Glasshouse in Virginia, height 6.3 in. (16 cm). The blue vase was acquired in Egypt in 1984, height 8.3 in. (21 cm). The central green vase has no definite attribution—somewhere on the north Mediterranean coast is one possibility, height 6.3 in. (16 cm). Glass from the same workshop is often seen in antique shops; whatever the shape it always has the standard engraved ship with oarsmen and is always pale green. It may have been made in the 1960s.

[3]
Two transparent-enamelled beakers in Biedermeier style but made in the late 19th and early 20th centuries. They should be seen as part of a continuous tradition of an extremely popular style originating in the early 19th century, rather than as fakes or forgeries. The glass on the left probably comes from Steinschonau in Bohemia and is late 19th-century. The other beaker is enamelled with a panel reading "L'Inspiration Favorable" and signed with the initials "FLF" which stand for Fürchtegott Leberecht Fischer. Born in Vienna in 1866, he had an atelier at Währingergasse 133, and died in 1954.

continued from page 92

## Glass in the USA

Glass is collected in America with an enthusiasm and vitality reflected in the large number of clubs and societies covering every specialized topic. These organizations have done much to keep track of forgeries and reproductions. For example, in 1985 the Heisey Glass Club purchased all the Heisey moulds on the closure of the Imperial factory to prevent them from being used to make forgeries.

Pressed glass has been the mainstay of the American glass industry since its introduction in the 1820s. In widespread use today, it has created problems for collectors. In writing his book on milk glass, E. McCamly Belknap felt the chapter on fakes was the most important to help differentiate between antique and reproduction. For example, the Westmoreland Glass Co. in Pennsylvania continued to make clear pressed and milk glass reproductions of early American originals alongside their own creations from 1889 onwards. The later addition of the initials ''W'' or ''WG'' helps to trace their products. A similar situation arose with the works of John E. Kemple in Ohio. In 1949 Kemple had acquired 150 old moulds and very quickly unsigned milk glass appeared from the factory and was sold through two large outlets.

Fortunately moulds do eventually wear out, so production is limited to some extent. But old pressed glass can still be difficult to attribute because the companies who supplied the moulds often sold copies of the same mould to factories in America and England. In view of the many complexities, the best advice to the aspiring collector is to join one of the many glass societies and get to know the subject by talking to fellow collectors.

In the area of blown glass the classic American style is the blown 3-mould. In 1941 the McKearins bought a group of glasses supposed to come from the Mutzer family early in the

**Mary Gregory**
In her book on 19th-century art glass, Ruth Webb Lee confirms that a lady called Mary Alice Gregory was a decorator at the Boston & Sandwich Glass Company during the 1870s and 80s. She lived most of her life in Sandwich, Massachusetts where she died in 1908; white enamelled figures of boys and girls are supposed to have been her speciality. The same decoration appears on late 19th-century Bohemian glass and the name should be used to cover all glass of this kind rather than seeking to restrict it to the work of this one American lady.

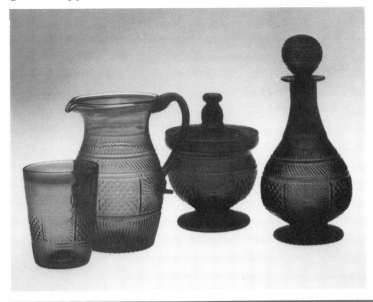

[1]
A selection of Mutzer fakes, c. 1920-29.

[1]
A Burmese jug imitating 19th-century Mount Washington glass. The shape is right but the poor colour and texture are not.

19th century. After some initial doubts the group was proved to be fake, possibly made in Pennsylvania between 1920 and 1929. About 50 pieces have been located since. In New Jersey the Clevenger Brothers Glassworks made reproductions which could be ordered by mail as late as the 1970s. Other typical American patterns like the Lily Pad or the Hobnail are prime targets.

Copies of art glass include the expensive Peachblow and Burmese. Imitations of "Wild Rose" Peachblow from New England were made in 1950 but not in original patterns and with poor chalky colours of white shading up to red. Burmese imitations, shading from a weak pink to yellow, suddenly appeared in antique shops in England in the 1970s. Of a grainy, sugary texture, they probably came from Murano.

### Some American Reproductions

The complicated array of forgeries available, including historical flasks, is too large to cover in a short space but this list details some of the items available recently in American shops:

- Diana the Huntress candlesticks, clear with satin finish; 10.5 in. (26.7 cm)

- three dolphin blue milk glass candlesticks.

- scroll flask (7 in.—17.8 cm) and Washington & Taylor flask, (8 in.—20.3 cm); both flasks made by Clevenger Brothers

- milk glass banana boat compote turned up at the edges; 14 in. (35.6 cm) across

- purple slag rabbit: 5.4 in. (13.7 cm)

- carnival glass hen dish; purple or marigold; 8 in. (35.6 cm) long

- blue milk glass robin on nest, the bird forming the lid; 6 in. (15.2 cm) high

- "Jumbo" match-holder; clear, blue and dark amber: 5.4 in. (13.7 cm)

- "Monkey" spoonholder; clear, ruby and vaseline: 4.8 in. (12.1 cm)

- General Grant plate: 9.2 in. (23.4 cm)

- child's ABC plate: clear, ruby, vaseline and amber; 8 in. (20.3 cm)

- Uncle Sam on battleship; 6.5 in. (16.5 cm)

- cannon on drum; 4.3 in. (10.8 cm)

- daily bread plate, oval, by the American Historical Replica Co., Grand Rapids, Michigan; 12.5 in. x 9 in. (31.8 cm x 22.9 cm)

- "Thousand eye" goblet: clear glass

- Hobnail cream pitcher: rose-opalescent; 3.5 in. (8.9 cm)

- shoe on roller skates: blue

- star with dewdrop salts; salmon pink and green; originals only in clear

- Westward Ho! lamp and goblet

- dolphin compote: stem in clear, bowl in opaque blue

- gypsy bottle on three feet: daisy and button pattern

- Hobnail vase: opal glass

- baskets with crimped rims and rustic handles with bizarre colour combinations

- lion goblet

- three-mould toilet bottle with panels of sunbursts and diamond quiltings: amethyst glass, stamped imitation pontil mark

- Lily Pad pint pitcher: brownish-purple

[2]
A late 19th-century (?) Hobnail jug with shell handle of a type that is still in production.

## Bubble Glassware

In most antique shops one can find a piece of glass made of very bubbly metal, often slightly irregular in shape and purporting to be "old". The idea that all such glass is antique is based on a vague notion that 17th- or 18th-century glassmakers lacked technology and skill and therefore their products would be obviously imperfect. In fact, most of the bubbled glass that appears today should be considered as 20th century until it can be proved otherwise.

It was only at the end of the 19th century that the idea of using bubbles as decoration resulted in the conscious imitation of ancient Roman glass. In the 1880s Christopher Dresser designed the "Clutha" range for Couper and Sons of Glasgow which featured deliberate imperfections, bubbles and irregular handles and rims. Following the success of Clutha, Stevens and Williams used "Caerleon", the name of the Roman site in South Wales, for a range of bubbled and iridized vases.

By the 20th century bubble glass offered a profitable market, especially as it could be melted easily and quickly and did not require highly technical finishing skills or machinery. The cruder and simpler it looked, the easier it was to sell. Green is the predominant colour achieved naturally by using low quality sand with a high iron ore content.

In 1927 in America, the Consolidated Lamp and Glass Co. patented "Catalonian Old Spanish Glassware" in a range of about 40 different pieces, mainly vases, plates, salad bowls, iced tea and water sets, and sugars and creams. The range was offered in "brilliant" colours of Emerald, Green, Spanish, Rose and Crystal or in "soft" colours of Honey, Amethyst and Jade. Characteristic features are swirling ridges and small bubbles, with larger distinct bubbles scattered at random through the glass. By 1928 the Diamond Glass Ware Co. of Indiana, Pennsylvania advertised "Barcelona Glass—A Reproduction of Early Spain" which imitated the wrinkled look of "Catalonia". In September 1932 Henry Beach, a direct importer in El Paso, Texas, advertised Mexican Bubble Glassware, noting that it had "all the charm of true craftsmanship, made in Mexico by the peons in the age-old manner of their ancestors—but produced under the supervision of our own agent". Another "El Mexicano" range from the Morgantown firm was advertised in a Marshall Field catalogue of 1933 in green or frosted glass. At the same time, Bryce Bros of Mt Pleasant, Pennsylvania, introduced "El Rancho" pitchers, vases, salts and peppers in reddish orange or greenish blue milk glass.

## Makers' Marks

Glass is marked less frequently than pottery and porcelain simply because any lettering would detract from the appearance, especially of clear glass. The most famous glass mark is the applied raven's head seal of George Ravenscroft, which was used literally as a seal of approval for his new lead glass.

E 5431
Height 13½"
Dia. 12"
AMBER
WILLOW GREEN

[3]
An example from the 1934 Hill-Ouston catalogue, which showed a range of bubbly glassware with enough of an air of "old country glass" to be passed off as early 19th-century Nailsea or Wrockwardine. The supplier is unknown.

**End-of-day glass**
This phrase is applied quite wrongly to glass that is decorated over the whole surface with bright mottled colours; the suggestion is that the glassmakers were using up leftover glass at the end of each working day. Molten glass is a precious commodity and if it is not used in one day it can be kept at a constant temperature for the following day's work or alternatively ladled out into cold water and reused as cullet.

There are too many "end-of-day" pieces for them to have been made sporadically at the end of the day; they were actually a commercial line, mainly from factories in America during the late 19th and early 20th centuries.

### Kite Marks

Patent Office registry marks, often known as "kite marks", are extremely useful for dating British glassware of the mid-19th century. Kite marks can also be found on ceramics, furniture, metalwork and so on of the period and indicate when the design was first registered.

The system was introduced in 1842 and until 1867 kite marks were arranged as follows: at the top, the class, below it the year letter; left: the month; right: the day; at the bottom, the parcel number. In 1868 the system changed and until 1883 the information was given in a different order: the year letter moved to the right, the parcel number to the left, the day of the month to the top and the month letter to the bottom.

The code letters were as follows:

| 1842 to 1867 | 1868 to 1883 |
|---|---|
| **Years** | **Years** |
| 1842 — X | 1868 — X |
| 1843 — H | 1869 — H |
| 1844 — C | 1870 — C |
| 1845 — A | 1871 — A |
| 1846 — I | 1872 — I |
| 1847 — F | 1873 — F |
| 1848 — U | 1874 — U |
| 1849 — S | 1875 — S |
| 1850 — V | 1876 — V |
| 1851 — P | 1877 — P |
| 1852 — D | 1878 — D |
| 1853 — Y | 1879 — Y |
| 1854 — J | 1880 — J |
| 1855 — E | 1881 — E |
| 1856 — L | 1882 — L |
| 1857 — K* | 1883 — K |
| 1858 — B | **Months** |
| 1859 — M | Jan — C |
| 1860 — Z* | Feb — G |
| 1861 — R | Mar — W |
| 1862 — O | Apr — H |
| 1863 — G | May — E |
| 1864 — N | Jun — M |
| 1865 — W | Jul — I |
| 1866 — Q | Aug — R |
| 1867 — T | Sept — D |
| **Months** | Oct — B |
| Jan — C | Nov — K |
| Feb — G | Dec — A |
| Mar — W | |
| Apr — H | |
| May — E | |
| Jun — M | |
| Jul — I | |
| Aug — R | |
| Sept — D | |
| Oct — B | |
| Nov — K | |
| Dec — A | |

(*R may be found as the month mark for 1st-9th Sept 1857, and K for Dec 1860.)

In the 18th century factory marks are non-existent but engravers' and enamellers' signatures do appear—usually of well-known and "expensive" names such as William Beilby and Isaac Jacobs.

In the 19th century trademarks became more common. As these marks are studied and recorded they can be of great assistance with accurate dating, particularly where company records still exist.

The diamond registry mark of the Patent Office (and after 1883 the Registered Number) is used to provide a key to the date of registration and the name of the manufacturer. On pressed glass the diamond mark is not always an infallible guide because there are known discrepancies between marked pieces and the lists at the Patent Office. Although the diamond is seen mostly on pressed glass, it can also appear as an engraved mark. By the 20th century trademarks had become much commoner. Some of the best work done in this field of research is by Cyril Manley, who has listed his finds in his book *Decorative Victorian Glass*. Dr Helga Hilschenz in *Das Glas des Jugendstil* provides similar lists of Continental marks and signatures.

The obvious place to look for marks is on the underside of the foot, but it is worth examining every inch of the glass in case they have been placed in some hidden corner. On cut glass the foot may be so ornate that the mark may be placed at the top of the stem of a wineglass or at the base of a jug's handle. Badged marks applied with acid or sandblast are often so faint as to make them almost invisible. Wear and tear on the foot can erase all or part of a mark whether it is painted, engraved or etched.

Any signed or marked glass is worth collecting even if initially there is no information about the maker. That information probably does exist somewhere and by locating it a glass that seemed of no consequence may acquire added significance both in historical and financial terms.

## Glass Paperweights

Every collector and dealer has different views on how to spot fake paperweights. The quick rules-of-thumb regarding correct identification are usually best taken with a large pinch of salt. The best advice is that given by Paul Hollister in his excellent book on weights published by the New York Historical Society. He notes eight main points which cover buying from dealers, rarity and uniqueness, use of the ultraviolet lamp, identification by profiles and profile condition, regrinding, buying for pleasure rather than investment, and forming a balanced collection.

There is really no substitute for hard work in learning the characteristics of cane formations and profiles from each factory. The profile of the weight—that is, the shape of the high dome of clear glass—helps to suggest provenance but should also be examined for possible alterations. Scratches and chips accumulated over the years can be ground and polished leaving noticeable irregularities, unlike the original fire-polished finish. Deeper bruises can be removed by cutting facets into the surface. Hollister also mentions deliberate vandalism, where coloured grounds have been cut away or coloured overlaps re-cut to produce a "fancier" example. Original facetting is sharp and will always have at least a few scratches and marks. The use of an ultraviolet lamp is suggested in some books as a method for identifying different factories. However, variation in fluorescence is so slight that when coupled with the variations within each factory's weights, the method becomes unreliable.

The shortage of documentation about paperweight manufacture has resulted in many incorrect attributions when a name is needed to help sell the weight. In recent years the Stourbridge attribution has become a favourite, but there is no known mention of weights being made in the Stourbridge district in any of the available 19th-century literature about the area. The Islington Glass Works and Bacchus in Birmingham made weights from mid-century and it is assumed that some rival attempts appeared from Stourbridge, but there is certainly no evidence to support this supposition. However when the collecting of weights began in earnest from about 1900-1920, Birmingham and Stourbridge were quick to "assist" with an increased supply, including 1848 specimens. The Richardson pattern books illustrate a scent/ink bottle, a salt and two weights in millefiori. In the Hill-Ouston catalogue a perfume/ink bottle and a weight dated 1848 may be from the Walsh Walsh factory which worked until 1951 and continued to produce weights during this time.

A letter from Mr H. Parkes, who was one of the workmen at Walsh, Walsh and later became manager, gives vital clues to distinguish these imitations. Each number of the date was set in a separate cane; the blue numbers against white opal were inserted in the second outer ring. The pontil mark was left on and the bottom was scratched with a coarse pad. The firm also made millefiori stoppers for decanters. The letter comments that "All the experts fell over each other to buy the genuine millefleur [sic] paperweights" and it points out that "the old British craftsman could equal and very often surpass your Bigaglias, Saint-Louis etc . . .".

## Modern Factory and Museum Reproductions

Present day reproductions capitalize both on the wave of nostalgia for bygone ages and the vanity of buyers who, in purchasing these glasses, identify with elegance, good design, the investment value of prized possessions, discriminating taste and an appreciation of craftsmanship. Thomas Webb and Sons used this approach in the leaflet advertising their reproduction Bristol Blue series. It was echoed more recently by an Israeli firm who issued this statement about their miniature vases: "The hand blown vases of Ha'oman (which means artisan) are made by the same methods used in biblical times, each piece being blown and painted individually with colours mixed to

1 *above*
Daisy pattern millefiori bottle from the Hill-Ouston catalogue.

2 *above*
An original green Bohemian jug, painted in the Mary Gregory style, *c.* 1890-1900—height 7.1 in. (18 cm).

3
Antique Moser glassware of the kind that is still being produced. This late 19th-century bowl is in dark blue glass with an etched and gilt border of female figures.

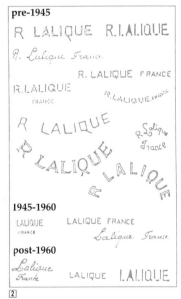

Lalique glass. The vase on the left is signed "R. Lalique France" but the lettering is back to front—this is almost certainly an innocent mistake at the factory, as no faker could afford to be so negligent. The dahlia scent bottle on the right is marked "Lalique France" and is still in the catalogue.

The vast majority of Lalique articles, but not all, bear a mark, some examples of which are shown here. The style of the mark varied with time, though facsimiles of René Lalique's signature appear in all periods. The marks were variously moulded, sandblasted and wheel cut; if moulded marks appeared indistinct, an etched mark was often added for clarity.

The full mark, "R. Lalique France" dates from before 1945, though the "France" was not always added. "Lalique France" dates from 1945 or after. The size and shape of all the marks can vary according to the size and form of the object being marked.

give the textured effect of an archaeological find, making each a collectors piece." If the collector can acquire these publicity leaflets he will have the best record of what is available now and in the future. Regular visits to glass and china shops will keep one up-to-date with new developments.

"Mary Gregory" imitations, mainly in ruby, have been exported from Czechoslovakia for a number of years. Removed from a trade stand display and seen amongst other antiques these vases could be deceptive.

In the 1930s the London firm of John Jenkins introduced a range of pressed glass known as "Barolac". The firm has now reintroduced the series in these patterns: Palm Trees, Cherries, Aquarium, Sea Horse, Pansy, Poppies and Trees. Vases and bowls are not marked but are very close to the frosted milky appearance of the originals.

Moser of Czechoslovakia base some of their current lines on their 19th-century designs. After studying antique examples in books and museums it should be easy enough to spot the new copies, which tend to be larger-than-life caricatures. One range to be wary of however is that of ruby and brown vases with a continuous band of etched and gilt classical figures.

The German firm of J. Oertel is presently marketing a number of 18th-and 19th-century styles. They have a selection of good quality *transparentenamel* beakers in Biedermeier shapes. *Schwarzlot* decoration is copied as well as the gilt vermicelli decoration first introduced in the early 19th century. The technically brilliant process of *Zwischengoldglas* has also been successfully attempted, but prices of modern versions are higher than those of 18th-century examples.

In America the important firm of Fentons uses many processes which echo the late 19th century and also include Burmese and Carnival glass of the early 20th century. A selection was introduced into England in 1986 and it is only a matter of time before it arrives in the antique trade. Ruby or cranberry glass is made in Czechoslovakia under licence from English firms. Fentons also produce a "splashed" series of red baskets with frosted twisted handles.

The one area of reproduction which can create difficulties in accurate dating is the continuous production of a design over many years. In Finland the Iittala glassworks have made the famous Alvar Aalto vases since they were designed by the architect in 1936. The 1967 Orchidea and Alpina designs of Tapio Wirkkala are similar examples.

Lalique glass has maintained its high reputation for sophisticated design since the 1920s. However, many of those shapes are still continued and dating them means relying on 1930s publicity and pattern books, details of signatures and reference to the most recent catalogues. Modern patterns come in clear or frosted glass. Joblings of Sunderland imitated Lalique between 1930 and 1934 with a high quality range of bluish opalescent vases, candlesticks and animals which had the trade name "Opalique".

Museum shops have created a wave of museum-originated reproductions. The Metropolitan Museum of Art in New York sells an imitation early American mould-blown tumbler, stamped with the initials "MMA". At the reconstructed 1608 Jamestown Glasshouse in Virginia, the visitor can buy twelve glasses "of authentic 17th century English design" (*Ill. 2*, p.96) The green bubbly effect of the Jamestown replicas can be achieved by melting Coca-Cola bottles. At least one studio glassmaker in America has been approached to make "old" glass without any signature.

## The Repair of Glass

The question of repairs is a subjective matter and everyone must decide their own priorities about alterations. Collectors tend to prefer not to have any visible signs of damage, whereas museum curators would rather show the object in its original condition. Repairs can be acceptable provided the proportions are not destroyed: for example, on 18th-century glass the foot will always be larger in diameter than the bowl; anything less should cause suspicion.

Over the years the techniques of repairs have changed—the old way of trimming a foot went vertically through the rim, giving a flat edge. When the underneath of a foot is chipped or flaked, instead of trimming the edge the underside is skimmed out. This results in a thinner foot with some loss of the original striations and loss of wear marks. Any artificial wear produced by rubbing on emery paper will show random scratches often going inwards from lines of natural wear. One Midlands factory is said to have employed a retired glassmaker to grind the feet of 18th-century reproductions on the back doorstep. When trying to ascertain if wear is genuine, consider which part of the glass could have been in contact with the surface. If the scratches are generally deep, look unnatural and go too far inwards, then the glass has been altered.

"Marriages" of two separate glasses, such as the bowl of a wine glass joined onto another stem, can be passed off as a genuine glass. The stuck join has to be at a definite joint—probably where the stem joins the bowl or the foot—which helps to disguise the deception. Removal instead of addition also takes place: a rummer with a broken foot can be transformed into an acceptable tumbler by cutting away the unwanted glass stem and leaving a ground out pontil.

The introduction of modern glues and resins specifically for glass has been of immense benefit both to the bona fide restorer and the forger. "Superglues" set hard on exposure to the ultraviolet rays in ordinary daylight, but on coloured glass the colour filters out the ultraviolet and the adhesive does not form a strong join. It may be that these glues are not as long lasting as epoxy resin glues.

Wax and silicone rubber moulds used with polyester resins have revolutionized the restoration of ancient glass where a considerable amount may be missing and requires an infill. Certain resins have an inherent abraded look that suits ancient items; others may discolour. More importantly, they allow the work to be reversible.

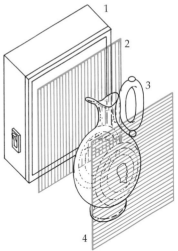

**3**
A polariscope, used to reveal the flow lines of glass and therefore able to show interruptions to those lines where a break has been mended or where parts have been added.

The box (*1*) holds a light source behind a diffusing surface. The light then shines through a polarizing screen (*2*). The sample (*3*) is set between this sheet and the analyser (*4*), a second polarizing screen with its axis set at 90° to the first.

**The ultraviolet lamp**
An ultraviolet lamp will help to identify the composition of glass. The complex nature of glass chemistry can create difficulties and therefore the readings are not completely infallible. But as a general rule it will help to distinguish between soda and lead glass. A lead content will give a light blue tinged with purple, whereas soda shows a distinctive green-yellow.

# 7: BASE METALS

THIS CHAPTER IS CONCERNED with several metals — Pewter; Copper, Brass and Bronze; Iron and Steel — but the general approach to authenticating objects made in any of them is similar. It can be divided into five areas, as follows:

**Method of Manufacture** Over the centuries the techniques of making all forms of metalware have varied, some methods declining while others rose in importance. A sound knowledge of how objects were made at various times in history is a great asset when seeking to date metalware. For example, the types of seam used in copper and brass work are good guides to dating.

**Makers' and Other Marks** This is perhaps the easiest check where reference works illustrating makers' marks exist. Only a small proportion of objects do have makers' marks however. But there are other marks which can be useful: housemarks, ownership marks and initials, full coats-of-arms or crests engraved on items can all help with dating. To give but one example, coats-of-arms have been rendered in different styles according to their period; establish the style and you can begin to date when the work was done.

**Style** This is a dangerous area if knowledge is used inflexibly. Similar objects were made over several decades and it is often not possible to establish a nice, neat, chronological order. Nevertheless, patterns do emerge and identifying the style of a piece already suggests a broad period during which it might have been made.

**Observation** You can learn a lot by feeling an item as well as by looking at it. Handle it, feel its edges, turnings and hinges. Run your fingers over all the surfaces. Try and identify where the wear is. While you may come across a 17th-century object in pristine condition the odds are against it; no wear usually means little age.

**Alloys** For economic and technical reasons the alloys used by coppersmiths, brassfounders, braziers, blacksmiths and pewterers have varied over time and a knowledge of the alloys can provide definitive answers. This is the hardest check to carry out however as it requires access to analytical equipment.

There is a sixth aspect of authentication which no book can teach — experience. No amount of advice, no list of facts, no practical guidance can give you the experience that is needed to make sound judgements. The more metalware you handle the more you will see and understand, for it can never be sufficient just to apply a set of rules and come out with a dogmatic judgement. Assessing an item is a matter of balancing the probabilities. If all the indicators point one way then you can be reasonably sure of your attribution, but where the evidence is conflicting you will have to be more tentative.

[1]
The coppersmith: an 18th-century Dutch print showing a hammerman at work raising a pan.

[2] *opposite*
1920s reproduction pewter candlesticks from the Pearson-Page catalogue. These items, now 60 years old, have acquired some of the appearance of age and can be deceptive.

There are two sources of potential difficulty: genuine fakes, which were carefully made to deceive; and reproductions, once offered for sale for what they were, but now either deliberately aged to deceive or which have achieved genuine age and wear. True fakes are rare and are difficult to spot, reproductions are easier to identify even if artificially aged. Cupidity is the danger: the natural desire to make a ''find'' can lead one into dangerous waters.

# PEWTER

Pewter is an alloy of tin. For 450 years or more it was one of the most important metals found in the home. People of all classes used it for eating and drinking, and about the house. The rich man might have had many dozens of plates and dishes but even the pauper owned a battered pewter plate.

Being a soft alloy, pewter had a comparatively short working life; as soon as they needed replacing, damaged objects were usually traded in for newly worked pewter. Hence there are few survivors of the tens of thousands of items that were in daily use. Seventeenth-century pieces are the earliest that can normally be found. This was the period of maximum production in Britain and Europe, but the manufacture of pewter continued at a high level in the 18th century and in the United States it reached a peak in the 40 years after the War of Independence. Pewter continued to be made in the USA into the 19th century, at a time when the craft was in great financial difficulties elsewhere. During the 19th century a variation of pewter — a hard alloy of tin made with the help of steam driven machines and known as Britannia Metal — became

3] *above*
Examples of a plate and an inkstand from the Pearson-Page Company pewter catalogue, 1920s. The factory was in Birmingham but these wares were also held in stock in New York and Montreal by Pearson-Page's North American representatives, the Skinner-Hill Company.

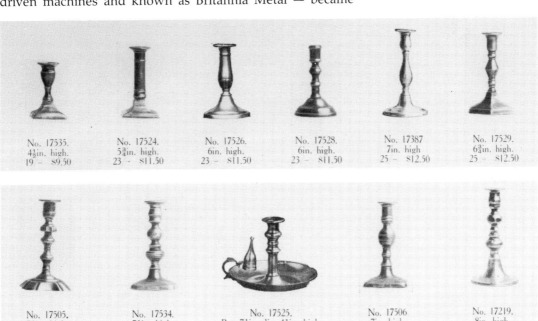

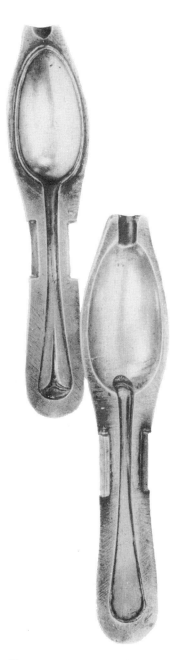

[1]
An 18th-century brass spoon
mould.

increasingly popular and was widely used.

Most commonly found now are 18th-century pewter plates and dishes, 19th-century drinking mugs and Britannia Metal tea and coffee pots, but almost anything one can think of which was used in the home has been, at some time or other, made in pewter.

Pewter was first collected in Britain in the 1900s, so no earlier fakes exist. Most British fakes were made in the 1920s. They are well made, often carefully "repaired" to set the collector's mind at rest. Unless it is polished almost daily pewter soon develops a patina or film of thin oxide which is difficult to replicate and this type of oxidization is one of the things collectors look for to confirm age. Unfortunately it is possible to fake oxidization and all good fakes have this simulation of age carefully applied to their surfaces. Collectors should familiarize themselves with the appearance and colour of authentic patina.

Because the fakers wanted to make money they nearly always copied the more valuable objects, such as 17th-century candlesticks and flat-lidded Stuart tankards. In contrast, reproductions of quite ordinary items were widely made from the 1920s onwards. These were perfectly fairly offered for sale for what they were, but time has aged them and the unwary can be deceived. Unscrupulous people have also set out to age reproductions. For example, in recent years a flood of acid-stained black pewter of little age has been offered for sale in auction rooms and has often been wrongly identified as old. Reproduction pewter is widely stored in France among grass cuttings to give it a kind of patina, and other methods of dulling surfaces and making them look old have been tried.

Another category of fake with which great care has to be taken is the genuine item which has been "improved" to increase its value. Genuine late 17th-century plates can have their value increased threefold by adding a wrigglework decoration; plates from the workshop of Alderson, George IV's pewterer, can be made into "Coronation" plates by the addition of the scroll: "GR IV". In the USA the faker has taken genuine antique plates and added copies of American marks, thus greatly increasing the plates' value.

## Methods of Manufacture

Most pewter is cast in moulds. These were often made of bronze but moulds were also made of iron, wood, clay and stone. Simple shapes such as plates and spoons could be cast in a two-part mould, but complex forms, such as tankards or flagons, needed multi-part moulds. The various parts of a casting had then to be soldered together. When a casting came out of the mould it had a rough, unfinished appearance. Surplus metal had to be trimmed off and the rough surface polished down on a wheel, using a hard tool or abrasive.

Pewterers tended to complete the undersides of their pieces carefully, using a wheel and turning off the metal in a widening concentric ring. So look for evidence that the object

has been cast in a mould, not raised over a form or stamped out from sheet metal; look for quality craftsmanship on the seams and turning; be sceptical about anything that has not been turned off on the bottom or under the base.

One way of bringing together small parts for fastening was to cast a part of an object directly on to the rest of it — for example, a porringer ear onto the side of a porringer or a lid onto the thumbpiece of a flagon or tankard. To do this the mould was clamped into place on the partly completed object with a pair of pincers protected by a piece of linen. The joint was then poured and the impression of the linen remains.

Flatware — that is plates, dishes and chargers — needed to resist heavy use and it was found that by hammering them round the booge (the area between the rim and the bottom of the plate) a stronger metal could be obtained. In Britain most plates were hammered, but American flatware is less frequently hammered. Few reproductions are hammered.

Rarely did the reproduction makers follow the old skills; they needed modern machines for quick production. Virtually all reproduction pewter falls at this hurdle.

## The Styles of Pewter

To be able to date pewter you have got to be able to put a provisional period to an object from its appearance. This will not be an exact date, for stylistic changes did not occur in a smooth, even way, but its shape and appearance ought to suggest to you a likely period in which an object would have been made. Reference books (Cotterell and Hornsby, for example — see the Bibliography) are invaluable in this regard, to professionals as well as to amateurs, and the more illustrations they have, the better; but they need to be complemented by experience in handling objects.

## Makers' and Other Marks

Fakers and reproduction makers have used "genuine" marks on their work, so a mark by itself is no safeguard. Likewise, genuine pewter was often not fully marked, so fine things may lack the proof of who made them.

The nature and size of marks usually struck has also changed. Early marks are very simple, basic shapes with two

[2]
A spoon as it comes out of the mould and another that has had a preliminary scraping but awaits finishing.

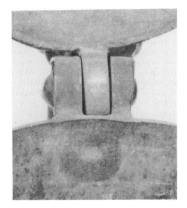

[3] *above*
An 18th-century "Jersey" flagon, showing the linen marks where the handle was cast directly onto the body.

[4]
A late 17th-century hammered pewter plate. Most plates were hammered in the booge to strengthen them, but this has been struck all over the surface as well, for decoration.

1 *above*
Dating by the style of armorials. The same coat-of-arms in 19th-century style (top) and as represented in the 17th century.

2 *above*
Nineteenth-century capacity marks, required by law to be stamped on measures used in the sale of ale or dry goods, are valuable pointers to age.

3
A 17th-century plate showing knife cuts, general wear and patches of oxide. It is very difficult for the faker to simulate the naturalness of genuine wear.

initials, usually small; they were struck on handles, the front rims of plates and so on. By the late 18th century large, complex marks with full names and even addresses were being used and these appear, because of their size, underneath plates. Stuart tankards normally have marks struck either on the lid, if it is flat, or inside the base, but during the early 18th century a tendency developed for marks to be struck on one side of the neck, close to the handle. In the mid-17th century a secondary system of marking became popular — pseudo hallmarks. These were normally struck four times and they are useful both to help identify a maker and offer confirmation of the period. It is not possible to establish a set of rules — makers tended to put their marks where they wanted — but by handling pewter, examining where marks are struck and looking at illustrations of pieces a working idea of styles of mark and where they normally appear will emerge.

Other useful marks found on pewter are those placed there by early owners. These ownership marks take three common forms: a small group of housemarks, often obscure in meaning, struck on early pewter — generally before 1600; a triad of owner's initials widely punched on pewter from the early 17th century into the 19th but less common after 1750; and crests and coats-of-arms.

With some experience you can usually identify the period in which initials were struck. Just as with handwriting, so punches followed the letter forms of the day. The way in which coats-of-arms were ornamented followed the broader style of the period. Not only can the style of an armorial help to date an object but if the arms can be identified important provenance is added to the piece.

When an object was made for use in a tavern or market its capacity had to be confirmed by the authorities. Pewter and brass mugs and measures are often found with these capacity checks stamped on the rim and they too help to confirm the period in which an item was used.

## The Condition of Old Pewter

Look at every surface of a piece of pewter. How did it get its bumps and bruises? Are they consistent with real wear? Fakers tend to bang away, adding marks of wear without regard to the way an object is naturally used. A pattern of even wear over the entire surface is unnatural. If it is a plate. is there an irregular pattern of knife cuts, or are there just a few, evenly marked across the surface? Are the edges, bottom, hinges and neck of a flagon or tankard worn soft with use or are they sharp and even?

Most alloys of tin will oxidize over time but it takes at least 50 years for genuine oxide to develop. Is the oxide where you would expect? In damp parts of an object or where it got less use? Real oxide can erupt into unpleasant bubbles and these are very hard to fake. Likewise, genuine light oxide cannot be copied properly. Most attempts to create oxide are poor although the true faker of the 1930s did obtain some skill. Fake

**4** *left*
A pair of fake pewter candlesticks in Charles II style. The stems show too regular an appearance, with little wear, and the decoration on the drip pans and bases lacks the quality one would expect to find on a genuine example. They are also much lighter and less robust than authentic candlesticks of the period.

The bases have been partly turned off, but they lack signs of wear and there is no genuine oxide to be seen.

**5**

A bulbous measure with spout.

It is not easy to find the exact form in reference books. The round-bodied shape is however typical of many Continental examples and there are some ale jugs of the late 18th and early 19th centuries which follow approximately this form.

The method of manufacture might also cause some disquiet. Instead of the horizontal seam one would expect on old pewter, there is a vertical seam behind the handle. The seaming technique is very different from that used on the flagon on the next page, where there is a narrow band applied within and behind the pieces — here a strip of solder has been put between the two parts which have then been melted together.

There is a maker's mark by the neck but it is not to be found in the standard works. It includes the initials ''NR'' — initials used by one of the reproduction makers of the 1930s.

The body is well finished off, with some evidence of turning, but there is no wear to be seen. The

thumbpiece has not left a mark on the handle and the hinge (right) does not have the loose feel or worn appearance of age. Both the thumbpiece and the lip are sharp to the touch.

This is clearly not a genuine piece of old pewter — in fact, we can say with some confidence that it dates from the 1920s or 1930s.

oxide is always found with small holes in it rather than rounded eruptions. This is because it was put there with a fine drill and acids, rather than occurring naturally from within.

## The Alloys

The traditional alloy of pewter most widely used into the 17th century consisted of tin and copper with small amounts of other elements. In Britain and Europe all objects, such as flatware, which needed to stand up to hard use contained above 90% tin with perhaps 2–6% copper plus some lead and antimony. Measures, flagons, balusters and the like, with their more complex shapes needing careful casting, were made of a softer alloy with less tin and more lead. Apart from Roman pewter few items contain more than 20% lead. Later in the 17th century the proportion of copper gradually decreased and a popular "hardmetal" appeared with a high tin content and some antimony or bismuth. In the United States, for historical and economic reasons most new pewter was made from old metal and a slightly lower quality alloy was common for flatware. Although the guilds governing the manufacture of pewter did lay down firm rules these were only minimum standards and anyway, they were not universally obeyed.

[1] *left and right*
A test case, or how to apply the method of authentication.

The shape of this flagon can be found in reference books. It is known as a "Beefeater" and was widely used in the period 1650–1700. There are four hallmarks on the lid and there is a maker's stamp in the base. These can be looked up—they are the marks of James True of London, who died in 1681.

The base shows turning marks, as does the inside of the lid. The piece has been cast in several sections and the joints, completed with a thin band of solder, are visible inside the body. The method of manufacture seems to be authentic and would be consistent with the date span provided by the style and the maker's marks.

It remains to look at overall condition and signs of wear. It would be reasonable to expect the hinge to have worn—which it clearly has (right). Also, when the lid is opened, the thumbpiece falls back against the handle and should have left a mark—this too is present.

Another small point to look for on flagons is some slight denting to the front of the base. The natural way to set down a full flagon is not perfectly flat on its base but front edge first. And, of course, there should be no roughness or sharpness—pewter is too soft an alloy to retain sharp edges, even if the maker had left them thus.

All the signs then from shape and style, marks, method of manufacture and condition point to authenticity.

# COPPER, BRASS AND BRONZE

Copper by itself, although suitable for some tasks, is too soft for many purposes; it is also difficult to cast. Alloys were therefore adopted, each based on a different hardening agent. The most common were bronze and brass.

Bronze is made with tin added to copper and brass has zinc in the alloy. In practice, other elements are also found and "pure" brass or bronze was seldom used in the past. The lines of division between alloys are not as easy to establish as was at one time thought.

An enormous range of objects used in the home or workshop was made in brass, bronze or copper from the Middle Ages into this century. Most commonly found these days are 18th- and 19th-century brass candlesticks, 19th-century copper and brass kettles, and 19th- and early 20th-century copper saucepans, jardinieres and boxes. In addition there is a mass of reproduction brass and copper of the 1920s and 1930s; some of the pieces are copies of earlier designs, others are more loosely based on earlier styles.

In the Middle Ages Britain had sufficient tin but was obliged to import both copper and zinc. The first British copper appeared on the market in late Elizabethan times but it was not until after the restoration of Charles II that the British copper mining industry expanded. It did so very speedily and by the early 19th century Britain was supplying nearly all the world's copper ore and British centres such as Birmingham were making millions of brass and copper objects for export. Pewter manufacture was always based on small scale local production by craftsmen. Brass, bronze and copper manufacture started out in this way but by the late 18th century was becoming increasingly mechanized and factory based. In America copper and brass were imported from Britain in substantial quantities, both as raw materials and as completed goods. As a result it took some time for local manufacture to become established, but by the 19th century large quantities of brass and copper were being made in the USA.

Until after the Second World War there were few fakes of British or American copper, brass or bronze pieces as the originals had little value. Plenty of popular reproductions were made in the years between the wars however and many of these have now acquired genuine age and wear.

In Europe metalware was popular well before the 1914–18 war so European fakes a hundred years old do exist. In addition, several museums offered for sale first class unsigned replicas, copies of important objects, in the late 19th century. Fakes are currently thought to be being made in Spain and Italy and include copies of wall sconces, alms dishes, ladles, candle moulds and other popular and valuable forms. These are well made and are excellent facsimiles.

[1]
Reproduction brass skimmers and roasters from the catalogue c. 1925 of Cyril E. Jones, Birmingham. The firm advertised "Fine Reproductions of all Periods" in silver, copper, pewter, brass, iron and wood, some of which could well have been made to precisely the same patterns for well over 100 years, since the firm was founded in 1810.

1 *above*
Brass jardinieres from the 1927
Pearson-Page catalogue.

2 *above*
A brass tobacco box offered by
Pearson-Page in 1927.

3 *below*
A selection of reproduction candle
brackets and tray candlesticks from
the Cyril Jones Period Brass
Foundry, Birmingham, *c.* 1925.

## Methods of Manufacture

The main alloys of copper — brass and bronze — each fulfilled
certain purposes especially well. Bronze was easy to cast,
useful for goods that had to withstand extreme heat but less
satisfactory if placed under pressure or hammered. Pots,
saucepans and other cooking implements were mostly cast
from bronze. Examine any medieval cooking pot and the way
it was made is clearly written on its surface. They were
normally cast in boxed sand moulds or clay *cire et perdue*
moulds and the marks where the moulds joined show clearly.

Brass objects could be made by casting, but most were raised
from sheets of metal. At first brass or copper sheet was made
by hammering, by hand, and this gave a thickish, uneven
sheet. Later the thinness of the sheet was improved by using
water-powered trip hammers, and by the 19th century sheets
of copper and brass were made by steam power and rolling
mills. With this technique really even, thin sheets could be
made for manufacture into household items. In the same
period increasing use was made of stamping machines, which
punched out small objects or parts from sheet metal.

For every item of late 17th- or early 18th-century copper or
brass still surviving, you will find hundreds or even thousands
of examples of 19th-century workmanship, so it does not take
long to become familiar with the range of products raised from
the sheet.

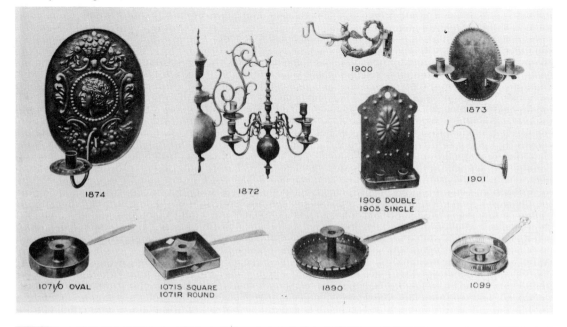

[4]
A page of reproduction brass candlesticks from the Pearson-Page catalogue for 1927.

[1]

A selection of reproduction brass trays; Pearson-Page, 1927.

Joins in hand-raised objects were created with a series of dovetail joints; when fitted together these were hammered to make the joint watertight. Another widely used method was to rivet two objects together, hammering the top and bottom of the rivets firmly into place. Little use was made of solder or other types of joint. By the 19th century however most joints were soldered or folded over. These folded seams were made by bringing together the edges of the piece to be joined, folding them over each other and then hammering the joint to make it strong. This technique is not normally found on articles dated before 1750 and seldom before 1800. Old skills such as the dovetail seam continued to be used by craftsmen right into this century.

Early cast objects were carefully finished off with chisels and then turned off on a wheel to make a smooth surface underneath. Foot lathe turning tended to be uneven — modern turning is much more regular. A craftsman of the 16th or 17th century would never leave his candlesticks or other objects unfinished, but reproduction makers of this century often did not bother with the finishing of lower quality products and many objects of Georgian style were produced with rough sand cast bases. These can be distinguished at a glance. Recent fakers seeking to age candlesticks made in this way are turning them off in the base, but the surface they leave tends to be very smooth and new looking.

Screws are frequently found on copper alloy objects and these can help to date pieces. Machine-made modern screws cannot date from earlier than the mid-19th century, while hand-cut threads are a good indication that an object was made before or during the industrial revolution.

It was not until the 18th century that brassfounders learned the technique of casting hollow candlesticks. Until around 1730 or so they were cast in two parts and carefully seamed together vertically with solder. Always look at such hollow objects for evidence of seams (breathing on the surface can

*2 above*
A 19th-century copper coffee pot, showing both the dovetail seam and the crude riveting of handle and hinge to the body.

*3 above*
The inside of the base of an original 18th-century brass candlestick, showing the kind of finish to expect.

*4*
The underside of a Gothic brass candlestick showing the riveting of stem to base.

*5*
An example of a folded over joint, on a late 19th-century watering can.

*6*
The base of a kettle marked with the catalogue number of the Army & Navy Stores for 1910 but still made with dovetailed seams.

A copper saucepan and lid with iron handles.

These flat based and topped saucepans were made in the early 19th century and continued in use until the early 20th. It has clearly been raised by hand from thick sheet metal. The base is folded over to join it to the sides and the riveting of the handles is slightly crude.

The inside is tinned, suggesting the pan was made for use (copper cooking vessels have been tinned since the late Middle Ages for safety) and the article looks well worn, with plenty of workmanlike dents. There is no reason to doubt that it is what it seems — early 19th century.

help to reveal them). Until the 19th century it was difficult to make objects of any length in hollow form so candlesticks were made of two or more parts fastened together horizontally. By the 1830s manufacturers had learnt how to produce long thin hollow cast tubes of brass — it was these that formed the gas tubes of the 1880s.

## The Alloys

While the alloy from which an object is made can seldom confirm by itself whether the article is old or not, knowing what an object is made of is a very useful dating tool. We can confirm whether it has the same kind of composition as is found in other genuine examples. The alloy used can also help to identify the national origins of some obscure objects, as different nations appear to have used different alloys according to local costs and the availability of raw materials.

In the case of brass however analysis can take us a stage further. Before 1770 mineral zinc was not available — only calamine, an oxide of zinc. Combining calamine with copper was difficult, as the zinc tended to evaporate when added to the crucible. Until the discovery of mineral zinc it was not possible to make a brass alloy with more than 30% zinc and to get the level above 20% was very difficult. A simple test for the proportions of zinc may therefore tell us at once whether an object was made before or after 1770. Most 18th-century brass has several trace elements in addition to copper and zinc; "pure" brass is likely to be modern.

## Makers' and Other Marks

Few copper, brass or bronze objects, other than the mass-produced items of the 19th and 20th centuries, are marked by their makers. Little help is offered therefore by makers' marks alone, although naturally the makers of some objects have been identified and recorded. Some 18th-century brass-workers and a number of 17th- and 18th-century skillet and mortar makers are known.

As with pewter, some help may be offered by inscriptions, owners' initials and house marks. Care must be taken however with inscriptions found on copper and brass. Reproduction makers made their products more interesting by adding inscriptions and false owners' names to many objects. For example, there are dozens of tobacco and snuff boxes with dated inscriptions to be found, all modern. Look at the nature of the lettering and try and compare it with genuine inscriptions on objects in museums. Modern letters appear rather thin and scratchy and often far too sharp.

## The Condition of Old Metalware

②
Until around 1730 candlesticks were made in two parts and joined with a vertical seam, as shown here.

Take an object and run your fingers over all its surfaces. Is it smooth where it would naturally have worn? Are there rough corners and edges? Are there clear signs of wear and are they

3
Reference works and pattern books show this candlestick pattern was introduced in the mid-19th century. This example is therefore Victorian or a later copy. There is no sign of a seam, so it was cast in one piece — this confirms that it can be no earlier than the 19th century. The composition is rather thin — unusual for early workmanship.

A cork pusher for helping to extract the candle suggests that this article was made for use, but there has been no attempt to finish off the base — the sand casting marks are clear. This suggests that it is not a 19th-century example.

The candlestick has been well used and is indeed a bit battered, but the turning marks on the surface are still sharp. Each cut can be felt, though the base edges are not unusually sharp.

All these indications suggest that this is a Victorian-style candlestick probably made *c.* 1910–30.

where they ought logically to be? Your fingers can often tell you more than your eyes. Where there are repairs, try and work out how the damage took place. Is it plausible?

By and large people prefer their copper and brass polished, so some of the evidence of age, offered by the patina and so helpful in pewter, is not always available for copper and brass.

Some late 17th-century and early 18th-century brass and copper objects of high quality were originally silvered. It is wise to check all the crannies of a piece for evidence of this as it confirms an early manufacture, even if it means that the object is now not as it was originally made. Later brass and copper pieces were sometimes silver plated and still later they were electroplated — again it is worth looking for evidence of this type of treatment.

# IRON AND STEEL

Until the 19th century steel was hard to make; its use was limited to cutting tools, weapons and some jewellery. Gradually, improved manufacturing techniques led to the more efficient combination of carbon with iron and from the early Victorian period onwards steel was easily made and extensively used. It speedily drove out wrought iron as the principal ferrous metal.

Iron has been used in both its cast and wrought forms from the earliest times, but until the 18th century iron for casting tended to be brittle because of an excess of carbon and other impurities in the alloy. Although cast iron objects were made they were limited in purpose: there are a few fine medieval

[1] A small fragment of 16th-century cast iron, part of a set of gates.

French cast iron mortars and in the 17th and 18th centuries fine decorated firebacks were cast in the Sussex and Kentish Weald.

The invention by Abraham Darby early in the 18th century of blast furnaces able to use coke rather than charcoal lead to a rapid improvement in the quality of iron. Production expanded dramatically. Cast iron was widely used in industry and construction and many domestic tools and objects were cast in the ironworks that developed in many British coalfields. Until the mid-18th century it is broadly true that most ironworks were local, small in scale and in the hands of blacksmiths. The ability to use coke for smelting opened the door to large scale factory production.

Until the industrial revolution by far the most widespread use of iron was in its wrought form. Every town had its blacksmiths who, by heating, hammering, re-heating and shaping made a range of useful domestic and other tools. Candle holders, rushlight holders, grease pans, cutting tools, ladles, forks, jacks and chimney cranes are amongst the objects most frequently found in wrought iron. Large quantities of gates, fences and decorative ironwork were also created.

Excellent fakes of lighting devices have been made in Spain in recent years and even better copies are now coming from Nepal and the Far East. These include copies of designs illustrated in standard reference works.

The reproduction industry did not seize on wrought iron as it did on pewter, brass and copper, but individual copies were made by local blacksmiths everywhere throughout the 19th century and even until the 1940s. It was possible to buy cast firebacks too in the 1920s and 1930s. These, being made in the same manner as the originals with similar ore and the same skills, are naturally difficult to detect.

## Methods of Manufacture

Wrought iron was worked in a forge by the blacksmith. Joints were made either by fusing the iron bars together under intense heat or by riveting them. Shapes were created by bending the hammered bars round angles on the anvil. Everything was individually produced and each item, however skilfully made, differed slightly from the next.

Each blacksmith would make his own bars for further shaping into the tools and objects he wished to make. Thus all the iron used was hand made and slightly uneven, whereas modern wrought iron is made from pre-shaped bars of a high quality and evenness. Reproduction work usually makes use of very even wrought iron bars but Asian blacksmiths making fakes tend to follow the old methods and make their own forged iron.

[2] A fireback as advertised in the Cyril Jones Ltd reproduction catalogue, mid-1920s. It bears the date "1588" and is described as "Sussex hand cast iron".

When iron was cast into household objects some were made in moulds but widespread use was also made of open sand casting. Firebacks, for example, were made by stamping the decoration in casting sand and pouring the melted iron directly into the open boxes. Early firebacks are generally very thick — an inch or more — but modern founders were more sparing with their ore.

## The Metal

It is possible to analyse iron and steel and determine the proportions of carbon they contain; this helps with dating. The nature of the impurities iron holds can also identify the fuel used in its forging and thus help to date the hearth used in its manufacture. Wrought iron is hard to date by analysis as the methods used remained the same over a long period and only the use of modern iron now distinguishes today's black-smith's work from earliest productions.

## Makers' and Other Marks

Many 19th-century and earlier blacksmiths signed their work but there is no book which can help identify where or when they worked. Local records have to be consulted if a particular blacksmith's mark has to be identified. Owners' initials, marks or inscriptions are seldom found on ordinary objects.

## Condition

Iron tends to oxidize rather speedily, so it is not difficult to give a wrought iron object the appearance of age. However wear is not so easy to copy and fakers often simulate it indiscriminately. Look for wear at the points where an object would have been put under maximum use.

The surface of wrought iron ought to be genuinely worn by a combination of oxide, cleaning, repainting and wear, the cycle being repeated freqently over the object's working life. Genuine wrought iron usually has a pitted and mottled appearance, even if it has been cleaned (see *Ill. 3*). Look for evidence of use and decay: most reproduction iron will be rusted but not worn, impacted and corroded.

3
The authentic appearance of the effects of wear and oxide on wrought iron — a detail of a 17th-century processional cross.

4
A wrought iron candleholder. This is clearly hand made — the arms have been fused rather crudely into place and the whole is uneven and roughly constructed. Such articles are known to have been used from at least the 16th century until the 18th on cottage walls, in outhouses and farm buildings.

The arms are now thin in places and the piece has a slightly frail appearance. The sharp edges that might be felt when handling it could plausibly be the result of wear and oxide.

The style, method of manufacture and appearance all suggest that it is old. It probably dates from before 1700, but with wrought iron it is hard to be any more precise.

# 8 : SHEFFIELD PLATE

SHEFFIELD PLATE properly describes a process of fusing silver and copper that was accidentally discovered by Thomas Boulsover in 1742. It was applied to the manufacture of domestic articles from the 1750s to the 1850s, and no article may legally be sold as Sheffield Plate unless it is made both by the precise process and within the period.

Not all Sheffield Plate was made in Sheffield however. Large quantities were made in other manufacturing towns in England and the process was copied abroad. Russia, Poland and France all produced fused silver items, though their quality and style were generally sufficiently inferior to make them easily recognizable. To date there is no evidence of any large scale production in Ireland or North America.

Boulsover enjoyed some success with his discovery, but not enough. By 1769 he had given up making fused plate, but Joseph Hancock, now known as ''The Father of Sheffield Plate'', had taken up the process for the manufacture of domestic items. Matthew Boulton established his Birmingham factory in 1762, and with his partner John Fotherfill produced high quality work. Boulton was among the first platers to adopt the sterling silver thread process, invented by Roberts and Cadman, by which a silver wire was soldered to edges to hide the raw copper that would otherwise show through. Such pieces Boulton stamped with the words SILVER BORDERS and his marks, the double or single rayed sun.

IOS<sup>H</sup> HANCOCK SHEFFIELD.

The maker's mark of Joseph Hancock, ''The Father of Old Sheffield Plate'', and right, the mark of Boulton and Fothergill. It is rare that makers' marks on Old Sheffield bear anything more than a fleeting resemblance to silver hallmarks. This is about as close a parallel as is normally seen.

[1]
A set of three tea caddies from the mid-1760s. Seams, when the construction required them, can be difficult to trace; on these items they should be discoverable inside, at the corners.

## The Process

The first form of Sheffield Plate was arrived at by binding with a brass wire an ingot of sterling silver to an ingot of copper that was hardened with about 25 per cent brass alloy. The bound ingots were then heated in a furnace until they fused; when cool they were rolled into thin sheets. This was single plating. After 1770 however, double plating came in. The method was similar, but now the copper ingot was sandwiched between two ingots of silver. The resulting sheets accordingly showed silver on both sides and could be used for making articles such as sauce boats and entree dishes that required silver to show inside as well as out. Where a surface was unlikely to be seen but nonetheless required a finish it was tinned. Original tinning is steely grey in colour and if it is in good condition counts as a plus point.

Fused plate articles were made in much the same way as their solid counterparts. This created a problem, the solution to which presents us with a guide to authenticity. The hammering and annealing required to raise a seamless vessel contributed to the edges of the work fraying. Makers masked this by cutting the sheet at an angle, allowing the upper or outer edge to be drawn over and under (''lapped'') to keep the edge tidy and conceal the raw copper. It is thus only on the very earliest examples of Sheffield Plate that a raw copper edge can be seen. This problem also existed on items produced by seaming and die-stamping. The application of a hollow silver wire or

[2] *above, left*
A candelabrum of the type for which Matthew Boulton was justly famous, with applied heavy silver and lead-filled borders. It dates from about 1800.

[3] *above, right*
One of a pair of wine coolers, dating from about 1800, with a rubbed-in engraved armorial. Had this been a very early piece of Sheffield Plate, the engraving tool would have revealed the copper underneath the silver skin.

thread (after 1785) proved an effective alternative. Wire was applied until the mid-1820s, the technique having run concurrently with applied decorative borders — first the bead, then the gadroon and finally the foliate and shell motifs — since the 1790s. These borders were made of stamped silver filled with lead.

A major innovation in 1768 was the production of plated wire, which enabled the construction of delicate wirework baskets and other decorative containers. The refined effect of wirework was a natural partner to the elegant designs of the Adam period; work of this period was enhanced by piercing, bright-cut engraving and the application of either stamped out or applied reeded wire or bead borders.

**Electroplating** The technical innovation that hastened the decline of the Sheffield process was the introduction of German silver, in which a mixture of nickel and brass was applied between the copper and the silver. By 1836 a refined nickel called Argentine was used as a total replacement for the copper. Then in 1840 a patent was registered for an electroplating process which was to prove the end of Sheffield Plate.

However, by the end of the 19th century there was a considerable demand for the Old Sheffield look and electroplating onto copper as well as Argentine became popular. This is where mistakes can occur. When silver has worn through to expose the copper underneath (called "bleeding") it has been assumed that the article must be Old Sheffield. But this can only be so if the silver is of sterling standard — electroplating is done with pure silver. Initially the sharpness of colour and the feel may be a guide, but the forger can now create an old "skin" or patina. In the last resort a solution of nitric acid dropped on the surface will decide — it will turn sterling silver blue but has no effect on pure (electroplated) silver. A replated Old Sheffield item can be told by its slightly greasy feel.

Most of the Sheffield Plate that appears on the market is in relatively good condition, whereas much 19th-century electroplate is very much the worse for wear. This is in part because the method of making Old Sheffield articles — annealing and raising — actually strengthens the metal. If an article can be easily impressed or dented it is unlikely to be Old Sheffield.

## Style and Decoration

Gradually, Sheffield Plate became as popular as silver — and not just because it was cheaper. In some homes, plated articles were used in preference to their equivalents in sterling silver. For Sheffield Plate to be this popular it had to be as fashionable as silver: shapes and forms of ornament had to be fully up to date and every bit as stylish as their sterling counterparts. An item that is offered as early Old Sheffield that is not stylistically true to its period is unlikely to be authentic. This rule of thumb does not however apply throughout the whole period of Sheffield Plate: in the last two decades of the process, fused platers kept their expensive Regency steel dies in use.

[4]
These two figure candlesticks are so fluid as to appear cast, yet they are Old Sheffield dating from c. 1815. The front and back of each figure are made separately and soldered together — a seam is therefore detectable.

[5]
An early Sheffield Plate two-handled cup c. 1760, by Thomas Law. The quality of the work shows an important aspect of Sheffield Plate — that it was in many cases made by silversmiths, who made fashionable items either in silver or in Sheffield Plate as the market required.

[6]
A collection of Sheffield Plate coffee pots dating from c. 1760 to c. 1810. The one on the left shows the marks of Tudor and Leader, punched "silver style". The change in patterns over the period is quite evident and a reminder that all Old Sheffield made prior to about 1830 should be made to a completely authentic pattern for the period from which it purports to come.

# 9 : AMERICAN SILVER

Aмerican silver of the colonial period—with the temporary exception of that made in New York until the mid-18th century—relied very heavily for its designs on English models (in New York Dutch influence was stronger). The possibility instantly arises of wrong attribution in some cases if one is judging by style alone. A substantial number of pieces could have been made in either country.

The fact that America did not adopt the hallmarking system could lead one to suspect all sorts of malfeasance. If, under the strict supervision of the Goldsmiths Company, English silversmiths could perpetrate deceptions such as those described in "English Silver" (p.127), what could American silversmiths not have got up to without any form of regulation?

## The Marking System

To forge an English hallmark requires the making of four, five or even six punches. American silver of the 18th century however normally bore only a maker's mark. This might be the maker's full name stamped in a rectangular punch or it might be just his initials, but either way, it is a great deal less trouble to forge these marks than those of an English assay office.

There is no simple way to gauge whether a marked piece is genuine. Comparison with the mark on an article known to be genuine by reason of its provenance can help to confirm the authenticity of a mark or to raise doubts about it. It is in the end largely a matter of experience, however; of establishing whether the marks look right—whether they have been punched where one would expect, whether the silver looks new or has the patina and wear appropriate to a piece that is 200 years old.

There are three main ways to fake silver with American marks. The first is to make a copy of something that one would expect to find made in the Colonial or Federal periods and stamp it with a fake punch, thus making an out-and-out fake. The second is to take a piece of English silver of the period, erase the hallmarks and add an American maker's mark with a forged punch. This is rather more difficult to detect than the first deception as the piece will be authentic in every detail of style, wear and patina. The third is to find a beaten up but perfectly genuine American spoon, cut out its mark and solder it into a larger piece; a thin line of solder can usually be seen however when this has been done.

Wrong attribution of marks is another possibility. There is a not inconsiderable amount of antique English silver stamped with a maker's mark only. Such items judged by their style alone could often have been produced in either America or England. If found in America, it is a natural assumption that they are American until proved otherwise—an assumption that may be made innocently or by turning a blind eye.

### Makers' Marks

1 *above*
The makers' marks of the 17th-century firm of Hull and Sanderson, Boston.

With reasonable technical ability for die-sinking such punches can be simulated. The more one can examine authentic punched marks therefore, the more likely it is that a wrong one will be spotted.

2
Marks used by John Coney, Boston.

3
Marks used by Peter van Dyck or Dyke. Their relative simplicity and minor variation indicate how easy it would be for a skilled forger to simulate them.

4
Maker's marks used by Jacob Hurd of Boston, recorded from 1723. Some makers used their initials only, others their surname, yet others marked their work with initials and surname.

5
Marks used by Philip Syng Jr, of the famous Philadelphia family.

6
Two versions of Paul Revere II's mark.

7
Two of the several marks used by Samuel Kirk of Baltimore between 1830 and 1846. The figures refer to the weight of the piece. If Kirk's work were not so well known, the wide variety in his marks could be taken as an invitation to add to his catalogue.

## The Safeguard

Whereas in theory American silver was wide open to abuse, in practice there is a powerful safeguard. It is that comparatively little silver was produced in America during the Colonial period. Most of it is now in major collections and has been carefully scrutinized and recorded. An unrecorded piece coming on the market would be noticed immediately and would need, if it was not authentic, to be a very good fraud indeed if it was to get past the expert assessment it would undoubtedly receive. Despite the close regulation of silver in England, it would probably be easier to get rid of a dubious piece of 18th-century English silver than of its exact counterpart from, say, Boston, simply because it could be buried in yet another routine sale of antique silver.

## Proper Attribution

Silver should not be assessed from its mark alone—nor should the mark or marks be the first thing you look at, for they can prejudice a more balanced judgement. The overall design should be the first aspect to consider, followed by condition and then details of decoration.

In the matter of design, the student of American silver has some interesting and subtle problems to contend with. New England silver of the 17th century—to all intents and purposes Boston silver—is instantly recognizable to someone who is familiar with English silver of the period. Many of the 24 goldsmiths working in Boston in 1680 had served their apprenticeship in London and they brought on their apprentices in the same tradition. Not only were they London trained, but as well as making silver themselves they regularly imported pieces from London, as many extant bills and letters prove.

The prosperity of the Colonies meant more work for silversmiths and they established themselves in many New England towns, such as Newport and Providence, Rhode Island; New

8 *left*
A George I bullet teapot. Bullet-shaped teapots are rare and fairly important objects and at one time this teapot, bearing only the maker's mark "S.B." was optimistically believed to have been made by Stephen Burdett in New York about 1730.

Apart from the fact that it could be shown quite unequivocally that the mark was in fact that of Samson Bennett, and therefore the teapot was made in Falmouth, Devon, about 1725, the bellflower motif from which the spout springs is entirely typical of Exeter/Plymouth/Falmouth.

9
A coffee pot by Paul Revere II, Boston, 1781—the exact date is confirmed by his account books.

Whereas it is true that American silversmiths were following English patterns closely, there were on occasion time lags, of which this is one. The Rococo outline and very Rococo spout of this example would have been considered dreadfully outmoded in London at this date.

Note that with the exception of the contemporary coat-of-arms the pot is left entirely plain and unchased, as one would expect.

Haven, Hartford and Norwalk, Connecticut; Ipswich, Massachusetts; and many others. From the end of the 17th century the great city of Philadelphia was supporting a large number of goldsmiths, pre-eminent among them the first members of the Richardson dynasty. Outside New York, all these smiths were working in current English styles.

New York was a law unto itself, as it still is in so many respects. The names of smiths alone give one a good idea of what to expect: Cornelius van der Burch, Jacobus van der Spiegel, Cornelius Kierstede and Peter van Dyck were making items as closely patterned on Dutch models as the Richardsons' work resembled that of London goldsmiths. The descendants of these same smiths however were within a couple of generations succumbing to the fashion for English silver that dominated New England, but at the end of the 17th century and during the early years of the 18th, two styles were in production contemporaneously and were sold alongside virtually identical imported wares.

1 *below*
A tankard by John Coney, Boston, *c.* 1690.
A fine example of Coney's work. Note especially the cherub's head on the handle terminal: this is a feature that is particularly American and is very rare on English made tankards.
The position of the mark is also informative. American made tankards, mugs and cream jugs are usually marked on the left of the handle, while English made pieces are almost invariably marked on the right. If an example turns up bearing a maker's mark only and punched to the right of the handle, make doubly sure that it is not English of provincial make.

3 *above*
A teapot and stand by Paul Revere II, Boston 1787. Quite unlike *Ill. 9* on the previous page, this shows Revere working in up-to-the-minute London style.
Pots of this sort would generally have either engraved and bright cut decoration or none at all. If you find any form of chased-on relief on pieces of this type and period they are best left well alone.

2
A single-handled porringer by Ebenezer Moulton, Newburyport, Mass., *c.* 1790. The late date clearly demonstrates the extraordinarily long survival of these objects in America, long after they had ceased to be made in England. Like so many American porringers, it is marked on the handle only.

As the 18th century progressed links with London remained strong, but certain features became characteristic of American silver and help to differentiate it from English wares. The lions rampant and angel-head terminals applied to New York tankards and to the pierced galleries of the vase-shaped sugar bowls of the Neoclassical period are just two examples. Forms changed too—witness the unusually large (not to say enormous) Philadelphia coffee pots of the late 18th and early 19th centuries.

**Porringers** For some reason, there is one object made in Colonial and indeed in Federal America that steadfastly maintained its popularity despite its demise in England early in the 18th century—the single-handled porringer. Quite what these porringers were for is a matter for heated debate and various conyictions; what is certain is that they are attractive objects and very collectable.

Large numbers of American made porringers are marked only on the handle. This raises the possibility of removing a handle, taking several casts from it, making several more bowls and multiplying at a stroke the number of early porringers without undue difficulty. Marks that have been cast rather than punched tend to show a certain roughness however; a slight pitting to the background can be seen with a glass, whereas a punch leaves a cleaner impression.

**The 19th Century** The tendency to establish an indigenous style that was asserting itself in the latter part of the 18th century was disrupted in the first few decades of the 19th.

After the split with Britain it was natural that there should be some dissociation from English models, and this was accompanied by a leaning towards France in its Empire and post-Empire periods. This quasi-French style was not altogether successful however and rarely poses possibilities of confusion between French models and American adaptations of them. The style shows at its best in New York, but even there it was relatively heavy, lumpish and derivative.

From this period on, errors of attribution (and the possibilities of deception) arising from confusion between Dutch, English and French originals and their American counterparts become less likely. In mid-century a great surge of both design and technical ability, particularly in New York and Baltimore, led to the creation of an emphatically American style. Led by Joseph Kirk of Baltimore it reflected the European Rococo Revival and exhibited a marked penchant for robustly chased and cast work decorated with complex Classical architectural scenes. The enormous American water jug

4 *above and left*
One of a pair of water jugs by Samuel Kirk, Baltimore, *c.* 1850. A superb example of the high quality of the chaser's art in the United States in the mid-19th century. For some reason, elaborate Rococo chasing is very seldom found in America during the 18th-century Rococo period (*c.* 1740-70). If shown a mug or coffee pot from that earlier period with high Rococo chasing, look at it several times and prudent be. On the other hand, silver of the mid-19th century with high relief chasing can be accepted with relative confidence. Left: a detail of the chasing.

1

This relatively modest cream pitcher by Thomas Arnold (Newport, Rhode Island, c. 1760) is a perfect candidate for later decoration. It would be more than reasonable to expect an English example of this date to be chased but rare indeed to find a genuine American one.

probably came into style at this time. The lavishness of their decoration together with the size of many of the more distinguished examples of this period mean that these pieces are unlikely to be fraudulently reproduced or made up.

Later in the 19th century both Tiffany and Gorham were responsible for a great deal of silver and base metal work made in the Aesthetic taste; their forays into Art Nouveau were equally successful. This period of silversmithing in America has been ignored by collectors until relatively recently, when there was a dramatic surge of interest, with price increases to match. American silver of this period is arguably better made and more innovative than at any other, the technical skill displayed being some protection against faking.

## Alterations

A besetting problem in English silver, alterations can be made for reasons of innocent expediency or to enhance prices. The kinds of alteration to be found on American silver are, necessarily, similar to those effected on English silver: tankards to jugs, for example; see the following chapter.

While pieces of American silver that have been altered at some time in the past exist, it becomes progressively less likely that alterations will be made now or in the future. Authentic items from the 18th century now fetch such high prices that they will be preserved as they are, which incidentally means that the would-be "improver" has to pay a fortune for his raw material and is therefore most unlikely to be able to make a profit from his work.

In parallel with alterations to the form of pieces, a great deal of relatively plain American silver was chased up in the mid-19th century with fruit and flowers. This was done merely to update pieces and with no intent to deceive, but the embellishment can be so obtrusive as to render the qualities of the original invisible.

## Training The Eye

Because of the way that American silver developed—at first in close imitation of two European styles, then developing a domestic identity but remaining open to foreign influence— authentication by style alone can be quite difficult. The marking system is of value, but it leaves much unsaid. There is accordingly no substitute for looking at lots of silver and developing a feel for what is authentically American.

A knowledgeable dealer is the best assistance and protection a collector can have, for he or she will assist with their knowledge and protect with their reputation. Excellent collections, such as those at Boston, Yale, the Metropolitan Museum and Winterthur to mention but a few, were formed to inform and should be used accordingly. The third and indispensable source of experience is books, both the catalogues of major collections and more discursive works, a few of which are mentioned in the Bibliography.

# 10 : ENGLISH SILVER

THE SILVER HALLMARKING SYSTEM, introduced in the late 15th century in the form which has lasted to the present day, is one of the earliest types of consumer protection. The 20th-century dealer and collector is extremely fortunate to have this system to back up his knowledge of style and form. The hallmark will indicate to the purchaser that a piece is of sterling or Britannia standard, in addition to revealing its age. This provides a system for double-checking the instinctive judgement of a piece against the marks of one of the official Assay Offices. The faker of silver articles has to be that much more inventive than fakers in other areas of antiques, as he has to produce not only the piece but also the hallmark.

The ultimate guardian of honest trade practice is the Assay Master at Goldsmiths Hall. In addition to being responsible for the assaying and marking of all new wares, the Assay Master chairs the Antique Plate Committee which sits regularly to examine suspect pieces submitted for scrutiny. The Committee is made up of experts in the trade. As well as attending meetings their duties include informing the Assay Office of any suspect piece they may come across. The Assay Master will then require other members to examine the item and either confirm or contradict the original suspicion.

The focus of this attention naturally falls on the auction market, as that is where the majority of traders purchase pieces. Occasionally a piece will be withdrawn from sale because it is suspect. This makes London unique in that an amateur collector has unparalleled protection against being duped at auction. If a piece were to escape the eye of one of the Antique Plate Committee members, which is unlikely, the major auction houses have a reputation to maintain, and some of them give a five-year guarantee which offers additional protection. The Trade Descriptions Act can also be employed in extreme cases.

## The Categories of Fake Silver

There are two distinct categories of fake silver: articles with forged hallmarks and hallmarked pieces which have been altered or incorporated into others. The former, until recent years, were fairly easy to spot by comparing the marks presented with marks which were known to be genuine; the evidence now points to greater sophistication being employed by forgers to reproduce facsimiles of marks, and microscopic examination is sometimes necessary. The latter is usually detectable by diagnostic examination.

### The "Bekegle" Cup

An example of how much our knowledge of antique silver has improved is the "Bekegle" cup. Sir Charles Jackson, who produced his excellent volume of marks in 1905, illustrated this piece on page 632 of the first edition (page 685 in the second) and described it as *c.* 1690, made in Cork by Charles Bekegle, the Flemish immigrant who was Warden of the Cork Guild of Goldsmiths in 1693. Recent examination of this piece showed that the marks are fake and the decoration, combined with the shape, is quite wrong for the period.

[1] *right*
Never believe the hallmark implicitly. This tray bore the maker's mark "AC" and London hallmarks for 1895 when it appeared at auction in 1980. When examined in 1986 the original marks had gone and 1745 marks had appeared. The mixture of styles would point to alteration if the tray were truly 1745.

[2] *below*
A close examination of the marks on the tray however disclosed discrepancies when they were compared with a set of marks known to be authentic.

## The Analytical Method

The oblong tea tray above illustrates the kind of deceit practised in the 1980s. It appears to be mid-18th century; the hallmark is for London 1745 with the maker's mark "SW". On the face of it, this is a magnificent George II 20 in. (51 cm) tea tray. The experienced eye is however uneasy. Examining the tray in all its aspects the following points can be noted:

1. Gadroon borders are rarely, if ever, combined with chased decoration.
2. The band of flat chased decoration is too dense and tightly packed to be contemporary with the mark.
3. There are no co-ordinating stylistic factors between the dolphin feet (not visible), the border, the band of chasing and the armorial.
4. Armorials were not generally enclosed in drapery cartouches in 1745.
5. The quality of engraving is poor for the purported date.
6. Hallmarks are more commonly found on the underside of trays, whereas in this case they have been struck among the decoration to disguise discrepancies.
7. The hallmarks are in an unnaturally straight line.
8. The maker's mark is that of Samuel Wood, a caster and cruet frame maker who rarely employed chased decoration.
9. The shape of the shields around the three hallmarks varies and there are minute discrepancies in size.

Research in sale catalogues showed that this same tray had previously been sold with a different maker's mark and the authentic date 1895. But had the substitution of marks not been noticed and if the tray had been sold as George II rather than late Victorian it could have fetched as much as four times its proper price.

The questions to ask, after forming an initial impression based on style, are then these:

☐ *Do the hallmarks agree with your initial impression of date?*

☐ *Are all the marks there?*

☐ *Are they distorted or in an unusual position?*

☐ *Are any subsidiary pieces lacking the correct marks?*

☐ *Are there any signs of repair, such as patches or rough soldering where separately made pieces have been attached?*

**3** *left and right*
A late 19th-century conversion of an 18th-century mug into a jug. The hallmark is for 1768–9, the engraved date is presumably commemorative. The handle and foot are typically those of a mug, and the piece is both too large for an 18th-century milk jug and too small for a water or ale jug. The marks (right) are clustered. The decoration lacks coordination — the fluted rim is imitative of the William III-Queen Anne period, and whereas the birds among fruit and foliage of the Rococo era would coincide with the marks they are improbable with a plain handle and foot.

## Tankards

Perhaps one of the most common fakes is the conversion of an 18th-century tankard or mug to a more useful jug. This was done extensively during the 19th century and the illustrations show some typical examples.

The covered tankard became unfashionable in the 19th century and provided the innovative silversmith with an object that could be converted into a variety of items. The most common alteration was to a jug for hot or cold liquids. *Ill. 3,* p. 130 shows an 1870 conversion from a baluster tankard. The chased decoration is in the mood of Landseer, whose paintings and engravings were so popular at this period. This example is perfectly legal and saleable as the additions of spout and finial have been later hallmarked. Apart from the marks on the spout and finial, the outline form of the handle, the lid with thumbpiece, the body and the foot immediately suggest a tankard. The fact that there are four hallmarks on the base and inside the domed lid is also a clue. Tankards are the only pieces that have this combination of four marks on the base

**4**
The conversion of mugs and tankards to jugs became so commonplace in the late 19th century that silversmiths began to copy the fakes. This example was made and hallmarked 1899.

2 *right*
The marks on the base of the jug above are a giveaway: only tankards, mugs, coffee pots and the larger ale jugs have this cluster of marks.

4
A tankard in elaborate disguise, but the lid with thumbpiece, the handle and spreading foot are recognizably those of the original form. The mock William III-Queen Anne fluting is also a giveaway when combined with a hallmark for 1760. When this was converted about a hundred years ago very few people knew that the hallmark would reveal a date.

Although Octavius Morgan first demonstrated there was an annual date letter system to the Society of Antiquaries in 1851 it was another quarter of a century before people became familiar with the more detailed works of W. Chaffers and W.J. Cripps. Universal recognition of the British hallmarking system was certainly not apparent until the publication in 1905 of *English Goldsmiths and their Marks* by Sir Charles J. Jackson F.S.A., and probably not easily available until the first edition of Bradbury's (pocket) *Book of Hallmarks* was published in 1927.

1 *left*
The faked jug can occasionally be completely divorced in form from the mug from which it was made. But though its origins are well disguised, this jug, hallmarked 1768, arouses immediate suspicion by its large size and the style of its decoration.

3 *above*
No attempt has been made to disguise the shape of this tankard. This is an "honest" conversion from a plain piece with added mask spout, rocky finial, ivory fillets in the handle and chasing. The spout and finial, the only parts of silver added, have been assayed and marked 1870.

and lid as a matter of course.

The example in *Ill. 4* (left) is a less obvious alteration from a tankard, but compare the handle, lid with thumbpiece, and foot. Add to this the "Queen Anne" decoration and the 1760 mark and no further proof is needed, but one hundred or so years ago, when hallmarks were less well understood, this was not so obvious.

*Ill. 5* (opposite) is a conversion of a Queen Anne tankard with pseudo-Queen Anne decoration. A better attempt, but still obvious because of the retention of the original shape. The handle fillets are also wrong as these, in conjunction with silver handles, are not found on English silver until the 19th century.

The tankard on the left of *Ill. 8* is an authentic example. Note the thumbpiece which is needed for convenient opening of the lid: a finial in the centre of the lid is a more common feature for a pouring vessel. The coffee pot on the right in *Ill. 8* is a "legalized" conversion from a tankard. Note the similarity in size and taper with the tankard. The thumbpiece has been removed but the marks reveal a date of 1774, while the finial and spout are hallmarked 1831. The handle with fillets is again a feature which should prompt suspicion.

Genuine coffee pots can be subjected to the addition of decoration alone. This is not illegal and while in Victorian times it would have enhanced the appeal and value of a piece, today it will probably diminish it by a factor of five.

## Later Decoration

The alteration to or imitation of older styles was not just a phenomenon of the late 19th century. As early as 1810 the large manufacturing silversmiths of Garrards and Rundell, Bridge and Rundell were reproducing late 17th-century Baroque style and mid-18th century Rococo style pieces (see *Ill. 2*, p. 134). The pair of ornate jugs (*Ill. 1*, p. 132) is early

**8** *above*
A comparison between a 1766 tankard and a coffee pot made up from a tankard of the same period. The additions to make the pot were in this case hallmarked in 1831, but the shape in conjunction with the 1774 marks should have pointed immediately to a conversion.

**5** *above*
A better attempt at deception (compare the similar fluting on *Ill. 4*, opposite), but the tankard shape is still obvious, especially when the spout is omitted.

**6** *right*
Many pieces have been subjected to later decoration which is not against the hallmarking laws. Here a Queen Anne coffee pot of 1705 has been savaged in the second quarter of the 19th century.

**7** *left*
This jug is not only later decorated but is also converted from a goblet by adding a handle and the superstructure.

Its marks (below) reveal its origins in a goblet hallmarked in Edinburgh in 1818. The marks are on a level with the lower handle fixing, therefore near the rim of the original piece. The marks on an original jug would normally be near the base.

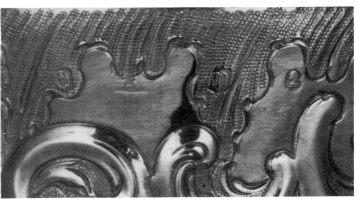

[1]
A pair of Queen Anne ewers given a "more authentic antiqueness"(!) for the early 19th-century dilettante. Originally very plain, their handles, finials, spouts and chasing were all added in Edward Cornelius Farrell's workshop in 1822.

evidence of the alteration of pieces to the "antique style" so avidly sought after by dilettanti in the early 19th century. The bodies are made from 1705 Queen Anne ale jugs which have been chased with mythological battle scenes. The spouts have been cast from a mid 18th-century piece and the handles modelled on the 17th-century caryatid type.

## Cream Jugs

In the past, cream jugs or boats were created by converting a number of obsolete objects. The most common are caster to pitcher cream jug (*Ill. 4*, below), punch ladle bowls to small cream boats (below), and pap boats to similar but larger vessels by the addition of feet and handles.

[2] *above and below*
Two punch ladles, ripe for conversion, one plain London 1766 and the other with contemporary decoration, London 1753.

[3] *right*
A punch ladle bowl to which feet and a handle have been added to make a cream boat. The double lipped variety is found with two handles and four feet added. Pap boats are also subjected to this alteration.

## Teapots, Stands and Kettles

Teapots were rarely converted to other objects but were often modernized by adding decoration, a new spout, finials and handle. These can usually be spotted by following the analytical method.

Teapot stands, which were common in the late 18th and early 19th centuries, have been used to manufacture "antique" teapots. Nearly all the stands are hallmarked in a straight line and not at the points of the compass as on the base of a teapot. Teapot lids should be hallmarked, and if these marks are missing or differ from the base mark then warning bells should sound. Small bullet teapots of the first half of the 18th century also need careful examination, as it is now known

[4]
Small baluster casters have been converted to more useful pitcher cream jugs by the addition of handles and spouts. Occasionally they are very difficult to spot, but usually poor craftsmanship, discoloration of the skin or heat marks where the additions have been soldered should point to a conversion.

*continued on page 136*

1 *left*
A pair of cast silver candlesticks, made by Samuel Tingley, New York, *c.* 1760-65. Cast candlesticks made in America are extremely rare.

It would appear that most American goldsmiths used to import English candlesticks for sale, and there is no doubt that these two are cast from an English model. On the undersides of the bases it is possible to see the slight impressions where the hallmarks were on the original.

To create such objects today would not be technically too demanding. It would be relatively easy to remove the English marks on an English made pair of cast candlesticks and substitute an American mark, thereby increasing their apparent worth several times. To sell such an item would be considerably more difficult however. There are so few surviving pairs of American cast candlesticks that a hitherto unknown pair would automatically require the closest possible inspection by experts of the first rank.

2 *right*
A Tiffany silver milk jug in the Japanese style with applied motifs in mixed metals, *c.* 1890.

The prices of spectacular Art Nouveau and Aesthetic items by Tiffany are now so high that in theory a substantial opportunity exists for the faker. In practice, however, each example coming on the market will be checked with extreme thoroughness; any attempt at deception would have to be exceedingly good.

By contrast there seems as yet to be no significant premium on more modest Tiffany items. These are therefore scarcely any more prone to the faker's attentions than other objects of similar quality, design and period.

1
The épergne, or centrepiece, enjoyed a period of popularity in the 18th century. A number have been dismantled at times when their popularity has waned, with the result that the small dishes have been sold as sweetmeat baskets. These are not always fully marked, and can be easily spotted, not only by style but by lack of date letter and town marks.

2 *below*
Making honest replicas had a brief period of popularity in the early 19th century. The sideboard dish was made in 1814 for Garrards in the 17th-century Baroque style, though there is some stylistic confusion as the engraving is a copy of mid-18th century Rococo.

The cup on the other hand is a straight replica of a George III race cup, the form of which is based on designs by Robert Adam of 1763. It was made in 1857 by Hancocks from the silver of the 1856 Doncaster Cup, which the recipient was presumably not pleased with as the original was an equestrian statuette of Napoleon III.

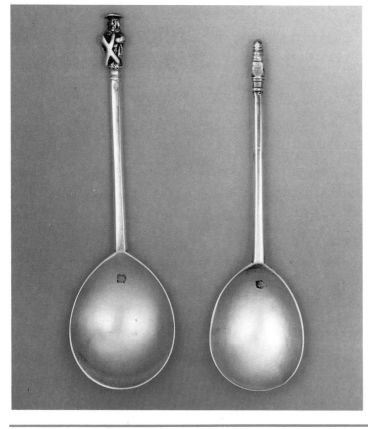

3 *above*

Collecting silver reached fever pitch in the decade and a half before the First World War and there was not enough antique silver coming on to the market to satisfy the demand. This encouraged manufacturers to produce replicas of earlier pieces and in some cases to produce fakes.

The silver-gilt monteith bowl was made for the firm of Wakely and Wheeler in 1903. This style, a copy of a piece dating from about 1690, was copied extensively, sometimes with 17th- or 18th-century hallmarks to deceive the collector.

The ewer is a copy of an early 18th-century example made for Carringtons in 1910.

4 *left*

Two spoons, apparently of the same period, one hallmarked 1630, the other 1628. The apostle spoon is a modern forgery and a very clever one, but there are certain features which betray the deceit. The proportions are slightly wrong — notice the slightly larger bowl. The detail of the finial figure is very stiff, especially the treatment of the nimbus with holy dove. The lack of any wear at the edge of the bowl is disconcerting, but of course not always a sign that a piece is a forgery.

*continued from page 132*

**1**
A brandy saucepan with the handle removed makes an ideal small sugar basin.

**2**
Add a handle to an example with a spout and a cream jug is created.

**3** *below*
A Plymouth or Exeter type cream jug. These have been suspect in the past because they are so like conversions from brandy saucepans.

that some were made up by unscrupulous use of the silver and marks from a mug or tankard.

Tea kettles, like teapots, were often updated, but are not commonly faked. Always make sure that all separate parts are correctly marked and there should be little chance of being fooled. On one type of fake however the marks from an 18th-century tankard base have been let in to the base of the kettle while the tankard lid is used to make a burner, which is fixed to the tripod stand. The test here is to look carefully for any distortion of the hallmarks, to make sure the lid has a good mark, and, if the burner is removable, to check for a hallmark on the stand. The burner, which is small compared with a tankard lid, is the place where the marks will be most obviously distorted if it is a fake.

Tea/coffee or hot water urns are sometimes found made from a cup and cover by adding a tap; alternatively urns are occasionally found converted to cups by the removal of taps.

The wine funnel (left) has been subjected to various adaptations. The most common is calling the bowl of the funnel a tea strainer. By blocking the perforations in the bowl it can become a small sugar basin or salt cellar. The replacement of the spout by a pedestal foot can make a goblet. If the foot is not made so tall, and a spout and handle are added, a milk jug can be made. It is highly unlikely that these adaptations would be made now that wine funnels are fairly rare and can fetch several hundred pounds at auction.

## Sugar Basins, Argyles and Brandy Saucepans

Large sugar basins were needed for unrefined sugar and the size of these is such that with the addition of a handle, lid and

**4**
How a wine funnel was converted into a tea strainer, a goblet or a milk jug.

[5]
A pair of candlesticks, Ebenezer Coker, London 1769, cast from a pair of Queen Anne candlesticks. Although these are genuine, having been re-marked, examples are found cast from originals without being re-marked. Always check to see whether the marks occur in identical positions on each candlestick, look for granulation in the mark and look for identical flaws in both sticks

spout a small teapot can be created. The argyle (gravy pot) with internal insulator removed is occasionally found passed off as a rare bachelor's teapot.

Brandy saucepans are sometimes found with their handles removed to be sold as sugar basins. Spouts can be added to early 18th-century examples or replaced on later examples. There has also been controversy in the past about a type of cream jug that looks like a 1730s brandy saucepan with its turned wood handle removed and a simple wire scroll handle added. These have now been accepted as genuine, but only if they are made by Exeter or Plymouth silversmiths who used this style.

## Candlesticks

Until the third quarter of the 18th century the majority of table candlesticks were cast. It is possible to make a mould from a candlestick that has been hallmarked and thus achieve a very accurate replica, including marks. The innovation of electrotypes in the mid-19th century added yet another dimension to the art of copying.

Candlesticks cast from one another, including marks, can be spotted by careful comparison of the placing of the hallmarks and any obvious flaws. With loaded candlesticks there is a possibility that marks have been "let in" to the edge of the base. The "let in" mark is most likely to have come from table silver, and if a maker's mark is visible it will probably be identifiable as a "spoonmaker's". Seams where the piece has been soldered in are also likely to be visible. The detachable drip-pan or nozzle should always be marked with maker's and duty marks to match the stick.

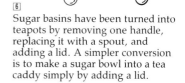

[6]
Sugar basins have been turned into teapots by removing one handle, replacing it with a spout, and adding a lid. A simpler conversion is to make a sugar bowl into a tea caddy simply by adding a lid.

*right*
Candlesticks and tapersticks were intentionally reproduced in earlier styles from the early 19th century onwards. These reproductions are recognizable by their smaller bases and fatter stem proportions. On the left is a Victorian taperstick of 1848, a copy of the 1762 example on the right. In the centre is a copy of an early George II example made by Bradbury's in 1908, again of dumpier proportions than the original.

2 *above and below*
A chamber candlestick formed from an inkstand bottle holder with added handle, sconce, base and feet.

Always examine candelabra carefully as an old trick is to solder the nozzle sleeve to a branch so that it bears the same mark as the candlestick. Candelabra branches should be marked with date letter, standard, duty, town and maker's mark, depending on their period. All detachable parts should also bear corresponding marks.

Chamber candlesticks are now popular again as they are ideal for small dining tables. Again, check the detachable pieces. Hallmarks will not appear on them if the chamber stick has been constructed from an epergne dish (especially period 1720–60), a wine funnel stand, salt cellar stand or counter tray. Wax jacks are also known to have been made up from these same items.

Snuffers and their accompanying trays have been comparatively free from interference by fakers but are occasionally subjected to the addition of handles and feet. They are also convenient style converting into inkstands by the addition of simple rings to hold the glass inkwells. The absence of or difference in hallmark on the inkwell covers will reveal the truth.

## Trays and Salvers

It is not often that one comes across tea trays that are wrong (though see *Ill. 1*, p.128), but when viewing a potential purchase check the mark to see if it is distorted at all or struck too close to the border. Either of these factors could reveal reshaping or additions to the borders. Tea trays are sometimes made up from oval salvers or meat dishes by the addition of handles and feet. In these cases the handles will often not match the design of the border, which they will normally do on a ''right'' example.

The most commonly found alteration of a salver is from a plain Georgian example to a decorative Victorian presentation piece (*Ill. 3*). If an inscription does not coincide with the mark, or if the style is not quite what one would expect, then check carefully to see if there are any odd creases or seams which might denote an added border and/or feet. Occasionally one

will find that the border has been hallmarked at the time of the addition. The marks are usually tiny and difficult to spot, but must be there if an altered salver is to be sold legally.

In the second half of the 17th century and the first quarter of the 18th there was a vogue for the salver on foot, or tazza. When the fashion for tazzas waned many had their central "trumpet" foot removed and three or four small feet added at the borders. These are usually discernible by an examination of the centre on the underside where some sign of the position of the central foot will remain. I have also seen these conversions reversed. It is therefore important when examining a salver on foot to see that it is struck with the obligatory lion passant or leopard's head erased mark. This should always be the case except on some provincial or late examples of the second quarter of the 18th century onwards.

## Plates and Dishes

Dinner plates, soup plates and meat dishes, which were produced in their thousands for affluent 18th-century families, were usually of plain circular design until 1740. After this date the vogue was for shaped circular plates with gadroon borders, and many plain services were returned by patrons to their silversmith for updating. If they were not re-marked, the original marks will have been distorted and partly lost during the refashioning.

Another inventive use for the dinner plate during the last hundred years has been re-hammering them into more saleable and appealing rose bowls and strawberry dishes. Again, stretched marks will give this away. More difficult to detect is the conversion of soup plates into dinner plates by removing the centre of the plate, cutting it down, re-hammering and soldering back into the border. An original scratch weight is always a useful check, as soup plates tend to be between $7\frac{1}{2}$% and 15% heavier than dinner plates.

Entree dishes have been remarkably free from tampering, but the addition of decoration and the replacement of detachable handles should be watched for.

3 *above left*
Salvers were sometimes refashioned as presentation pieces. This example from the 1850s is typical, but the hallmark is for 1787. The original would have been plain circular with a reeded or beaded border. Some salvers that were altered in this way were sent for re-assay and a Victorian hallmark will be found on the border and added feet. If these marks are not visible then the piece contravenes the hallmarking laws.

4 *above right*
A 1775 salver with lap-over border. This type is peculiar to two periods in England, *c.* 1735–80 and, revived by Rundell, Bridge and Rundell, *c.* 1805–1815. A check should always be made to see if the lion passant and/or maker's mark is stamped on the border. If not, then it is probably an illegal alteration.

1 *right and below*
An 1803 cigarette box! Probably made around 1900 using a spoon mark with the maker's mark cleverly removed.

Soup tureens and sauce tureens are in the same category, with the following additional points: look out for let-in marks on pedestal feet, and make sure a full set of marks appears — otherwise the piece may be a converted liner. Soup tureens made in the period 1805–1840 often had detachable liners. These liners will have the same set of marks as the tureen except that the town mark (leopard's head or mask in the case of London) will have been omitted.

The faker has in the past found a variety of uses for both the tureen liner and the wine cooler liner. Whilst the former can be turned into baskets, bowls or tureens, the latter can, by the addition of lids, become biscuit barrels or ice buckets. Cake/dessert or sweetmeat baskets are extremely popular and apart from converted liners mentioned above, dismantled epergnes (*Ill.3*, p. 135) and converted goblets are the two most common deceptions.

## Cow Creamers and Porringers

Popular interest in collecting silver was immortalized by Bertie Wooster's antics with cow creamers and porringers. The cow creamer in its original form was almost exclusively made by John Schuppe in London between 1750 and 1775, while the ''modern Dutch'' replicas were made from the 1880s onwards. Eighteenth-century examples are clearly identifiable from the hallmarks: claims for those without should be given a wide berth. However, the modern Dutch cow creamer is worth one-tenth the value of an 18th-century English one.

Porringers on the other hand need careful examination if one is to avoid buying a fake. Many William III/Queen Anne style examples decorated with curved lobes and fluting below a corded girdle have been created from Georgian mugs and tankard lids. Careful examination of the hallmarks for distortion and signs of a seam where hallmarks may have been let in will reveal the truth in most cases.

Beakers are not very common in English silver and caution should be taken over 17th-century examples that bear the hallmark on the base. There is a chance that these may have

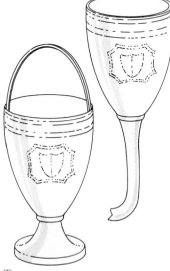

2
A goblet can be converted to a sweetmeat basket. Another possible conversion to look for is a goblet bowl into a wine funnel.

been rebodied. Be careful to compare the wear and colour of both body and base.

Other conversions and fakes to be looked out for that are not quite so common are:

- ☐ tankard lids converted into bleeding bowls

- ☐ dish rings with marks from a spoon let into the rim

- ☐ wine coasters converted to soy frames by the addition of a handle and feet

- ☐ cruet frames converted into wine coasters by the removal of handles and feet

- ☐ wine coasters converted into decanter wagons by soldering two together and adding carriage wheels

- ☐ punch ladle bowls converted into salt cellars

- ☐ salt cellars converted into mustard pots by the addition of lids and handles

- ☐ snuff boxes turned into vinaigrettes by adding grilles

- ☐ vinaigrettes converted into pill or cachou boxes by the removal of grilles

- ☐ teapot stands converted into toast racks by soldering on bars.

[3] *above and below*
This mustard pot has genuine 1791 marks, probably taken from a spoon. Notice the maker's mark is missing and that the lion passant mark is eroded in a peculiar fashion not consistent with normal wear. Apart from the style being wrong for the date, a mustard pot of this type would normally be hallmarked on the base in the 18th century.

## Cutlery

The novice silver collector will often use cutlery as his springboard — surely an area free from fakes and forgeries you may think. Certainly the ordinary spoon and fork is not often the focus of a forger's attention, but some of the rarities or specialist collecting fields are. For instance, caddy spoons have been a specialist collectors' area for decades and some of the common fakes are made by soldering the top of a Georgian teaspoon handle (with its marks) to a bowl of fancy design.

The first English design cutlery to be popularized was Hanoverian rat-tail pattern in the early 18th century, hence the aim of many is, or has been during the last hundred years, to own a service of this design. A limited amount has survived however, and therefore later 18th century Old English pattern items have been converted to supply the demand. Spoons with added rat-tails can usually be spotted because they appear on post-1740 examples, at which date the design was practically extinct. In addition the rat-tail is frequently of poor proportion and there is a visible seam. The accompanying fork of this pattern was three-pronged and these too are nowadays extremely valuable. Shams of these are more difficult to spot in isolation but many conversions were made from mixed bundles of spoons, which were made and have survived in greater numbers. If one comes across a dozen three-pronged forks, all with differing marks, then caution should be exercised. Always test the strength and length of the tines/prongs against a good example if possible.

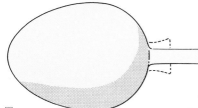

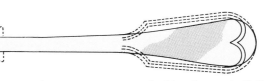

[1]
The removal of Fiddle pattern flanges to form Old English pattern — a legal alteration.

These conversions of table silver are all illegal, but one which is not is the alteration and matching up of patterns as long as no extra metal is added and as long as the form is not changed substantially. Fiddle pattern is not as popular as Old English, so it is not unknown for the former to have the shoulders at the top and base of the stem trimmed away to form the latter. Old English pattern in turn is not as sought after as the more decorative forms of the same design. It is, for example, not impossible to "manufacture" Old English Thread, Feather-edge, Beaded, and Bright-Cut engraved patterns from the plain form.

## Spoons

In the Victorian era there was a vogue for presenting "Berry [strawberry] Spoons". The majority of these are plain spoons which have been embossed with foliage, fruit or flowers in the second half of the 19th century. Their value is, strangely, usually double that of the plain spoon, reversing the price trend that is followed by later-chased holloware (mugs, tankards, coffee pots, etc.). The "modern" strawberry was not cultivated and popularized until the early 19th century, but a lot of these spoons are marked pre-1800. Sauce ladles have occasionally been treated in a similar fashion and sometimes pierced to form sugar sifters.

The doyen of cutlery is the apostle spoon, which was revered as an object of curiosity by antiquarians as early as the late 18th century. They were made over a period of two centuries in England, achieving their highest production during the late 16th and 17th centuries. Various types of forgeries occur of which the commonest is also the easiest to spot. This is the reshaping of a plain 18th-century tablespoon *Ill. 4*, p. 135. Another form that is also easy to spot — on close examination but not superficially — is a casting from an original. The test for this is to apply pressure to the stem: if it bends easily it is not an original. Apostle spoons are generally the most expensive of a group that includes seal tops and slip tops, as well as lion sejants, maidenheads and other finial types. It is therefore prudent to check carefully all finial spoons to see that they have not been changed. A good rule of thumb is to check the way in which the terminal has been jointed on. On London spoons it will be with a "V" and on provincial spoons a lap or "L" joint.

Clever fakes are still being produced to add to the deceptions practised in the past. But collectors should not let themselves be put off — genuine articles outnumber the fakes by more than a hundred to one. A good knowledge of the genuine article will automatically develop and extend into an instinct for that which is not, and instinct is one of our most valuable senses — manufactured reasoning to contradict it must be comprehensive.

**"Duty Dodgers"**
A few early 18th-century silversmiths occasionally dodged duty by making an item and incorporating marks from an older piece. "Duty dodgers" were produced mainly between 1719 and 1758, when the duty was sixpence per ounce. Typical candidates for this evasion were coffee pots, teapots, two-handled cups, casters and sauce boats on spreading feet. These are nearly always marked on the base and give the opportunity to insert a disc of silver with an earlier mark.

It is essential when first examining a piece to check both that marks coincide with dating by style, and that the marks appear in the correct places. Coffee pots, teapots, cups and casters are, more often than not, hallmarked in a cluster on the base in the same manner as mugs. If three or more base marks are in a straight line the likelihood is that a disc has been inserted. Coffee pots with straight tapering sides are ideal for this as the base is made as a separate piece and soldered in. The other four categories require further silversmithing ingenuity by soldering in a disc within the depth of the applied foot. This would otherwise be visible from the interior, where the solder line would show. A double base of this type can be detected by giving it a sharp tap with a pointed instrument. If a pimple appears on the inside then there is no double skin.

# 11: NETSUKE & OKIMONO

T HE NETSUKE IS A SMALL OBJECT, usually in wood or ivory, designed to suspend a pouch, pipe case and/or *inro* (set of miniature boxes) from the *obi* (sash) holding together the pocketless kimono formerly worn by Japanese men and women. To fulfil its function it could not be too large or it would be uncomfortable to wear, nor could it have projections that might get caught up in the kimono. This sorts out a true netsuke from the later *okimono* (standing figures) or groups carved by the same *netsuke-shi* (carver), either for indigenous collectors or more often for export. Okimono started to be produced when Japan was opened up to Western influence after Commander Perry of the US Navy sailed into Yokohama Harbour in 1853. Okimono continued the netsuke tradition of two holes *(himotoshi)* in the base but were obviously too large to be worn.

## The Materials

To tell fake from genuine netsuke you need some familiarity with the materials from which authentic pieces were made. The numbers of original netsuke carved in ivory and wood were about equal, but there are more forged ivory carvings on the market. There are several reasons for this. First, up until about five years ago ivory netsuke were more highly regarded and more expensive. Second, the patina of wooden examples, both that put on by the original carver and that developed through age, is a great deal more subtle than on an ivory of comparable date and therefore harder to recreate. Third, the availability of plastic to simulate ivory.

Ivory is not indigenous to Japan and was introduced only in the 19th century. Strictly speaking, the term should be applied only to the tusks of elephants, either those we know today or mammoths', though a wider definition includes the teeth of the hippopotamus, narwhal and walrus, of which only the third is a consideration here. Tusks are incisors from the upper jaw and are entirely formed of dentine. This is composed of innumerable minute longitudinal tubes which are, when fresh, filled with oil. This oil enables ivory to take on its characteristic polish and is slowly lost with age.

Faint longitudinal stripes are a sure guide to identifying the simulated ivories that appeared at the turn of the century with the stripes built into them. If the suspect ivory is held near a light source so that the stripes are visible and then revolved slowly horizontally through 90 degrees, the light and dark stripes on genuine ivory will become less pronounced or disappear. On the simulation, they will be visible at any angle; they also tend to be wider and more regular than on the genuine article. This test takes some learning but once learned is invaluable. The colour of these simulations is also revealing: they are not stained but an even white all over — too white. The forgeries made about 1900 are in casein (made from milk)

[1] *above*
Okimono of a peasant (5 in.; 13 cm), moulded in plastic.

[2]
Manju netsuke with silvered metal purse attachment (1.9 in.; 4.7 cm). It displays light and dark stripes simulating ivory, but they do not disappear when the piece is revolved. Early 20th century, made from similar plastic to *Ill. 1*.

1 *left*
The base of the plastic peasant figure illustrated on the previous page, showing the characteristic parallel lines of simulated ivory and the moulded signature.

3 *below*
The base of a walrus ivory (2.6 in.; 6.5 cm maximum width), showing the granular, translucent appearance of the core disguised by lotus leaf carving. The slight darkening at the edges is typical of walrus. Signed Gyokuzan infilled with red.

2 *above*
The base of an elephant ivory figure (2.6 in.; 6.5 cm maximum width) showing the radiating, intersecting lines forming minute lozenges and the concentric rings of lighter and darker colour. The nerve canal has been inset with a red lacquer panel signed Kosei.

and other plastics and occasionally have the "signature" of the "carver" moulded into the base. The base also displays the same striping as the sides, whereas a cross section of ivory shows concentric lozenges.

Another substitute for elephant ivory is walrus tusk, which can be distinguished from true ivory by its core of granular dentine, though this is often disguised by cross-hatching or similar patterning. Walrus ivory is formed of different layers and so is less stable than ivory and more prone to cracking.

A cheaper and readily available material which is often passed off as ivory is bone, and netsuke in this material are at large to trap the unwary. Bone, unlike ivory, is provided with a blood source and therefore, even in small pieces, has minute pores and channels through which the bone is kept alive. They appear on a carving as small brown or black spots or channels.

**Casting in Plastic Resin** Since the mid-1970s large numbers of deceptive netsuke and figures have been produced by casting in plastic resin using a flexible mould. These are extremely difficult to detect as they are taken directly from originals, usually those of okimono type from the second half of the last century, and the process is so sensitive that it picks up every detail of the original, including undercutting. After casting they are stained in a deep sepia, which is thinner on the proud surfaces and gives a realistic impression of wear. They can be found in antique shops, antique fairs and country auctions, frequently with the lower portions retaining quantities of dust, suggesting that they have come from an old, neglected collection. In fact dust is blown into the interstices from the wrong end of a vacuum-cleaner as part of the finishing. Turn-of-the-century plastic netsuke and okimono are lighter in weight than the originals but this problem has been overcome with the modern copies.

There are two ways of distinguishing the modern products. A chip on a genuine ivory shows an irregular new surface of similar colour but perhaps slightly paler in tone. The modern resin chip is more akin to glass, with a shiny white surface. The other aid to identifying the plastic forgery is temperature. Ivory feels much colder than the reproduction as it conducts heat away from the skin far more readily.

The definitive temperature test is burning. If you have ever had a tooth drilled you will know the characteristic smell of burning tooth. Hold a pin in a pair of pliers and heat it glowing hot and then stick it in some inconspicuous part of the carving. On ivory the pin will barely mark the surface but there will be a burnt-tooth smell; on the plastic it will enter readily with a puff of smoke and throw up a burr at the edges of the hole. There will be a strong smell of burning plastic. Some experts with a very good sense of smell say that it is enough to rub a plastic reproduction vigorously on a piece of fabric or clothing — this warms it enough to release volatile oils and therefore the smell of plastic.

## Signatures and Attributions

Once the material has been established as ivory it may still be necessary to consider the matter of attribution in some detail before deciding that a carving is altogether genuine.

East is East and West is West and the twain certainly do not meet over their attitude to imitation. The 18th- and 19th-century netsuke-shi were not regarded as artists but as craftsmen of a very lowly order; only rarely did they achieve any recognition for their skills. As such, they frequently did not sign their work, particularly in the 18th century. Those that achieved a degree of fame were unashamedly copied by their contemporaries, with or without the originator's or their own signatures. The successful carver would be unable to supply the demand for his work and would employ pupils who would copy the master's work as closely as possible, starting by roughing out the shapes until skilled enough to undertake the

4 *above*
Section of a figure composed of carved bone parts. The lower centre displays brown-black flecks and pin holes and a larger brown canal. These have had leaves and a floret carved over them in an attempt to disguise them.

5 *above*
A modern resin netsuke (1.8 in. ; 4.5 cm), made in a flexible rubber mould from a poor original; sepia stained.

6
The base of the resin boar above, showing the moulding, rather than carving, of the signature.

[1] *top*
A modern resin netsuke: the chip on the prow has exposed the white, glass-like material. The whole is stained a deep sepia "worn" on the extremities and there is considerable dirt in the recesses.

[2] *above*
The base of the same boat showing the moulded signature "Tomochika" and the age cracks of the original. The wear to the left of the himotoshi is visible.

whole carving on their own. Occasionally a pupil would subsequently set up on his own, but many continued to work in a master's studio. As a result, there were not only a great many unsigned pieces, but pieces were originally signed in ways that now can be confusing.

The Japanese, as in the West, have a surname (written first) and a given name, but these are only infrequently their working names. It was much more common to adopt a professional name (*gō*) which could be changed several times throughout a craftsman's life: Kaigyokudo Masatsugu, for example, signed variously: Masatsugu, Kaigyokudo, Kaigyoku and Kaigyokusai; he also used an adoptive family name. A pupil would adopt one character of his master's name, which aids the tracing of a particular school, but overall it is difficult to attribute all but the greatest carving with certainty.

The matter is complicated by the Japanese love of travel within their own country — the carvers would have been influenced by work from other centres that they passed through. Attributing netsuke to a particular artist working in a particular centre is therefore fraught with difficulties. All that we can do is propose likelihoods.

There is a trend in connoisseurship to make the mistake of believing that a netsuke carved in the style of a master and bearing his signature but which is in some way less powerful or inventive than one might expect must perforce be either the work of a pupil, partly worked by a pupil, the work of a follower, or an out-and-out forgery. But great artists do not always turn out masterpieces. The muse deserts them, they have off days, financial pressures enforce second-rate work. One has only to look at some of the rubbish turned out by Picasso to see the truth of this, but no one doubts his standing as the major artist of the 20th century.

There seems to be a preference for signed netsuke over unsigned, although the quality may be no better. But the preference is sufficient to tempt fakers to indulge in a little "attribution" and sign an unsigned piece. This may spoil a good piece as most collectors, when told that their perfectly genuine Tomotada bore a later signature, would rate it less highly. It goes without saying that only the signatures of major artists are liable to be forged.

## Modern Copies

Now that a netsuke has fetched over £44,000 ($66,000) at auction and one is rumoured to have changed hands at $200,000 (£130,000) privately, the urge to copy pieces in a quasi-authentic manner is irresistible to the unscrupulous. There are two levels at which a forgery may appear. One is in the rarefied atmosphere at the high end of the market, say over £5,000. Here the forger must provide his highly skilled carver with a model which is uncommon, or better still unknown, give him as much time as is necessary to carve one or two meticulous copies and then sell them to collectors long on money and short on experience. Such an operation is both expensive — the money invested in the genuine example is tied up for a long period and the carver will not come cheap — and risky — the dud piece cannot be released via a major auction house but must wait for passing trade. With this in mind, exercise the *utmost* caution in buying from galleries and shops on the tourist routes, including that most expensive of operations, the hotel shop.

**Identifying recent restoration**
Recent restoration, invisible to the eye, can sometimes be detected by the nose. Many modern adhesives have a lingering smell; smoke may have been used to darken a part and this too is detectable for quite a while afterwards. And the acidic, vinegary miasma that accompanies chemical staining can drift around a piece long after it has left the workshop.

3 *below, left and right*
A very good ivory copy of a sleeping boar by Kaigyokusai Masatsugu. The carving is highly skilled and only the over-large (but not impossible) size and the less careful handling of the hair marking suggest at first sight that something may be wrong.

The signature supplies a further clue. The first character is badly engraved and hesitantly formed, the second slightly better, the third better still and the fourth is carved with considerable bravura, probably indicating the trepidation with which the forger embarked upon his work and his increasing confidence. It must be said, however, that the first character in Kaigyokusai's signature is never as well formed as the rest.

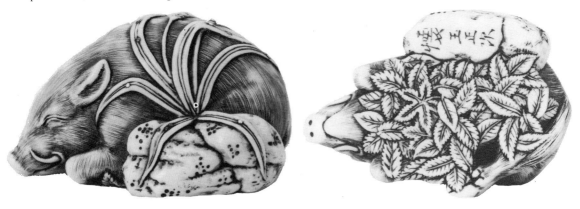

**1** *above*
A modern resin copy of a Japanese ivory hunter (13 in.; 38 cm). This is a flexible rubber moulding carrying considerable conviction and reproducing well the engraved patterning, weight and colour.

**2**
The base of the hunter (*Ill. 1*) with the signature of Seiko or Masahiro. The basket was engraved at the time of carving to disguise not the granulation of walrus ivory, but the already appearing stress cracks. The mould has caught the details brilliantly and dirt has been blown in to add further conviction.

There is a safeguard, however: a copyist is not a creative artist; were he so he would have no need to copy and run the risk of prosecution. He therefore takes a borrowed model from a bent collector or dealer and in reproducing it almost always loses the vitality and often the attention to detail of the original. In one noted case, a forger copied an instantly recognizable rabbit and its young by Okatomo from Bushell's *Netsuke*, but not having an illustration of the reverse he left the back of the carving almost flat. A knowledge of reference books is therefore of great value when a rare netsuke is being sold for what appears to be a bargain price.

At the other end of the scale is the tyro collector, the tourist after a souvenir or the small-time dealer hoping for a snip. To satisfy this demand, China is supplying quantities of ''hand-carved'' netsuke, in ivory, but produced in very large numbers. They make no pretence to having any antiquity or pedigree, although some are artificially stained. I have not encountered any with signatures that could lead to confusion with a collectable carver. They can be found in profusion at airports, hotel shops, fairs and small dealers and are remarkably cheap. They are, however, carved from new tusks (old ivory becomes too hard to work) and in numbers too great to be supplied from the strict quotas now in force to protect elephants. Purchasing them can only lead to further slaughter.

**Signs of Wear** The old netsuke, those made in the golden age between the late 18th century and the middle of the 19th, show over a century of natural ageing and wear to their surfaces. This will include, as the pieces were in everyday use, wear to raised portions and particularly to the cord holes, the himotoshi. This wear is almost impossible to reproduce realistically and the forger, if he considers it at all, fails to make the smaller cord exit hole display more wear than the larger hole which accommodated the knot. If the holes were originally of similar size one will display more wear than the other. In addition, a patina builds up from constant handling and exposure to the air, which is never perfectly reproduced. As ivory ages it darkens, but in a haphazard fashion. The staining with sepia dye on reproductions is consistent, unrealistic and generally with an unpleasant pinkish tinge.

General characteristics of these modern netsuke are the crudeness of the carving and the use of black staining to emphasize details such as facial features to cut down on carving time. They frequently bear signatures in crude characters, albeit finely engraved. The subjects are usually those that can be carved with the minimum expenditure of material and time and include human figures and simple animals such as snakes and birds.

Despite the fact that the netsuke is no longer a useful object, honest examples are still being made and there are a number of superb modern carvers whose pieces are avidly collected. As their work is very expensive and obtainable only through particular galleries, the chance of forgeries of their work being offered for sale is small, but no doubt they will come with time.

The only advice that can be offered here is the same as with early netsuke — be familiar with the carvings of the artists that interest you. One of the greatest of these modern artists, Masatoshi, has written a biography with the aid of his mentor Raymond Bushell, and amongst the wealth of pertinent information is the astonishing fact that a satisfactory polish can take up to twelve hours' work and six different materials. While it is unlikely that all earlier carvings had that amount of time expended on them, it is a fact that modern forgeries do not have the deep patina obtained through hard work. In fact, so rapidly have many of them been produced that fragments of ivory scrapings and dust can often be found in the crevices.

The genuine netsuke sits comfortably at the waist and presents itself logically. A horse, for example, should hang in an upright position. This is rarely considered by the faker, who places the himotoshi without thought. A little time spent working out how the netsuke would sit is time well spent. The placing of the signature can also be used as a guide. On a genuine example it was never placed where it could be seen when in use and if the netsuke is viewed head on and then turned up to view the underside the signature should appear the right way up. The forger is frequently unaware of this.

The larger Japanese carvings in walrus and elephant ivory made after the market for indigenous netsuke collapsed in the 1860s have not been reproduced in resin to any great extent although it is difficult to say why this should be so. Large Chinese ''carvings'' of Immortals and the Emperor and Empress abound, so there can be no technical reason for reproductions to be limited to netsuke or small okimono size. Only one large piece has come to notice, purchased in an auction by someone who had not viewed the piece, which was added to the lot at the last moment.

③
Wood netsuke of a rabbit (2.2 in.; 5.5 cm), copied from an illustration in *Collectors' Netsuke* by Raymond Bushell, 1971, p. 32, no. 24. The copyist has engraved the hair markings very crudely and the reverse side, which was not illustrated in the book, is still less well carved. The original, by Okatomo, has a fine patina which the forger has imitated with a stain of almost black colour, now worn off in patches to expose a much paler body.

## Inlaid Carvings

So far we have looked only at okimono carved from single pieces of ivory. There was however a long established tradition of netsuke with small details such as the eyes inlaid in a different material — tortoiseshell into wood, for example. Over the years, through degradation of the glue or a knock, an eye may have been lost, so both should be checked to see that they have the same amount of wear and patination. The smart restorer replaces both pupils and if this is done well there is unlikely to be any great loss of value. Later netsuke, figures and works of art could have considerable amounts of inlay in mother-of-pearl, amber, coconut, tortoiseshell and stained ivory. Again, these may have been lost over time and replaced. A careful comparison with the colour and tone of remaining inlay may reveal discrepancies. Inlays into lacquer grounds are particularly difficult to replace accurately and usually show a gap between the ground and the inset; when they were first made the ground was applied up to already fixed inlays. The resetting, as opposed to replacement, of loose pieces is not in any way a detraction if it is properly done.

**Buying ivory netsuke at auction**
Always be suspicious of any auction catalogue description that fails to include the word ''ivory''. The piece is being sold with the full knowledge of the auctioneer that it is not genuine.

The same applies to dealers' price tickets. Always ask for a written receipt that includes mention of the material and the date.

## Sectional Figures

Towards the end of the 19th century, as the market for ivories exported to the West increased, sectional figures were produced made from separate pieces, many of which were offcuts sold by the makers of large carvings. These figures often mixed walrus and bone and there are two distinct grades of them. The first is of exceptionally finely carved groups which had to be constructed from several pieces as no single tusk would be large enough to accommodate them. What should be watched for here is the replacement of a lost part by one newly carved. The most obviously delicate sections such as pipes, tools, arrows, small boxes etc. should be examined for changes in colour or texture of the ivory, a down grading of quality or slight changes in scale. A substitution of a lost piece by something appropriate from a group too damaged to be of use but of comparable quality is undetectable and as such will not affect the value.

Many of these sectional groups were signed on a small red lacquer panel let into the base, and the belief seems to have arisen that a lacquer reserve indicates quality. Alas, both the best and the junk can have this feature, so look for the care with which the signature has been engraved and beware of the thin, spidery hand. New lacquer signatures have also been noted on originally unsigned groups.

The Tokyo School carvings produced from the end of the last century up until the First World War, usually from a single large tusk, have risen in value dramatically over the last few years. The major carvers, such as Ishikawa Komei and Yoshida Homei, are now becoming recognized. There is no likelihood of reproductions of their work ever being made as the skills are no longer around to produce them, but carvings bearing Ishikawa's name (though too poor to be by his hand) were produced contemporaneously. These are on the market and have deceived people who paid too much attention to the signature and not enough to the quality of the piece.

[1]
Plastic rickshaw group (3.8 in.; 9.5 cm) of very poor quality. It has built-in stripes to imitate ivory but is far too light. Moulded in parts as the original would have been constructed but with, for example, the shafts and the runner in one piece, which a genuine example would not show.

# 12 : POTTERY & PORCELAIN

TODAY NO-ONE WOULD REGARD a Bow blue and white copy of a Chinese or Japanese exportware plate as "fake"; nor would they regard a Qianlong crackle-glazed Guan dish copying a Song Imperial original as a "forgery". We use these words "fake" and "forgery" when discussing deceptive 19th- and 20th-century copies of earlier pieces, yet there was almost certainly less interest in the differences between Chinese and Japanese or Chelsea and Bow in the 17th and 18th centuries. Such niceties were the province of an extremely small group of cognoscenti, a circle including such celebrated collectors as the Duchess of Portland and Lord Holland.

Manufacturers recognized that their customers were for the most part concerned with what was fashionable, whether in the Chinese or the Meissen style, and that utilitarian qualities were of secondary importance. As long as the "china" looked right and up-to-the-minute, that was sufficient. Although a few manufacturers, such as Derby, chose Meissen as their criterion, most chose Chinese porcelain, as can be seen from the patent applied for in 1744 by Thomas Frye and Edward Heylyn. These gentlemen wished to make "a certain material whereby a ware might be made of the same nature or kind, and equal to, if not exceeding in goodness and beauty, China or Porcelain ware imported from abroad". In this enterprise they eventually succeeded, but in some cases they also attempted to copy a Chinese reign mark as additional evidence of authenticity.

## The First Fakes

Faking porcelain—as opposed to merely copying or working in a particular style—probably began in the late 18th century, when Paris enamellers purchased large quantities of Sèvres porcelain, painted them in the factory style and added the conventional interlaced "L" marks. Such specimens are everywhere and this has led to some erratic attribution, since the bodies are perfectly "right" and the enamels and gilding can be very good. Some of the Sèvres blanks were bought by Thomas Martin Randall of London and Madeley, who also decorated them in the factory style. A few examples of Randall's work have in the past proved good enough to be displayed in a major museum as factory decorated Sèvres.

The advent of the Industrial Revolution and the consequent redistribution of wealth among the expanding middle classes created a demand for both antique and fashionable china such as Sèvres. Since supplies of old porcelain and pottery were limited, factories such as Merkelbach and Schiffer in Germany, Samson in France and Cantagalli and Doccia in Italy catered for the demand by producing very deceptive copies. Some of these pieces appear not to have been marked, or if they were marked, the marks have since been removed in order to deceive (see *Ill. 3*, p. 169).

[1] [2]
Two lead-glazed pottery copies of an 18th-century "The Squire" Toby Jug, probably late 19th century. The first has been covered in a wash of bluish glaze in an effort to reproduce the appearance of the originals, but it is far too intense to be convincing. The second has a turquoise jacket, a colour which was never used, and a translucent off-white crackled glaze which ironically is not blue enough.

[1]

A pair of early 20th-century copies of Wei dynasty tomb figures. Soon after tomb figures first reached the west at the beginning of this century, forgers both in China and Europe took the opportunity to replicate the simpler unglazed types such as these.

At first these forgeries fooled many collectors who had little experience of early pottery, but eventually they were detected by comparison with the genuine excavated pieces. The copies are in general stiffly modelled and heavier in construction, although some are good enough to require a thermoluminescence test to confirm a late date. Tang pottery is made of a pinkish buff clay but Wei is almost black. These figures are made of a coarse red brick-like material cunningly covered in a black slip.

[2]

The fake Wei figure presented to A. J. B. Kiddell in 1923.

With continuing demand for rare items in the late 19th and early 20th centuries, forgers had a field day. In porcelain and pottery, connoisseurship was in its infancy, as can be seen by contemporary publications such as W. W. R. Spelman's *Lowestoft China*, in which the author illustrates at least 60 items which are not from the Lowestoft factory. This does not mean that collectors were ignorant of the faker's art. There are also many references to dubious pieces. Captain Price, for example, in his *Astbury, Whieldon, and Ralph Wood Figures and Toby Jugs*, published in 1922, refers to the many fakes of the "Squire" toby jug.

In the field of English pottery, the 1920s were arguably the most active years for the forger. One of the most celebrated cases is that of the Astbury or Astbury-Whieldon figures and groups, which began to appear towards the end of the decade. Such figures were then, as now, very expensive collectors' pieces and would naturally merit the attention of the forger. In 1929 Herbert Read wrote, "I am not acquainted with any forgeries of the Astbury-Whieldon type. The delicately coloured glaze would not be easy to imitate." But they were imitated. As Ross Taggart observed in his article in *The Arts Quarterly*, "It would seem that it was at virtually this precise moment that the forgeries began to appear."

In a saleroom on 4 June 1931, three Astbury figures and a pew group marked "Wedgwood" were entered as lots 66 to 69, "The property of a Collector". All sold well and no-one was suspicious, that is until the following year. Ross Taggart writes, "When these were first known, they were in no way suspected by the leading auctioneers, reputable dealers, and discriminating collectors. It was Mr Kiddell (of Sothebys) who first began to doubt them in the light of another pew group that was shown him and was undoubtedly wrong. When this was brought to the attentions of Messrs Rackham, Honey and Elliot, the 'Wedgwood' pew group was still passed as genuine. It was only with the appearance of the 'Wood' piece that the true character of both became apparent."

It was also around this time that the first pieces of Tang tomb pottery arrived in Europe, and within less than five years the forgers were busy not only replicating this period but Sui and Wei pottery as well. Without the benefit of thermoluminescence testing, attribution, especially of the unglazed figures, must have been extremely difficult. It was A. J. B. Kiddell again who managed to ferret out the duds from the genuine. For his pains he was presented in 1923 with a specially commissioned fake of a Wei pottery equestrian figure which is currently stabled in Sotheby's celebrated "Black Museum".

## Spurious Marks

The use of spurious marks was widespread. In England the Meissen crossed-swords mark was copied or parodied by Worcester, Bow, Longton Hall, Lowestoft and Champion's Bristol in the 18th century, and by Derby and Minton in the early 19th century. In France the interlaced "L"s of Sèvres and

*continued on page 157*

 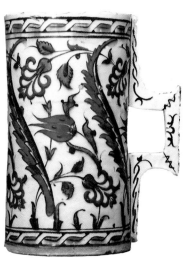

① *far left*
An authentic late 16th-century Isnik tankard, decorated in a typically bold palette under a brilliant transparent glaze. Both Cantagalli in Florence and Samson in Paris produced copies of this kind of ware. Compare *Ill. 2.*

② *left*
A copy of a late 16th-century Isnik tankard—compare *Ill. 1.* It is probably from the Cantagalli workshop but the mark (normally a punning singing cockerel) has been deliberately gouged out of the base.

The tankard is covered in a typical European tin-glaze, rather than the brilliant glaze of its model. The palette is also less bold—the green is too grey and the blue is a rather sticky looking ultramarine. As with most copies, the painting is weak and lacks detail when compared with an original.

This piece should properly be designated a fake rather than a mere copy as it has been altered to enhance its desirability.

④ *above*
A Doucai stem cup from the reign of the Emperor Chenghua (1465-87). The subtle palette is painted in a slight, feminine manner, reflecting the influence of the Empress on Imperial taste. The use of underglaze blue in combination with several overglaze enamels is an innovation of this period. The rather smoky ivory appearance of the glaze distinguishes Chenghua originals from the copies made in the reign of Kangxi (1662-1722).

The term Doucai translates literally as "contrasting" or "clashing colours".

③
Tang dynasty tomb figures (618-906 A.D.).

The expansion of the Chinese railway system at the beginning of the present century involved a considerable amount of earth moving, which resulted in the discovery of ancient tombs and the excavation of pottery figures which had been put there to accompany the deceased on their journeys in the afterlife. These figures caused quite a sensation when they arrived in the west and were exchanged for very large sums of money. Within five years fakes had appeared.

**1** *left*
A late 14th-century dish decorated in underglaze copper red. The reddishness of the unglazed portion of the dish is a characteristic of early Ming porcelain. Qing wares (those from the late 17th century onwards) are generally white or grey, but if they do oxidize a little, it will be to a brown or honey colour rather than this strong russet.

Qing wares are also covered in a glaze of uniform depth: the Kangxi period (1662-1722), for example, is noteworthy for its thinness and pure white colour. In porcelains of the late 14th and early 15th centuries, such as this dish, the glaze is generally thicker and bubbled, with the result that it looks slightly bluish or greenish and any underglaze decoration can sometimes look slightly blurred or out of focus. The glaze was rarely applied evenly and this led to pooling and dribbling, which can be seen more clearly at an oblique angle under strong light.

**2** *above*
A late 14th-century jar (*guan*). Another feature of early Ming porcelain is that the footrim is knife-pared and, except on the finest small objects, little effort has been made to smooth away the facets left by the knife. Qing porcelains, on the other hand, are almost always smoothed after trimming.

Throughout the dynasty the footrims on Ming porcelains are a little taller than on later wares, and they are often undercut, indicating that they have been formed by hand rather than with a mould or a profile cutter, which was common practice after the mid-17th century.

**3** *above*, **4** *left*
Two early 15th-century ewers of Islamic metal form. Early 15th-century blue and white is epitomized in the perfect balance of design and form in these two pear-shaped ewers. Like the Guan jar (*Ill. 2 above*), the ewer with fruit pattern (left) has blackish areas on the blue decoration. This is where the pigment has been applied thickly and has burnt in the firing. The effect is known as "heaped and pile" and was copied with little success by Chinese potters of the 18th century.

**5** *far left*

A Ming "Chicken" cup of the Chenghua period (1465-87), painted in Doucai enamels. These very rare cups are regarded by many as the finest wares produced during the Ming dynasty.

**6** *left*

A copy of a Chenghua Doucai "Chicken" cup made during the Kangxi period (1662-1722). The Emperor Kangxi encouraged not only the development of new glazes and techniques but also the revival of the classic wares of the Song and Ming dynasties.

**7** *above*

"Peach-bloom" wares such as these were one of the innovations of the Kangxi period. Their manufacture involved the use of copper oxide fired in a reducing atmosphere in the kiln. The red that this produced was a rich mushroom pink of variegated appearance suffused with areas of mossy green.

The glaze was used only on a small number of shapes, including a tall oviform vase, a beehive-shaped brush washer and boxes and bowls like the two illustrated here.

**8** *right*

A late Ming Wucai saucer dish of the Wanli period (1573-1620). Wucai translates as "five colour". It is a bold palette which uses underglaze blue and several (but not necessarily five) other colours. The designs are generally more loosely drawn and less sophisticated than those executed in the Doucai palette.

Wucai evolved in the late 17th century into the "famille-verte" palette, in which overglaze blue was used rather than underglaze blue.

1 *far left,* 2 *left*
Two ''famille-verte'' vases. The smaller bottle-shaped vase is a genuine example of Kangxi (1662-1722) porcelain. The taller oviform vase is a Samson copy of an early 18th-century Kangxi export-ware original, made in Paris around the turn of this century. Even when they are set side by side, it is difficult for all but the expert to tell which is genuine.

3 *above*
A ''famille-rose'' vase of the Quianlong period (1736-95) decorated in Chinese taste. These wares were made for the domestic market and were not intended for export.

4 *left*
A Worcester mug, *c.* 1753. The early polychrome wares of this factory were painted in a delightful hybrid palette partly based on Chinese ''famille-verte'' but also borrowing from contemporary Japanese enamels. The grooved handle with kick-back terminal and the slightly spreading foot are typical of Worcester in the 1750s.

*continued from page 152*

the ''VP'' monogram of the Marseilles factory were universally abused, doubtless for commercial gain. The Meissen crossed-swords were copied by a large number of minor Thuringian factories in the late 18th century.

**Reign marks** The situation as far as Chinese and Japanese porcelains are concerned is quite different. Few pieces of Chinese porcelain or pottery made prior to the 14th century bear reign marks and those that do should be viewed with great circumspection. It was not until the early 15th century that the practice of inscribing the Imperial wares of Zhingdezhen with the reign mark was adopted.

There is only a small number of pieces with the mark of Yongle (1403-1424); it was during the reign of Xuande (1426-35) that the number increased dramatically. These marks were usually written in underglaze blue enclosed within a double circle or more rarely a double square (the Japanese, incidentally, almost invariably used only a single circle). Towards the end of the 15th century we see retrospective marks for the first time, when a small group of slightly provincial-looking wares were given the mark of Xuande.

During the 16th century the sanctity of the reign mark or *nien hao* was generally observed, but the second half of the century saw the advent of non-imperial marks. These include the use of dedicatory inscriptions, so-called ''shop'' marks, or even an animal such as a hare. In the 17th century the use of previous reign marks was commonplace, particularly the use of the six-character mark of Chenghua (1465-87) during the reign of Kangxi (1662-1722). Ironically it is Kangxi's reign mark that appears most frequently on late 19th- and early 20th-century exportware. The ubiquitous ginger jars painted with prunus blossom on a cracked-ice ground will, if marked at all, nine times out of ten bear his four or six reign characters.

Another way of writing the reign mark is the use of stylized characters arranged within a square seal. This is rather like using capital letters as opposed to normal handwriting and we are therefore faced with much greater difficulty in ascribing

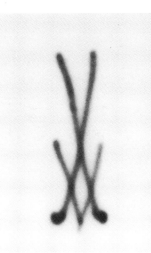

[1] *above*
Crossed-swords: a genuine 19th-century Meissen mark.

[2] *above*
A copy of the Meissen crossed-swords mark.

[3]
A blue and white bowl bearing the mark of the Emperor Xuande below the rim.

[1] *above*

A Chinese saucer dish, early 20th century.

Reign marks on Chinese porcelain should be treated with caution since 90 per cent are purely retrospective. The most common mark is probably that of the Ming Emperor, Chenghua, who reigned between 1465 and 1487, closely followed by that of Kangxi, who occupied the Dragon Throne from 1662 until 1722. These six-character reign marks usually appear on late 19th-century blue and white exportware painted with hawthorn or may blossom or with panels of tall elegant ladies (Long Elizas).

This saucer dish bears the four character mark of Yongzheng (1723-35), whose reign witnessed the zenith of ceramic achievement during the Manchu or Qing dynasty. The wares painted in ''Chinese taste'' were virtually unseen in Europe prior to the sacking of the Summer Palace in Peking in 1860. This dish is painted in this style, but it is a second-rate copy: the birds and the bamboo are poor, and the pink colour on the reverse is very harsh. The originals are brilliantly painted in a subtle and attractive palette, with a warm ruby back.

[2] *above, centre*

A seal mark of the Emperor Quianlong (1736-95).

[3] *above, right*

Conventional pseudo-seal mark by Samson of Paris, usually found on the ''Chinese exportware'' type of porcelain.

pieces. A thorough understanding of the idiosyncracies of each reign mark or seal is vital for sorting out the right from the wrong. One of the best guides is the section on marks in Sir Harry Garner's *Oriental Blue and White*.

The Japanese never employed a similar system of reign marks on their own porcelain. Instead they used a series of devices denoting ''good luck''. They did, however, copy Chinese reign marks from the late 17th to the early 19th centuries, mainly those of the Ming Emperors, Chenghua and Xuande. In the latter half of the 19th century any marks on Japanese porcelain will generally refer to the area or the potter but not to the Emperor.

## Methods of Dating

Every piece of pottery and porcelain possesses certain characteristics which identify it or relate it to a particular group or species. These groups or types have been located and identified by various methods, and each grouping is based on an accumulation of evidence garnered from many sources.

In the first place, crucial archaeological evidence has been produced by excavations of the Imperial Chinese tombs. Certainly until the early Ming dynasty most artifacts discovered in the burial chamber were more or less contemporary with the emperors' reigns.

We have also gained as much in recent years from marine archaeology: for example, from the expedition in 1976 to excavate the wreck of the Dutch East Indiaman, the *Witte Leeuw*, which sank on 3 June 1614 after her powder magazine exploded during an engagement with a Portuguese carrack off the island of St Helena. Among the cargo of this vessel was a consignment of contemporary Chinese export porcelain or *kraakporselein*, as it has been termed since. As this type of porcelain is never marked, the haul gave us an invaluable key to dating.

Many examples of similar kraakporselein and also of the ''Transitional'' family are found in old Dutch still-life paintings; this again helps with dating. Another important source is factory records listing what they manufactured and sold, such as those of Meissen, Sèvres and Chelsea.

4 *far left*
A late Ming kraakporselein dish, *c.* 1640.

5 *left*
A French fake of a kraakporselein dish.

Contemporary accounts of visits to factories are for the most part too vague to be of much use in indentifying exact forms or objects, but they can give an insight into conditions or current fashion. The visit to the manufactory at St Cloud by Martin Lister, court physician to William III, gives an account of the earliest French porcelain and a comparison with the Chinese variety.

Inscriptions on ceramics can often provide confirmation of origin and date, although it is salutary to remember that the celebrated Percival David Foundation vases had both date (1351 A.D.) and locality. These were presented to the temple at Hu-Qing-i, just over 100 kilometres (60 miles) from their place of manufacture, Zhingdezhen, but before World War II they were considered by most authorities to be wrong on the grounds of their complexity and sophistication. Now, however, they are accepted for what they are, namely the earliest and most important specimens of Chinese blue and white.

**Inscriptions** In Urbino, the great maiolica *istoriato* school of painters occasionally signed, dated and located their pieces. In the Wallace Collection in London there is a bowl painted with the descent of Orpheus into Hades and inscribed on the reverse "1152 *Alla Carothea Cimba arriva Orpheo*" [Orpheus arrives at the boat of Charon]; underneath the title is the signature of Francesco Xanto Avelli of Rovigo in the duchy of Urbino, the most important centre for such descriptive or istoriato wares. This is written in the distinctive manner of the

6 *below, left*
A Chelsea red anchor tureen described in the sale catalogue of the Chelsea factory for 22 March 1755, as "A very fine tureen, in the form of a RABBIT BIG AS LIFE, in a fine oval dish."

7 *below*
A late 19th- or early 20th-century Samson copy of the Chelsea tureen (*Ill. 6*, left). As is often the case, the Samson copy is smaller than the original. At 9 in. (22.9cm) in length, it is 5 in. (12.7cm) shorter. Details on both examples are fairly close, the most noticeable difference being the very fine brushwork on the fur of the Chelsea piece.

The Samson tureen is made of hard-paste porcelain which gives a definite metallic ring when tapped, unlike the somewhat duller sound of Chelsea. The base has the entwined "S" mark and it is also diestamped with the number 23. Chelsea porcelains are never impressed with numerals in such a manner.

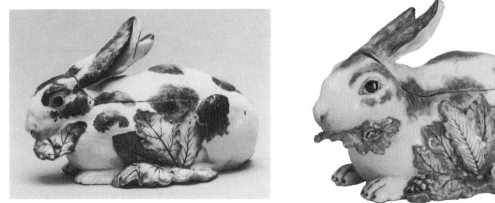

[1] *above*
An Italian Maiolica Drug Pot or Albarello, 19th century, a copy of a 17th- or 18th-century Savona drug jar.

These early wares are noted for the casual but freely drawn animals and flowers on a soft opaque white ground. The present vessel is very stiff and unnatural and the glaze has an uncharacteristic glassiness.

[2]
A porcelain reproduction, probably 19th century, of an 18th-century Doccia figure.

The figure, which represents Africa from a set of Continents, is almost certainly derived from a design for a baroque fountain by Giovanni Foggini. The extensive areas of degraded glaze, particularly in places unlikely to be worn naturally, leads one to suspect that an attempt has been made to give it an antique look by rubbing it with an abrasive.

Renaissance with all the spontaneity one expects from any individual's hand. The Cantagalli or Doccia copyists of the 19th and early 20th centuries were quite incapable of reproducing this feel and can be exposed from their handwriting alone. There is a lot to be learned from examining collections of maiolica in museums and paying specific attention to any inscriptions, for it is often on the apparently less important details such as handwriting that the faker comes to grief.

English delftware potters, who on the whole worked for a less aristocratic public than the porcelain manufacturers, inscribed pieces with references to topical events or causes such as the Popish Plot, Admiral Vernon's victory at Portobello or even an election issue. In some cases there are inscriptions of a localized nature which would indicate the probable source, such as the punchbowl painted with the Swedish ship *Wigelantia* and a reference to her docking at Bristol in 1765. But when a piece bears the name of a town, it does not necessarily mean that it was made there, as can be seen from all those little Goss commemorative pieces or the German tourist trinkets with "A present from Brighton" on them. We are on firmer ground, however, when inscribed pieces can be related to sherds unearthed at a particular kiln-site.

These identifying features are quite literally and irrevocably baked into the piece. This separates pottery and porcelain from most other materials in that it cannot be altered without seriously affecting its appearance. In contrast, the mahogany from a Georgian linen press can be used to make up an entirely different object. Many years ago I watched a restorer fulfilling an order from a client who had brought in a Hepplewhite dining chair which he wished to have copied in sufficient numbers to complete a set of 12. This same restorer related with some humour how he used to recognize many of his own and other craftsmen's fakes when paying one of his periodic visits to the London auction houses. Similarly with bronzes, oil paintings or silver, it is possible to re-work a piece with varying degrees of success.

The greatest difficulty in identification is experienced with the simplest types of unglazed pottery and porcelain, for one has to rely entirely on the appearance of the material and the form of the object. The difference between French biscuit porcelain and Victorian parian china is not always clear to everyone. Many northern European white tin-glazed wares pose a major problem to experts.

The more complicated a piece, the easier it is to attribute. A glazed and decorated piece says a great deal more about itself than an unglazed one, for it is not just a skeleton, it also has skin colouring and fingerprints. Every factory or type uses a glaze and a range of colours which together serve as this unique fingerprint. To consider solely the appearance of the glaze is extremely hazardous, since certain factories are quite similar. Ludwigsburg and Zurich for example, often have a pronounced smoky ivory appearance, which isolates them from their rivals at Frankenthal and Höchst, but they can cause some confusion between themselves. One is therefore

3 *left*
This large dish, a copy of a copy, is a curiosity for a number of reasons.

It is made of a hard-paste body with a gritty footrim attempting to copy the hybrid body of early 17th-century Kirman ware from Persia. The design originates in Ming porcelain dating from the second half of the 16th century. Similar pieces of porcelain were exported to India, Egypt, Turkey and Persia, and in the last two countries copies were made. The stiff and unnatural beast in the middle of the dish is supposed to be a kylin, a mythical Chinese creature which possesses the head of a dragon, the body and tail of a lion and the hooves of a deer. The Frenchman who painted this dish was certainly totally ignorant of what the original Chinese artist intended, since that had already been misinterpreted for him by a Persian 300 years before.

obliged to use other criteria in order to solve the problem.

The colours or enamels used on most pottery and porcelain are made from different metallic oxides, such as antimony, cobalt, copper, iron or manganese, which one might imagine should produce similar results anywhere, but they don't. For example, William Cookworthy of Plymouth achieved a strange mushroom pink quite unlike any other contemporary pigment. Some factories had enormous difficulties firing or fixing certain colours and as a result only used them sparingly.

## Methods of Manufacture

Just as the glaze and colours differ from one place to another or from time to time in the same location, so too the methods of manufacture can help us with classification. Chelsea porcelain wares, for example, are fired on small spurs, usually three, located on the base inside the foot, a method similar to that operated by the Arita potters but not used at other English factories. Factories used different methods of casting, Bow preferred to model by press-moulding, whereas Chelsea and Longton Hall used the slip-casting process. Press-moulding is the use of soft clay pushed by hand or with a tool into the various moulds which form the elements of the figure or group. This process usually means that the figure will be more heavily constructed than one made by the slip-casting method. The latter entails the filling of the main mould which forms the torso (and perhaps a leg or supporting tree-stump) with liquid clay or slip. This watery clay is left to dry out until there is a sufficient thickness of it on the interior wall of the

① *right*
A Samson copy of a Chelsea Billing Doves Tureen.

A good example of a Samson reproduction. The modelling is excellent, but, as always, it is lack of attention to detail that gives the game away. The original is delicately painted, particularly in the rendering of the plumage. But the applied flowers in the copy are stuck on with no sensitivity, a common failing with Samson. The paste and glaze on Chelsea of the ''red anchor'' period (1752-57) are among the most attractive on English porcelain and rival the finest French soft-pastes. Chelsea porcelain of this period has a silky feel and a creamy translucency, and sometimes, towards the end of this period, it has a trace of bluishness. Early red anchor is slightly opaque due to the addition of tin to the glaze.

The Samson porcelain is hard and unsympathetic with a very close-grained texture, as if the unglazed surface had been polished by a lapidary. The glaze is unevenly applied and has a greyish yellow tone. Perhaps one of the most revealing faults on this piece, and one which also occurs on many other late copies, is the maker's failure to smooth out the mould seams, which can be seen quite clearly on the heads of the birds. The great 18th-century factories of Meissen, Sèvres and Chelsea would never have allowed such shoddy finishing.

Worcester also produced a version of this tureen, probably in the late 1760s, of which there is only one recorded example. Like the Samson group it was also considerably smaller than the Chelsea original which measured 17 in. (43.2 cm). The Worcester example ironically bears a gold anchor mark, although the original was made only during the previous red anchor period.

mould to make the figure. The limbs of the figure, however, are still made by press-moulding.

Most Continental hard-paste porcelains are slip-cast, and a Bow model with an anchor and dagger mark which has been made by this method should be treated with much circumspection.

## Methods of Faking

Among the tricks practised by forgers is the decoration or redecoration of genuine ware. In post-revolutionary France a great quantity of porcelain was sold off from the Sèvres factory to Paris porcelain decorators. They were then painted in the manner of early Sèvres and suitable date letters and artists' marks were added to give them a little more authenticity. These pieces still cause tremendous problems today.

Another method of faking was by ''skinning'', or removing the enamelled decoration from an ordinary piece of right porcelain and enhancing it with a rarer or more sought-after pattern. A recent case in point was that of a plate apparently from the celebrated Sèvres ''Du Barry'' service. It was not until this specimen was viewed quite accidentally in a slanting beam of afternoon sunlight that the outline of a previous design could be detected. Instead of realizing several thousand pounds at auction, it was sold for a mere hundred or two. This technique was also used before World War II to great effect by Chinese dealers who redecorated genuine reign-marked period pieces with more interesting or costly designs.

② *left*
A Bow figure of a Sphinx, *c.* 1750, the decoration later.

An extremely interesting piece which, because of the crude painting, appears to be a very poor copy of an early Bow piece. The unglazed areas on the base and interior have a dry but close-grained texture which seems closer to pottery than porcelain. This, however, may be the result of underfiring. The thickly press-moulded figure has been covered in a greenish yellow glaze.

R.L. Hobson in the *Catalogue of English Porcelain in the British Museum* describes a similar figure, ''The piece appears to have been underfired, the glaze has crazed and the body being porous, has absorbed discolouring matter, giving the whole a dirty yellowish appearance.''

This figure, although glazed, has many similarities. It is a perfectly genuine piece, but it has been later decorated (many early Bow figures were left in the white).

A large number of fakes of English delftware were made in the 1920s and 30s. Some were direct copies of rare or early specimens, while others were perfectly genuine pieces ''tricked out'' or faked to enhance their desirability. The present wine bottle is an example of the latter. It is a ''right'' mid-17th century vessel which without a title and date would be fairly unexceptional.

The word ''Sack'' has been written in a totally unconvincing childlike manner, and the scroll or flourish beneath the date is hesitant and confused. Finally, the numerous craters in the glaze exemplify a phenomenon common to many re-fired pieces. In order to re-fire a pot successfully, it is necessary to dry it out in a warm oven over an extended period. If this is not done a sudden rise in temperature will cause the long-trapped moisture in or immediately below the glaze to expand too rapidly and explode through the surface as has happened here. This is an extreme case; the usual manifestation of re-firing is a speckled or ''peppered'' effect.

This deception of over-decorating or ''clobbering'' was used extensively on First Period Worcester porcelain to transmogrify mundane vessels by adding one of the highly desirable coloured grounds, especially claret or apple-green. These faked or ''tricked out'' pieces can usually be detected by the tell-tale black speckling on the foot or base.

In the late 19th century plain white English delftware wine bottles greatly outnumbered inscribed pieces; today the situation is completely reversed. There have been less than a handful on the market within the past 30 years and consequently prices for pure white bottles are very high indeed. It is worth remembering what A. H. Church wrote in *English Earthenware*, published in 1884: ''Of the wine jugs a large number of pint and half-pint are extant. Some of these are plain, but many are inscribed not only with the names of the wine they were intended to contain, but also with the date of their manufacture (or possibly the date of bottling). . . . However, there are many similar wine-pots of different sizes but perfectly plain.'' What happened to these ''many perfectly plain'' bottles is perhaps explained by another quote, this time from G. E. Howard's *Early English Drug Jars*, published in 1931. ''. . . John Hodgkin told me that his father maintained that in his day genuine plain Lambeth jars were exported to France or Holland, where inscriptions, dates or coats-of-arms were painted upon them, after which they were re-fired. He even asserted that he recognized actual specimens, which he had seen bought in sales by a certain individual, in their original undecorated state, and which, after a short period, reappeared on the market richly decorated. Some authorities, however, hold that it would be impossible to reglaze a jar in this manner.'' According to A. J. B. Kiddell this was precisely the sort of faking carried out by Gautier, the English delftware authority, who may well have been ''the certain individual'' mentioned by Hodgkin.

Another but much more unusual trick is to lute the base of an old but presumably broken vessel to a later vase. Some years ago I was completely taken in by two mirror-black vases which had been treated this way. Fortunately this kind of forgery is rare, as one would have to find vases and bases of similar dimensions in order to perform a convincing transplant.

A hard-paste porcelain fake of a Zurich plate, late 19th or early 20th century.

Zurich porcelain of the 1760s is distinguished by the smoky yellowish-grey glaze which is sometimes peppered with tiny pinholes. The paste is greyish white with the texture of very fine sand which can discolour rather like early Bow. Infrequently one finds kiln-grit adhering to the edge of the footrim or base. The flower painting at this factory can be extremely fine, approaching the quality of Strasbourg *fleurs fines*, but ordinarily the pieces are similar to the bread-and-butter wares of Ludswigsburg. The manufacturer's mark, which is a ''Z'' with a horizontal line through it, purports to place the dish between 1763 and 1792, the form, however, is not recorded in Zurich porcelain during this period. The creamy, glassy looking porcelain and the slightly warmer enamels indicate a 19th-century date.

A Yingqing Box of the Yuan dynasty (1280-1368), one of the forerunners of early blue and white porcelain.

# ORIENTAL PORCELAIN

Chinese porcelain was probably first produced in identifiable form during the 8th century A.D. The earliest pieces are the northern white wares, similar to the Xingyao type which have been excavated at Samarra, together with locally made copies in the Persian Gulf.

During the Northern Sung dynasty (960-1127) white wares were further developed in the province of Hopei, where a semi-translucent proto-porcelain called Ding-yao was made. This ware is distinguished by the warm ivory tone of the glaze, which tends to appear a greenish or even honey colour when it pools or dribbles. A characteristic of this ware also shared with the later Yingqing type is that dishes and bowls were fired upside down, leaving an unglazed rim which is then frequently bound with copper.

Both the Dingyao and Yingqing wares are mainly based on flower forms or lobed seed pods and are either decorated by moulding or with carving. The Yingqing type differs from Ding ware in that the glaze is a soft pale blue-green: the term Yingqing translates as "misty blue". It is from the latter type of porcelain and the closely related Shufu ware that the first blue and white evolved in the early 14th century. The earliest pieces of blue and white—and, for that matter, of copper-red—are composed of exactly similar paste and glaze, and the forms such as cuboid vessels, oil jars and double-gourd pourers and bowls occur in Yingqing, Shufu and in blue and red decorated pieces. This entire group of vessels, although much less sophisticated, is nevertheless akin to the pair of blue and white vases dated 1351 in the Percival David Foundation in London.

The David vases are the cornerstone of our understanding of early blue and white and are in turn related to a large number of vessels and dishes in Middle Eastern collections such as those in the Topkapi Sarayi Museum in Istanbul and at the Ardebil Shrine in Iran. The close trading ties between China under the Mongol Yuan dynasty and the Islamic world is underlined by the cross-pollination of form and design in the 14th century. These wares often follow Middle Eastern metal forms and are perhaps slightly more crowded than those of the succeeding Ming dynasty.

The spacious style of the reigns of Yongle (1403-1424) and Xuande (1426-35) was developed further and reached its apogee during the reign of Chenghua (1465-87). This period is regarded by many connoisseurs as the finest in Chinese porcelain, and the celebrated "Palace" bowls and the *doucai* (a palette of soft contrasting colours) "Chicken" cups are brilliant examples, which later Chinese potters of the Kangxi period (1662-1722) strove to copy (see *Ill. 5*, p. 155). A characteristic of this reign was the purity of the blue and the definite smoky ivory colour of the glaze, which is impossible to

A palace bowl of the Chenghua period (1465-87), an example of what many regard as the finest Chinese porcelain (see also *Ill. 1*, p. 173).

distinguish in an illustration but is quite clear when a piece is juxtaposed with one from any other period.

The 16th century was probably the watershed in the history of Chinese porcelain. The reigns of Hongzhi (1488-1505) and Zhengde (1506-1521) witnessed the changeover from the 15th-century tradition to the looser style which prevailed for most of the 16th century. The most attractive wares of the Zhengde period are brush-rests and utensils for the scholar's table, bearing either Arabic or Persian inscriptions. These were made for the Muslim eunuchs who effectively controlled the palace bureaucracy until they were themselves ejected by the succeeding Emperor Jiajing (1522-66).

3 *above,* 4 *left*
Two dishes from the second half of the 16th century, decorated in Mohammedan blue.

## Export Porcelain

In 1517 Vasco da Gama reached Canton and the first trade links were formed between China and Western Europe. Thereafter specific orders for porcelain were placed by Portuguese officials and there are several examples of such ware in the Victoria and Albert Museum with European coats-of-arms or inscriptions. The deterioration in the quality of potting and brushwork can be traced to this period, although there are brilliant exceptions. The use of the vibrant purplish cobalt called "Mohammedan blue", which was mostly imported, is one of the distinguishing features of 16th- and some early 17th-century porcelain.

The increased demand for porcelain in the West led to a further decline in standards. Now, in order to speed up the process, the designs were broken up into compartments so that less skilled craftsmen could cope with the smaller elements of the overall pattern—the beginning of mass

5 6
The reverse of a kraakporselein dish (below) with a plain French copy. Note the slightly burnt footrim and grit on the original.

A late 16th-century kraakporselein cover from Burghley House. Similar sherds have been excavated in Drake's Bay, California.

production. This ware is typified by poor throwing with much warping and the undersides were thinly glazed and showed the contour lines. The Japanese copies of this kraakporselein made in Arita in the second half of the 17th century are more heavily potted, with no kiln-grit and no tendency to flake on the rim as the Chinese originals do.

## Late Ming Wares

The late Ming reigns of Tianqi (1621-27) and Chongzhen (1628-44) are noteworthy for two entirely distinct but attractive groups of porcelain.

The first type, called *kosometsuke* by the Japanese, for whom they were intended, are freely drawn with sparse landscapes or with scholars meditating on the bank of a tranquil lake. Others from this group for the Japanese market are decorated with a combination of repeating diaper or patterns. Both these types were liberally copied in Japan in the 19th and possibly even the early 20th century as well. As the Chinese wares are very similar in body, glaze and kiln defects to the kraak-porselein group, copies should present very little difficulty.

The second type has been designated ''Transitional'' ware simply because it overlaps the decaying Ming dynasty and the incoming Manchu or Qing dynasty. This group is, in contrast to the slightly abandoned style of the previous group, painted in a more controlled, academic style with figures in idyllic cloud-wrapped rocky landscapes. Typical of this group are the use of plantain and horizontal swirling clouds. The effect of grass is achieved by a series of small crescent-shaped brush strokes, a method not used elsewhere. Another characteristic which can easily be overlooked is the use of lightly incised borders, appropriately termed *anhua* or ''secret'' decoration by the Chinese. This group of highly refined export porcelain has been reproduced within the last 15 or 20 years, using transfer-prints as well as hand-painted designs. The results are flat and lifeless and should not prove troublesome.

## Manchu or Qing Porcelain

A 20th-century Herend copy of a Chinese exportware plate of the Yongzhend period (1723-35).

The Manchu emperor Kangxi rebuilt the Imperial kilns after their destruction during the civil wars of the 1660s and 70s. As director, he appointed Ts'ang Ying-Hsuän, who proceeded to introduce a number of new monochromes and to revive techniques that had fallen into desuetude. The ''famille-verte'' palette was developed from the Ming *wucai* or five-colour enamel group in which green dominated. An important sub-division within this group was composed of the black ground wares naturally termed ''famille-noire'', which were highly prized in the 19th century and which as a result were widely faked. There are a number of examples of the forger's art extant where perfectly genuine but commonplace Kangxi pieces have been ''skinned'', i.e. their glaze has been removed to be replaced by the much more costly ''mirror-black'' or famille-noire colours.

③ *right*
A French hard-paste copy of a Compagnie des Indes armorial plate, late 19th century.

Chinese porcelain decorated with European coats-of-arms was first made in the reign of Chêng Te (1506-1655), but it was not until the 18th century that large orders for entire services were placed. England was the greatest importer of such wares in the 18th century. Painting in black or grey (known as *en grisaille*) was introduced in 1728, but this plate would have dated from about 1760, since the style of painting the isolated bouquets and sprays of flowers is taken from the fashionable *Deutsche Blumen* from Meissen.

The surface is almost oily to the touch and has a slightly tin-glazed appearance, probably because a thin bluish wash has been applied over the glaze in order to reproduce the appearance of Chinese exportware. This false lamina has been partially rubbed away with use, revealing the hard white porcelain below.

New monochromes appeared, including mirror-black, "clair-de-lune", apple-green and the so-called "peach-bloom" (see *Ill. 7*, p. 155). All these monochromes were copied extensively in China during the 19th century but the copies invariably lack the finesse of the original. "Famille-rose", a more sophisticated palette which naturally uses pink enamel, was introduced at the end of his reign. Rose pink ("purple of Cassius"), derived from colloidal gold, was originally formulated by Andreas Cassius of Leyden in about 1650. It was first used on German faience in the 1680s before appearing on Chinese porcelain towards the end of Kangxi's reign. By this time Europeans were placing orders not only for conventional blue and white and polychrome porcelains but also for services with their own coats-of-arms. These services often included hollowares based on contemporary European silver or ceramic shapes and copies of such pieces were made in the 19th and early 20th centuries by Samson of Paris.

During the reign of Yongzheng (1723-35) several other glazes were introduced such as "robin's egg", "tea-dust", sapphire blue and a variety of red soufflé glazes, but it was the revival of the fine celadon wares of the Song dynasty for which this reign is perhaps most noted.

The following reign of Qianlong (1736-95) at first saw a few new types, but there was still a dominance of retrospective design. It was during both this and the preceding reign that a number of copies and pastiches (see *Ill. 2*, p. 173) of early blue and white vases and ewers were made. The Yongzheng examples are possibly more successful, but both fail on the rather laboured brushwork. Towards the end of the reign there is a gradual loss of vitality and direction, with great emphasis on gaudy and over-elaborate decoration; this process of decay continued through the 19th century and into the early 20th. Traditional designs continued to be made during this period, but generally the materials are not first-rate and the painting is weak.

④ *above*
A Chinese forgery of a Tzu Chou enamelled dish of the Song period.

⑤
Monochromes of the Qianlong period.

## Samson's Oriental Reproductions

Emile Samson was certainly the most prolific manufacturer of reproductions, and his repertoire was enormous. He copied

French faience, Dutch delftware, Isnik and Persian pottery, German, French and English porcelains as well as Japanese and Chinese exportwares. He used a number of different bodies and glazes which approximated to the type being copied, although the most recognizable is a porcelain with an even bluish glaze and remarkably few flaws found on the ubiquitous "Chinese armorial" wares.

Samson was perhaps most successful in his attempts to replicate the larger Chinese and Japanese polychrome export-wares of the 17th and 18th centuries. These larger jars and vases generally had unglazed bases, which is unfortunate for anyone trying to pass off these French reproductions as "right", since the tell-tale bluish glaze gives them away. The very bold palettes, such as famille-verte, famille-rose and the sumptuous blue, red and gold of the Imari wares from Arita are particularly good.

The brushwork of old Imari porcelains is generous and sweeping, which is no surprise since most of these patterns were derived from contemporary Japanese textiles. The very free style was presumably intended to mesmerize the eye into disregarding detail. These rich wares were not meant as cabinet or collectors' pieces to be closely studied: they were made to stand as decorative complements to the tapestries and furnishings in the halls, stairways and apartments of grand houses such as Burghley, Longleat and Blenheim.

Since we do not examine the brushwork and tonal subtleties of the Imari palette in the same way as we would those on an early Kakiemon bowl, we can experience some difficulty when we are asked to consider such wares. It is worth remembering that some experts in Japanese porcelain are unacquainted with European porcelain or the enamels used on it and are some-times fooled. The problem is generally solved by peering into the interior of the vessel or the lid. If the glaze is irregular with numerous pinholes or other flaws then the piece might well be old. If it is perfectly smooth and a greyish blue, beware. Samson marked many of his oriental pieces with either a gibberish oriental seal or else a square mark (which is in fact a squared "S"), both in red.

② 
A Samson copy of an 18th-century "famille-rose" teapot.

① *above*
A Samson copy of a "famille-rose" tureen of the Qianlong period.

Copies of Chinese famille-verte and famille-rose porcelain present fewer problems, even if one cannot examine the glaze and paste, simply because the enamels alone should deter-mine their authenticity. The palette can appear to be quite close at a superficial glance, but a comparison, for example between a Samson famille-verte piece and a genuine Kangxi (1662-1722) piece, will show several differences. The late pieces never possess the luminosity and iridescence of the green and blue enamels, which also invariably develop a crackle. In the areas surrounding the blue on a genuine piece there is a zone perhaps no more than an eighth of an inch wide which has a matt appearance. This peculiar characteristic does not occur on 19th-century famille-verte or famille-rose porcelain. The yellow on Kangxi porcelain is very irregular with a dirty or muddy appearance quite different from the later chrome colour.

# EUROPEAN CERAMICS

## Italian Maiolica

A large number of reproductions of early Italian maiolica were made from the middle of the 19th century onwards. Some of these were shown at the major international exhibitions both in England and on the Continent. Many are painted in colours very similar to the Renaissance originals, but they generally fail to pass muster on the brushwork, for it is an extremely difficult task to paint convincingly out of one's time, to capture the spirit of an age or of a movement. Our Victorian forefathers were no exception and invariably rendered the faces of individuals in an idealistic, over-sweet manner. Correct attribution, particularly of the istoriato school of maiolica painters, is dependent on the ability to recognize the difference between the treatment afforded to a subject in the 16th century and those of the 19th and 20th centuries.

**Cantagalli** The Cantagalli factory was established in Florence in 1878, making reproductions not only of the istoriato school and other early Italian maiolica but also of Hispano-Moresque lustreware and the Isnik wares of Turkey. Their reproductions can be quite accomplished; the palette is close enough and there is little difference in the material. The Isnik wares are perhaps a trifle heavier and more slickly potted than the originals, but not always. As with many other copies, the most obvious fault is the failure to recreate the spontaneity. The copyist works in a tentative or groping way, as if trying to follow someone else's footsteps. His situation is analogous, but possibly less obviously so, to the efforts of the Bow and Worcester painters trying to copy the reign-marks on the backs of Chinese or Japanese dishes and ending up with nonsensical hieroglyphics.

Cantagalli pieces are nearly all marked with the singing cockerel, although it is not always easy to identify as such since it is sometimes rather cursorily or loosely drawn. Occasionally one happens upon a piece of maiolica or Hispano-Moresque

[3]
A close-up of the base of two Cantagalli (Florence) tankards, one with the usual factory mark, the other with the mark gouged out in an effort to pass it off as an early Isnik piece.

**1** *above*
An early 20th-century forgery of an early Caffagiolo roundel (*c.* 1510) by Ferruccio Mengaroni. The forgery is so good that for many years this roundel was exhibited in the Oppenheim Collection.

**2** *above*
A Mengaroni "resurrection" panel after an early 16th-century Faenza original.

where the glaze has been gouged or abraded away—beware, for the bird may have flown. There was probably a cockerel there once. The Doccia factory also produced reproductions of early Faenza and Urbino maiolica, but most are marked and are not in the least troublesome.

**Mengaroni** The most convincing faker of all was probably the brilliant Ferruccio Mengaroni of Pesaro, who was born in 1875. Until the time of his death in 1925, when he was accidentally crushed by one of his own monolithic creations, he produced highly deceptive fakes of the early masterpieces from Caffagiolo or Faenza. His work has duped many experts and will probably continue to do so.

Mengaroni took great pains both with the palette and with the detail of the subject, although the former is not quite as accurate as it should be. For anyone who is not well acquainted with his work and style, any of his pieces would be very hard to dismiss with confidence, particularly in a remote saleroom or a shop far from the Victoria and Albert Museum, where it can be checked.

**Molaroni copies** Vincenzo Molaroni, also of Pesaro, reproduced the classical wares of Urbino, mainly in the Castel Durante style. The flatwares are generally painted with rather sentimental renderings of figure subjects after Raphael, Correggio or Leonardo da Vinci. They are marked on the back with either painted or impressed marks in the form of a "VM" monogram or a plain "M" over "Pesaro", or with the manufacturer's full name in script.

Other notable makers of retrospective or "historismus" maiolica are the factories or studios of Achille Wildi, Bruno Buratti and the partnership of Guido Andreani and Giulio Patrignani, all of whom signed their work, the last using the letters "MAP" for Maiolica Artistica Pesarese.

## French Faience

The technique for making tin-glazed earthenware was introduced into France by immigrant Italian potters. At first the products of these denizen potters were, quite naturally, very much in their native styles, such as the "gothic" of Faenza or

**3** *right*
A reproduction of an Urbino maiolica dish of about 1535, painted in the manner of Francesco Avelli by Mengaroni.

**4** *far right*
A late 19th-century reproduction of a Gubbio lustred dish of about 1530 from the workshop of maestro Giorgio Andreoli.

5

A late 19th-century reproduction of a Faenza armorial dish of about 1520.

6

A late 19th-century reproduction of an Urbino istoriato dish in the manner of Avelli.

the istoriato tradition of Urbino, and it is sometimes very difficult to differentiate them from their Italian counterparts, particularly in the case of the work of the Lyons maiolica painters.

In the 17th century Nevers and Rouen were the most important potting centres in France. The former used a combination of contemporary Renaissance silver or metal forms but oddly enough painted in the Chinese "Transitional" style with figures in cloud-lapped rocky landscapes. An unusual variation of this was the use of a solid blue ground glaze over-painted in white enamel, vaguely reminiscent of Limoges enamel work, but probably derived from the 17th-century blue ground wares of Persia or late Ming export porcelain. This style has been termed *bleu persan*.

The middle years of the 18th century saw the rise of Strasbourg and Marseilles. By this time manufacturers had moved away from the restricted *grand feu* palette to the more sensitive *petit feu* or low-fired colours. This allowed the faience painter greater freedom. He was now able to compete with those who painted on porcelain. In fact some of the wares of the Sceaux factory are very close to porcelain.

The Marseilles factory of Veuve Perrin is one of the most commonly faked or copied in French faience. It is extremely difficult to sort out the tin-glazed earthenware, since the formula does not vary a great deal from one time to another, or for that matter from place to place. Without the help of decoration the extremely subtle differences between various factories can be nigh impossible to detect. This is especially so with Veuve Perrin, which was and is highly prized by collectors and as a result has received the unwelcome attention of forgers.

**Chantilly, St Cloud and Mennecy** Fakes or reproductions of French soft-paste porcelains are relatively easy to detect. Each factory had distinctive pastes, glazes and palettes unlike the late 18th-century Paris factories, which all produced very similar porcelains. Chantilly used tin in their glaze, which gives an opaque creamy-grey appearance resembling faience or *milchglas*—totally different from Mennecy, St Cloud or Vincennes, which are translucent or glassy. The silver-mounted "U"-shaped beaker (*Ill. 1*, p. 177) is painted in the Kakiemon style, which was very fashionable in the late 17th and 18th centuries—a fact confirmed by the great collections at

7 *above*

A Montagnon copy of a Nevers "bleu persan" sifter (*c.* 1900).

Without looking at the base, which is marked "Montagnon" it is easy to see from the fussy painting that it cannot be compared with the bold brushwork of old Nevers. The granular earthenware body on early Nevers is a soft pinkish buff colour: this piece is dense brownish red.

8

This double-handled dish is an early 20th-century copy of an 18th-century *grand feu* or high-fired Rouen. Apart from the painting, which is inept and wooden, the giveaway is in the very greyish dull glaze and above all the palette itself. One colour which seems to have proved elusive to recapture is blue. Early Rouen has a slightly greyish cobalt blue unlike that on these modern wares, which is a very bright Prussian colour.

1 *right*

A late 19th-century copy of a Marseilles (Veuve Perrin) plate.

The body and glaze are fairly good, but as is usually the case it is let down by the poor draughtsmanship. The trailing flowers on the rim are weed-like and lack detail, and the central figures are very stiff.

The enamels on Veuve Perrin are fresh-looking and sunny with a dominant milky pink. The palette on the copy is decidedly late Autumn, dull and grey.

2 *far right*

A Samson reproduction of a Marseilles (Veuve Perrin) jar and cover, probably early 20th century.

This piece is a straightforward reproduction of an early Marseilles jar. On the base are both the VP monogram of the Veuve Perrin factory—which is incidentally the most copied mark on French faience—and the entwined ''S'' mark of Samson.

Burghley House, Blenheim Palace and Hampton Court and by the collection of Augustus the Strong in the Johanneum. The Prince de Condé, who was patron of the Chantilly concern, was a passionate collector of this type of Japanese porcelain and a large proportion of the factory's production was made in this style. Chantilly Kakiemon wares are painted in a precise manner with the enamels carefully outlined in black, in contrast to the Arita or even the Meissen versions, which do not appear to be so well defined.

St Cloud made a large number of pieces in the white, relying on the form alone for decorative appeal. The shapes were taken from contemporary silver or from oriental ceramics. The body was similar to Chantilly, but the glaze, rather than being opaque, was glassy and of a creamy ivory tone comparable to Chelsea of about 1750. The Samson copies of St Cloud jars, however (*Ill. 3*, p. 177) were crudely potted and covered in a dull, widely crackled, greyish glaze on a granular earthenware body.

Small objects such as snuff-boxes, scent-bottles, étuis, cane-handles or other *galantriewaren* as these objects are designated, are especially difficult to attribute. The unglazed areas are usually impossible to examine because of the metal mounts, and one has therefore to depend solely on the glaze and enamelling (if any). *continued on page 177*

3 *above*

A tin-glazed copy of an 18th-century French faience vase, probably late 19th century.

The faience of Strasbourg is noted for brilliant rendering of naturalistic flowers which have a unique freshness and vitality. The present pot-pourri vase is fussily painted in flat enamels on a thin yellowish glaze in total contrast to the bold enamels and rich grey-white glaze of the 18th century. On the base is the monogram of Paul Hannong, proprietor of Strasbourg between 1753 and 1762.

4 *left*

An early 20th-century copy of a Chantilly flower holder. This is interesting for several reasons.

In the first place it is made of an earthenware or *faience fine* very similar to English creamware. The glaze which contains the opacifying tin is remarkably good but fails where it has pooled in the crevices or angles: here the glaze has become quite bluish and is cracked and much like pearlware. The enamelling has effectively captured the original feel and the flowers are well painted and delineated, the only evident weakness being the wheatsheaves and the butterfly, which are very stiffly drawn. This piece is signed ''Lefrond''.

1 `right
A Chinese blue and white Palace
bowl of the Chenghua period
(1465-87). The restrained, spacious
design is typical of this period,
which many connoisseurs consider
to be the zenith of Chinese blue and
white porcelain. Copies were made
during the reign of the Qing
Emperor Kangxi (1662-1722), but
they have the characteristic pure
white ground associated with their
period, which should not be
confused with the distinctive ivory
tone unique to Chenghua porcelain.

3 below
A Böttger stoneware lidded
tankard, c. 1710-15. Johann
Friedrich Böttger was unsuccessful
in his first attempts to make a true
hard-paste porcelain. By 1708,
however, he had manufactured a
porcellaneous stoneware
comparable to the southern Chinese
Yixing. Most Böttger stoneware
vessels are based on contemporary
metal forms and are embellished
with lapidary work or wheel-
engraved in the manner of Saxon
glassware.

2 above
An 18th-century Ming-style blue
and white vase. Although the form
is based on an archaic bronze
vessel, the decoration is derived
from early Ming blue and white.
Compared to the fluent and more
open appearance of earlier pieces, it
has a relatively stiff design.

1 *right*

A pair of Japanese vases painted in the Kakiemon palette, *c.* 1680-90. A similar pair of vases is included in the inventory of Queen Mary's collection at Kensington Palace taken in 1697. Copies of them were made at Meissen between 1725 and 1730, and again at Chelsea from around 1752.

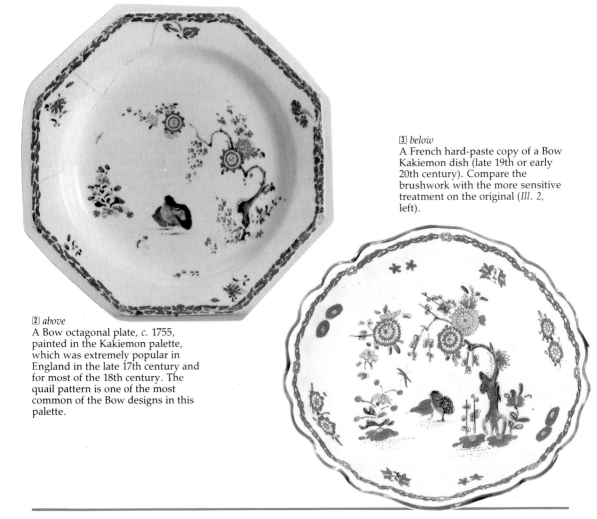

3 *below*

A French hard-paste copy of a Bow Kakiemon dish (late 19th or early 20th century). Compare the brushwork with the more sensitive treatment on the original (*Ill. 2,* left).

2 *above*

A Bow octagonal plate, *c.* 1755, painted in the Kakiemon palette, which was extremely popular in England in the late 17th century and for most of the 18th century. The quail pattern is one of the most common of the Bow designs in this palette.

4 *below*
An Hispano-Moresque lustreware
dish *c.* 1400 (Paterna or Manises).
The technique of adding lustre to
tin-glazed earthenware was
developed in the Middle East and
introduced into southern Spain in
the 13th century. The early wares
can show either Islamic influence,
as in the present example, or a more
European, Gothic appearance.

5 *above*
A Staffordshire slipware Charles II
portrait dish by William Taylor, *c.*
1670. The tradition of making lead-
glazed earthenware decorated in
slip in England began at Wrotham
in Kent early in the 17th century.
The finest pieces, however, were
made in the second half of the
century in Staffordshire by Thomas,
Ralph and James Toft and George
and William Taylor. Favourite
themes included the Pelican in her
Piety, Adam and Eve, mermaids,
cockerels, and royal portraits such
as this. A number of fairly accurate
copies were made earlier this
century employing similar
materials.

6
An Hispano-Moresque aquamanile
of the late 15th century, probably
Manises. These pottery vessels,
which were used for washing the
hands at table, are extremely rare:
only three others apart from this
one have been recorded. The tight
feathery scrolls are typical of
Catalonian lustreware of the 15th
century.

**1** *above*
A Meissen Commedia dell'Arte
figure of an actor, modelled by
Johann Joachim Kändler around
1737. Kändler was undoubtedly the
finest modeller at Meissen, and his
figures epitomize the vigour and
movement of the late Baroque. This
figure is perhaps the least known of
his minor masterpieces.

**2** *right*
A Meissen figure of Harlequin,
modelled by Kändler around 1738.
It is a brilliant example of his work:
the sense of movement is
emphasized by the strong enamel
colours which were typical of the
1730s and 40s.

**3** *right*
A Torquay forgery of an early
English porcelain squirrel, *c*. 1950.
The figure has a long genealogy.
The original was probably modelled
by J. J. Kändler around 1735, since
there are teapots of very similar
form recorded by him in May of
that year. This was subsequently
copied at Chelsea during the incised
triangle period (1745-49) and then a
little later at Derby, for which there
is an entry in William Duesbury's
*London Account Book* for 22 May
1751.

This piece can easily be identified
as Torquay by the dried out fissured
paste, the dirty looking crackled
glaze and the rather careless streaky
painting of the fur. The earlier
models, if coloured at all, are all
very finely brindled.

**4** *above*
The base of the Torquay squirrel,
(*Ill. 3*, left), showing the fissures
which make it look like one of the
early and faulty efforts of a newly
established 18th-century factory.

*continued from page 172*

1 *left*, 2 *right*
A Samson copy of a Chantilly beaker (late 19th or early 20th century) and a Samson copy of a small yellow ground Chantilly snuff box. On the beaker's base, marked in red, are both the hunting horn of Chantilly and the entwined "S" of Samson.

The beaker fails to convince simply because it is composed of hard-paste porcelain which strangely enough approaches the mid-18th century Meissen chalky body. It is covered with a very glassy glaze which is also peppered with small black pinholes, the latter probably contrived to simulate a characteristic fault of Chantilly.

The snuff box is unconvincing for the same reasons.

3 *below*
A Samson copy of a St Cloud jar and cover. The base is incised with both the St Cloud cipher and the Samson device.

## German Stoneware

Stoneware is a high-fired pottery, more often than not composed of clay and ground feldspathic rock. At very high temperatures—somewhere approaching 1400°C (2550°F)—the stone vitrifies, rendering it impervious to water and therefore obviating the need for a glaze (although in most cases after the 16th century a glaze was applied).

Stoneware was first made in China, probably during the Han dynasty or a little before, since it has an affinity with Yüeh ware, which is known to have been produced in the third century B.C. The early Chinese stonewares were generally covered in a thin translucent olive or sea-green glaze which resembled Celadon, but was not as unctuous or opaque.

It is unlikely that European potters learned the technique from the Orient. They probably discovered it for themselves in the early Middle Ages, perhaps in the Rhineland.

Some medieval stoneware is lead-glazed, but since it could not be fired at very high temperatures, the lead glazing was not always successful; it stratified and flaked away from the body. The solution was discovered in the 14th century with the introduction of salt-glazing. When the kiln temperature was at its highest, salt (sodium chloride) was thrown into the firing chamber. This immediately vapourized, the chlorine was exhausted from the kiln and the residual sodium combined with mineral elements present in the body to form a thin, close-fitting glaze.

Stoneware was produced in the Netherlands, Saxony and, from the 17th century onwards, in England, but the most important area of production in Europe was the Rhineland. The leading Rhenish centres were at Siegburg, Raeren, Cologne and Westerwald. Since the wares of all these centres were reproduced in either the 18th or the 19th centuries, it is important to give a brief history and description of each type. We can ignore 16th-century coiled wares since very few copies were made of them.

4
A Samson copy of a Chantilly knife handle. The small Chantilly and Samson marks in red on the butt of the handle could easily be missed, since they have been incorporated into an ancillary part of the design and are virtually hidden as a result.

[1]
A Hubert Schiffer copy of a Raeren stoneware tankard (*c.* 1880-90). Schiffer's products are generally marked with his monogram, "HS"; no early pieces are ever marked.

[2] *below*
A spirally-lobed Birnkrug with pewter mounts.

This is a copy of an Ansbach Jug painted in the so-called "green-family" style of the 1730s and 40s. The enamels are very dry looking and the painting is rather fiddly, quite different from the bold, confidently painted originals. The faces of the man and woman at the table look more like 20th-century comic strip characters.

What is more intriguing is the rather strange dull finish to the glaze on the outside of the pot. It is quite obvious that this piece has been deliberately abraded to simulate wear. Although the handle has been quite savagely scored, the surface of the glaze beneath it, where the fingers would quite naturally rub every time the pot was picked up, is absolutely untouched. The base is painted with marks normally associated with Ansbach.

**Siegburg** Sixteenth-century Siegburg (production ceased in 1632) is made of a fine greyish-white material. The decoration was invariably of applied oval or rectangular panels depicting the coats-of-arms of principalities or bishoprics; classical figures, perhaps symbolizing the Virtues; or biblical scenes, usually taken from engravings by Virgilius Solis or G. Aldegraver.

The most common form encountered is the tall slightly tapered cylindrical tankard *(Schnelle)*; these were copied at the end of the 19th century, particularly by the firm of C. W. Fleischmann. His products are far too wooden and precise, both in construction and design: they all look machine-made. Other spurious pieces, probably made to deceive, lack the crispness of the original. They are indifferently potted with a flat or nearly flat base (as opposed to a recessed or concave base), which is occasionally scored with grooves in a fairly unconvincing attempt to simulate the thumb-print marks found on some early stonewares. While many of this type were made of stoneware, there is a group which is made of fine earthenware dressed in a thin yellowish-white tin glaze.

**Raeren** Brown or very occasionally grey or yellowish brown in colour, Raeren stoneware was produced from the second quarter of the 16th century onwards. Early wares are very similar to Cologne, but those of the late 16th century are quite distinctive. The workshops of Jan and Peter Emens Menniken made fine tankards and jugs with a pronounced central bulge applied with a frieze of dancing peasants or biblical themes, such as Susannah and the Elders or the story of Joseph and his Brothers. The ancillary panels are of small circular medallions or bands of formal scrollwork. Good reproductions of this type were made by Hubert Schiffer and also by the Fleischmann concern during the last third of the 19th century.

**Westerwald** The third and most prolific region is Westerwald, situated between Cologne and Frankfurt-am-Main. Not much of importance was produced here until the arrival of the Knütgen family, the best of the Siegburg potters, in 1590. It naturally follows that their earliest pieces are indistinguishable from those made in Siegburg.

A little later the Mennicken family also migrated from Raeren, and brought their traditional style to Höhr in the Westerwald district. It was here that they developed fully the use of cobalt to enhance or highlight decoration. Towards the middle of the 17th century Westerwald stoneware became more mechanical and the more complex figural subjects were discontinued in favour of small, crudely applied moulded motifs and stamped repeating patterns. In the third quarter of the century manganese was added to the palette.

The most common form is the *Kugelbauchkrug* or, literally, "fat-bellied jug", which later was frequently applied with the device or bust portrait of William III or Queen Anne, or the monogram GR for either George I or II. Other popular forms were the *Humpen*, a short cylindrical tankard or mug, and the taller oviform jug with a narrow neck (*Enghalskrug*). These 17th- or 18th-century vessels were not made with great care and the potter's or workman's hand is usually in evidence.

Late 19th-century reproductions by Reinhold Merkelbach of Höhr-Grenzhausen are characterized by their over-neat potting, the slightly more stylized scratched foliage (even the late 17th-century pieces are fairly abstract) and the rather thin and watery royal blue that was used. The original's cobalt is a darker inky colour. Late pieces are sometimes impressed with numbers; early examples carry no marks at all.

3 *above*
A Samson copy of a Meissen figure, the Avvocato. The original is composed of a chalky paste and has a rich egg-yolk coloured enamel, but this copy has a flat "peppery" base and the enamel is a dull yellow (although on some figures it is a harsh chrome yellow).

The applied red rosettes on the cloak of this copy are simply modelled and, unlike those on the original, they have not been worked further with a knife to produce tiny veins. The base has been impressed with an S, but an attempt has been made to erase the tell-tale Samson mark.

4
A pair of Rhenish salt-glaze stoneware Bellarmines, made in the late 16th century at Frechen or Cologne and moulded with the arms of Queen Elizabeth I of England.

**Cologne or Frechen** made stoneware from the Middle Ages. Their most famous products are the brown-glazed globular jugs applied with a bearded mask on the neck, so-called "bellarmines", allegedly named after the notorious and much hated Cardinal Bellarmine. The majority of these vessels are applied with small medallions or an armorial device, which is sometimes the arms of Elizabeth I of England.

Similar but much cruder bellarmines were made in England at Fulham by John Dwight, who took out a patent in 1671. There are no convincing fakes of these wares since those produced by Merkelbach and others are too regular.

## Meissen Figures

Meissen single figures are among the more successful of the many types of porcelain and pottery which were copied by Emile Samson. The Commedia dell'Arte, which originated in the 16th century and was the ancestor of the modern Punch and Judy, was a continuing source of inspiration not only for the Italian porcelain modellers but also for Johann Joachim Kändler of Meissen and Franz Anton Bustelli of Nymphen-

5
A Samson copy of Tyrolean or Dutch dancers by J. F. Eberlein of Meissen, which was modelled in 1735. One of the most sought after models, it was copied in the 1750s by both Chelsea and Bow and, a little surprisingly, by the Chinese potters at Jingdezhen during the reign of the Emperor Quianlong (1736-95).

**Blue eyes and brown eyes**
It has often been said that blue eyes are never found on any 18th-century figure. In my experience this appears to be true, although Meissen did use a pale grey in both the 18th and 19th centuries, which is deceptively close to blue. Generally, 18th-century figures are painted with brown or very dark brown eyes.

① *above*
The Samson entwined "S" mark.

② *above*
A late 19th-century copy of an early 18th-century Augsburg hausmaler-decorated Meissen tea bowl and saucer.

③ *above*
A late 19th-century copy of an early 18th-century Augsburg lid (possibly a replacement) after an original decorated in the manner of Abraham Seuter.

④
A German hard-paste porcelain copy of a Fulda cup and saucer, late 19th century.
The cup and saucer would appear to be replacements for originals dating from the 1760s.

burg, the finest modellers in German porcelain. From the mid-1730s Kändler began a series of figures and groups based on such characters. Among them are Punchinello, Scaramouche, Dr Boloardo and the Avvocato, which was first modelled in 1748 (*Ill. 3*, p. 179).

**German Hausmaler** Large numbers of Meissen blanks were decorated outside the factory in the second quarter of the 18th century in the painting studios of *Hausmaler* ("house-painters"). Some of the finest work was done in these studios by painters such as Johanna Aufenwerth, Ignaz Bottengruber, J. G. Heintze or J. F. Metzsch, who mainly used coloured enamels. Elias Adam, the brothers Bartholomäus and Abraham Seuter worked principally in silver or gold. They were the most prominent of the Augsburg Hausmaler and specialized in chinoiserie subjects. Their method was painstaking and the results lacked spontaneity, but they were nevertheless a great deal more lively than subsequent fakes of their work.

Figure subjects on genuine Augsburg decorated pieces have a naturally fluid posture, whereas the graceless forms on the fakes resemble shapeless sacks. Beneath each chinoiserie vignette the pendant scrollwork or *ferronnerie* on the copy is crude and amorphous when compared with the controlled cursive ornamentation of the original. The gold on Böttger Meissen porcelains has a subtle coppery appearance with slight iridescence, unlike the gilding on the copy, which is dull and brassy. Differences between the glazes are also quite marked—Böttger Meissen is a warm smoky ivory or cream colour, in contrast to the hard glassy grey Thuringian porcelain of the late 19th century.

## Nineteenth-Century Copies

The increasing numbers and the growing wealth of the new bourgeoisie meant that by the middle of the 19th century more people could spend more money on more than the bare essentials. The new dynasts required that their houses be filled with fashionable artifacts and ornaments, which resembled—superficially at least—those in the houses of the aristocracy and the landed gentry.

The demand for decorative items in porcelain and pottery led to the foundation of a large number of factories. But from the end of the Neo-Rococo period, in about 1840, the greater proportion of this ceramic output was a re-hash of the porcelains made at the leading European factories, particularly Meissen and Sèvres.

The Neoclassical period, which included the so-called Empire style, gave way to a debased revival of the Rococo and with it ever increasing elaboration. This can be seen on vases, inkstands and other ornamental wares which were heavily encrusted with applied flowers. Figures took on a more sickly hue, all exposed parts of the body were painted in flesh tones and the faces were given an overall yellowish tone, in contrast to the more obviously rouged but more pleasing faces on most 18th-century figures (with the exception of some Italian and Thuringian factories, whose figures were often quite gaudily painted).

The greatest difference between, say, an 18th-century Meissen figure and a 19th-century copy is in the detail. Just a casual glance, for example, at the hair will immediately distinguish early from late. On the former it seems that every strand is picked out with an ultra-fine brushstroke, whereas on the latter the hair appears widely-spaced like the teeth of a comb.

Both Thuringian and Saxon factories in the second half of the 19th century followed the over-elaborate style which had developed in the second quarter of that century. The prolific Thuringian factories, most notably the Voigt Brothers of Sitzendorf and Schierholz of Plaue-am-Havel, used an insipid range of pastel enamels which included a pale pink and dull turquoise. The porcelain itself has a hard greyish appearance. Both these factories used parallel line marks crossed by either one or two diagonals, perhaps to simulate the crossed-swords of Meissen.

Other German factories were even less scrupulous and blatantly copied both the models and the crossed-swords of Meissen; and even if purists regard 19th-century Meissen as decadent, it is nevertheless superior to all other factories, with the possible exception of its neighbour at Potschappel. This factory produced some fine quality work in a palette similar to that employed at Meissen. Carl Thieme, the proprietor, used a ''T'' between crossed batons as his early factory mark, again causing confusion to the uninitiated.

**Copying in France** In France a similar situation prevailed vis-à-vis Sèvres and other lesser concerns. Many Parisian factories freely copied the interlaced ''L''s of the Vincennes and early Sèvres factories. It would not be exaggerating to say that over 95 per cent of pieces thus marked are later copies or forgeries. Apart from the usual differences in technical skill and the enamels used, the most obvious mistake is the use of a mark only found on early soft-paste when almost all later French porcelain was hard-paste.

## Dutch Delftware

The technique of making tin-glazed earthenware in the Netherlands was introduced by immigrant Italian maiolica potters early in the 16th century. With continued persecution in the southern Netherlands, they were forced to move from Antwerp northwards to Rotterdam, Haarlem, Delft and even across the North Sea to England. Delft became the largest centre for the production of tin-glazed pottery during the 17th and 18th centuries.

The major portion of the output was blue and white, loosely based on Chinese exportware, but polychrome wares in imitation of the fashionable Japanese or Chinese Imari wares were

5

These ribbed beaker vases are Samson copies of a Delft piece dating from the second quarter of the 18th century. Since some Samson pieces were masked or else have had their marks erased, these vases are very useful signposts; and a careful examination of the body, paste and decoration will give us a key to uncovering less obvious fakes.

The glaze is dull and off-white: early Delft is with very few exceptions, bluish. The unglazed areas show a very smooth close-grained paste, unlike the porous-looking buff or straw-coloured clay typical of Dutch Delft. The Samson brushwork is quite frankly, appalling. The faces of the ''Long Elizas'' are totally devoid of character and the scrollwork and foliage is extremely crude. The enamels are lacklustre and too thickly applied. There are two marks on the bases. One is PAK, the monogram of Pieter Adriaenson Kocks, the proprietor of one of Delft's most successful factories, De Grieksche A. The second is a variation of Samson's entwined mark.

6

A Japanese copy of a Dutch Delft dish, painted in the manner of Frederick van Frytom and made at Arita between 1685 and 1700.

3
A genuine 17th-century English delftware wine bottle on the left and a fake on the right, showing the difference in the shapes of the handles.

also made. It was the advent of Josiah Wedgwood's creamware at the end of the 18th century that signalled the demise of the tin-glaze industry, including Delft, not only in England but throughout Europe. Production, except for tiles and industrial wares, virtually ceased in the 19th century.

## English Delftware

A great deal can be learned by comparing a late 19th-century forgery of an English delftware wine bottle with a genuine bottle from the celebrated collection at Rous Lench. In the first place the genuine bottle is made of a buff-coloured clay, whereas the forgery is made of a dryish-looking, white chalky clay. The correct bottle shows no concentric throwing rings on the base, but the fake does. The glaze on the fake is dull and speckled with minute and barely visible spots of cobalt—no right bottle is ever similarly marked. The fake's glaze is also covered in a regular network of fine but pale, almost quadrangular crackle. Early pieces on the other hand have a thick, creamy, undulating glaze, which, if crackled at all, is a more obvious brown or buff colour.

The handle illustrates most clearly where the forger has gone wrong. Admittedly this fake jug is small, but nonetheless the handle is far too thin at the lower end where it is luted to the body and would not serve its purpose for long. The upper handle deviates from right pieces in that the handles of authentic examples are connected to the neck at a downward sloping angle in a natural manner, whereas the handle of the forgery is joined to the neck at a right angle and appears to have been pushed hard enough to form an awkward kink close to the body. Finally, the inscription looks passable at first sight, but it does not stand close scrutiny: the numbers and the flourish are fiddly and unsure.

As a postscript, it is worth quoting again from Geoffrey Eliot Howard's *Early English Drug Jars*. In his note on fakes he writes, ''Next come the commonest kind, which were made in France, probably about 50 years ago. [He was writing in 1931.] The whole jar is a clever imitation, made of 'white ware' in the exact shape of the Jacobean vessels, and with a perfect imitation of a Jacobean inscription. Two clues should guide the collector in detecting these. The body of the jar is composed of a much whiter clay than was used in Lambeth and very often rectangular cracks appear in the glaze such as are seldom found in genuine specimens.''

## Creamware and Related Wares

Creamware is a fine, lightweight pottery covered in a clear lead glaze. It involves the use of flint and gradually evolved from other Staffordshire earthenwares in the first half of the 18th century. The credit for its invention in the 1740s belongs to Enoch Booth, although it was Josiah Wedgwood who completed the process. Booth's formula enabled him to produce an attractive, creamy-looking, thin and crisply moulded ware at relatively low cost, and this allowed Wedgwood to compete with the more expensive and vulnerable delftwares. The success of this earthenware eventually led to the demise of the tin-glaze industry in Europe. By the end of the century, for example, all the delftware factories in England except Lambeth had closed, and even Lambeth had discontinued the manufacture of decorative ware in favour of more utilitarian and industrial items.

Creamware manufacture was also started not only by other Staffordshire potters but also at Bristol and at Leeds. Apart from flatware, which was made in all these areas, the Wedgwood and Leeds potteries made more ambitious pieces including centrepieces, cake stands and candlesticks, which were pierced to resemble lace-work.

Another form of creamware, also invented by Wedgwood, is "Pearlware". This is fundamentally the same material, but it has a greater proportion of white clay and flint in the paste. It has a decidedly bluish appearance to the glaze, doubtless contrived to emulate the glaze on contemporary Chinese blue and white exportware. Much pearlware is decorated in underglaze blue, either by hand painting or by transfer-printing. Examples of the former can be deceptively close in look to the less accomplished porcelain from Liverpool, since they are nearly as finely potted as porcelain. Pearlware, however, is completely opaque, unlike porcelain. The traditional "willow-pattern" almost certainly began life on this type of earthenware.

## Prattware

Prattware is associated with the creamware group in that it is made of the same material, although it is additionally decorated in high fired enamel colours, such as ochre, blue, green and manganese. The name derives from Felix Pratt, a potter from Delph Lane (Tunstall), Staffordshire, who produced classical figures, wall plaques and utilitarian items, including a tea-caddy moulded with so-called "Macaroni" figures, all decorated in this range of colours. This type of ware was not only made in Staffordshire but in Northeast England by Dixon and Austin of Sunderland, and in Scotland.

There have been few reproductions of any of the creamware group, other than the more elaborate Leeds pottery, presumably for the obvious reason that although it has a simple charm it is not much sought after.

## Teawares

The Staffordshire potters of the 1750s and 60s, among them Josiah Wedgwood and his former partner Thomas Whieldon, produced a number of teawares semi-naturalistically modelled after fruit or vegetables. The most common forms were the pineapple and the cauliflower. Generally speaking, the Wedgwood versions are superior since they are more carefully and thinly potted and have sharper detail.

④ *above*

A Leeds Pottery Cornucopia, *c.* 1880.

Early Leeds Creamware is noted for its sharp modelling and attractive creamy glaze. This cornucopia has little definition, the cobalt highlighting is clumsy and as mentioned before the greyish-cream glaze suffers from the too regular crackle. This piece is also impressed "Leeds Pottery" as most late productions are.

⑤

These elaborate pierced candlesticks are reproductions of early Leeds creamware, probably using the original moulds, which were acquired by Slee's Modern Pottery in 1888. They differ only slightly from the originals. The later body is a fraction lighter in weight, and the crackled glaze is more thinly and evenly applied, allowing the yellowish grey body to show through and giving an overall dull impression. In comparison, the early piece is an ivory-cream colour with a more lustrous appearance and with an "orange-skin" texture which can be seen when it is looked at in a raking light.

[1] *above*

A copy of a Staffordshire Tea Canister.

This is a perfect example of a copy taken from a genuine piece and not from the original mould. In the first place it is a fraction smaller than the original. Secondly there is a serious loss of definition, caused by taking

[3] *above*

A modern forgery of a Staffordshire model of Stanfield Hall (*c.* 1970).

[4]

A modern forgery of a Staffordshire group of Heenan and Sayers.

a mould from an already glazed piece. This has effectively disguised the "message" of the late 18th-century original, which was in effect a broadside against current fashion, being modelled in shallow relief with "Macaroni" figures sporting preposterous wigs.

All this is missed in the slovenly potting and careless application of these rather bright overglaze enamels. In contrast, the Prattware example would be painted in the typical palette of subdued high-temperature blue, green, ochre and brown on a bluish pearlware glaze.

[2] *above, right*

An early 20th-century forgery of a Wedgwood Whieldon teapot. It is thickly constructed and covered in a green and cream glaze. Both these colours differ from the original in that they are definitely greyish and hard-looking. The green on an 18th-century piece has a warm yellowish tone and a fine network of crackle,

unlike the later piece, on which the uncrackled green is dull and tends towards the blue end of the spectrum.

The modelling of the flower part of the vegetable on the early piece is very realistic, whereas on the late piece it is clear that the modeller has never examined his subject in nature. It looks more like the magnified surface of an orange. The intended deception is revealed when one examines the interior of this "teapot". The eight strainer holes are very small and all but two of them are blocked by glaze, rendering the vessel useless.

## Staffordshire Portrait and Flat-back Figures

Before World War II it would have been inconceivable for anyone to produce a forgery of a Victorian Staffordshire portrait or flat-back figure. The serious collector of pottery regarded little that was made after 1800 as worth considering, and there was no general interest in such primitive and relatively recent "fictile abominations" as they were called by one late Victorian Punch cartoonist. Nevertheless, reproductions of the more common types have been made more or less continuously up to the present day. These have been sold legitimately as reproductions with no intention on the part of the manufacturer to deceive. But once they have been circulated or passed through the original outlet, unscrupulous or ignorant people may well sell them again as genuine. This is when the reproduction becomes a forgery.

These modern copies of Staffordshire pottery include cottages such as Stanfield Hall, money boxes, and figures and groups, such as Dick Turpin, Grace Darling and the prize fighters, Heenan and Sayers.

What distinguishes them from the originals? In the first place, the originals were press-moulded, i.e. the clay was pushed into the mould by hand, which gave an uneven look to the interior of the figure, and the finger-prints were mainly obscured by the slightly greyish lead glaze. It was a process that required some skill and could be quite time consuming to the uninitiated. Most reproductions, however, were made by the slip-casting method, which needs little skill. The technique uses liquid clay or slip, which is poured through a small vent hole in each mould and allowed to dry. The longer the liquid clay is left in the mould, the thicker the walls of the object

5 *left*
A Staffordshire "Solid Agate" figure of a seated cat (1740-50).

6 *below, left*
An early 20th-century copy of a Staffordshire "Solid Agate" figure of a seated cat.

Low-fired lead-glazed pottery presents fewer technical problems to the faker, particularly if the piece to be copied is primitive ware such as this. One is forced to rely on more subtle clues in order to uncover the fake. There is little difference between the form or the general appearance of this figure and the original, although it must be said that the late piece is marginally thicker in construction, a fault that may not necessarily always apply. On almost all recognized right pieces, however, the simulated agate is defined by thin, "combed", striae, unlike the amorphous marbling on this fake.

7
A Staffordshire reproduction of an Enoch Wood portrait bust of John Wesley, late 19th or early 20th century.

This model, first made by Enoch Wood in about 1780, enjoyed great popularity which continued into the 19th century. There are numerous very late copies of which one should be wary. Anthony Oliver in his *Staffordshire Pottery, The Tribal Art of England*, writes ". . . it was copied by many other potters and some very late examples have appeared complete with a copy of Enoch Wood's original medallion mark impressed at the back." This is just such a bust, which has in addition been rubbed down with an abrasive material to fake wear.

become, and with very, very few exceptions these slip figures are much lighter than genuine 19th-century examples.

The moulds for these pieces are not themselves taken from the early moulds but from a genuine group or figure. There is obviously a great loss of detail, as the genuine figure is glazed and therefore less well defined than the mould cast.

When a figure is fired in the kiln it shrinks by approximately ten per cent. If taken from a Victorian figure, a reproduction will therefore be smaller by the same degree. The glaze on reproduction pieces is frequently given an artificially induced network of pronounced, fine, very regular crackle. This characteristic is often quite erroneously considered by the layman to be a symptom of antiquity and therefore of authenticity. The greyish but translucent lead glaze of Victorian Staffordshire pottery is crackled but not nearly as obtrusively; it runs erratically and is widely spaced. The dry wiped or brushed look of the clay on the unglazed foot is also a feature unknown on true Victorian pottery, which is usually partially glazed and with traces of kiln-grit.

## Longton Hall

Porcelain and pottery tea- and flat-wares based on vegetable or fruit forms were popular in England in the middle of the 18th century. Chelsea, Bow, Derby and Longton Hall all produced these wares, but it is the latter Staffordshire factory which is most closely identified with naturalistic forms. At their best they have a primitive charm, but more frequently they are clumsy or awkward. As the factory only ran for a period of ten years between 1750 and 1760, these wares are rare and command high prices, and therefore encourage forgeries.

8
A Torquay forgery of a Longton Hall melon tureen (*c.* 1950).

The Longton Hall body of the middle period which this is trying to emulate is fairly close-grained and white. The glaze has a distinct blotchy or irregular greyish appearance and has many pin-holes in the surface. In the palette, which can be a little muddy, there are a distinctive yellowish green and a greyish puce.

This copy on the other hand has a slightly more granular body covered in smoky off-white glaze. The most obvious fault, however, is the pale strawberry pink and rather washed out lime green, altogether too weak to convince. Finally, the faker has gone to the trouble of scoring the inside of the box in a deliberate circular fashion, whereas in the normal course of events there would never be such regular wear.

A late 19th-century forgery of a mid-18th century Bow plate.

A French hard-paste copy of a Worcester Neoclassical plate.

# PORCELAIN

## Bow

A large proportion of the production of the early Bow factory was utilitarian blue and white. The designs on these early wares were either fanciful chinoiseries or copied directly from the Chinese or Japanese export blue and white porcelains that were shipped in vast quantities, virtually as ballast. The painters even went so far as to simulate oriental reign-marks with amusing results.

The first example (*Ill. 3*, p. 174) is a fake of a Bow plate of about 1755 painted after a Chinese original of the Yongzheng (1723-35) or early Qianlong (1736-95) period. Bow porcelain of this date can be very heavily potted and opaque, even when held against a strong electric light.The glaze is thickly applied and suffused with air bubbles, which frequently give a slightly blurred effect on the blue decoration. Another characteristic is the bluish appearance of the glaze where it has gathered or "pooled" in the footrim. Finally, the unglazed paste tends to discolour to a brownish buff colour. The copyist on this plate has attempted to emulate these idiosyncracies, and, apart from some inept handling of the border, the plate only fails with the glaze itself, which has a thin, crackled, dull grey tone resembling pearlware. Bow is rarely crackled thus.

The second example (*Ill. 2*, p. 174) is a dish painted in the beautifully spare Kakiemon style with its distinctive palette of iron-red, cerulean, turquoise, gilding and black for outline. This palette was introduced in Japan by the legendary Sakaida Kakiemon in the third quarter of the 17th century. It soon became extremely popular among European aristocratic collectors, most notably Augustus the Strong of Saxony, the Prince de Condé, and Queen Mary, whose collection was inventoried at Kensington Palace in 1697. The style was copied at Chantilly, St Cloud, Mennecy, Meissen, Chelsea, Worcester and Bow, the latter particularly favouring "Quail" pattern.

A useful comparison can be made between the first dish, which incongruously bears the red anchor mark of Chelsea, and a genuine Bow dish of about 1755. The French dish has a deep glaze of greyish glassy appearance covering a white smooth paste with slight impressions left by kiln-grit on the unglazed base. Its colours are generally much more intense than those of the original, which is delicately but fluently executed in thinly washed colours. On the Bow octagonal plate the glaze has been very lightly applied, giving a creamier softer look.

## Worcester

The Worcester porcelain factory was established in 1751. Its earliest products were predominantly blue and white and a hybrid palette synthesized from Japanese Kakiemon and Chinese famille-verte porcelains. Unlike their contemporaries at Chelsea, Bow and Derby, who were most strongly influenced by Meissen, Arita and Blanc-de-Chine porcelains, Worcester designers based their work on a fanciful vision of China as an exotic country composed of pavilions and pagodas set among idyllic islands. Their delightful chinoiseries have an almost folksy appeal, in contrast to the more stylish and sophisticated efforts of their rivals.

By 1760 however, events on the Continent had had a profound effect on their output. In Germany the Seven Years' War had seriously disrupted production at Meissen and, perhaps as a consequence, the factory had lost its initiative in the markets of Europe. The leader of fashion was now the Sèvres factory under the patronage of the French King. Its sumptuous porcelains proved irresistible to the rest of Europe, and as a result almost all the leading factories adopted the Sèvres style. Worcester was among them, introducing an assortment of coloured grounds, including yellow, green claret and the very popular blue scale.

The little sparrow beak jug (*Ill. 4*, right) is an attempt to replicate a Worcester piece of the late 1760s or early 1770s. While the overall impression is pleasing, it differs from the original in several respects. First, a Worcester example is entirely hand-painted in rich enamel colours which, in spite of a tendency to sink into the glaze, as they do on most soft-paste porcelains, nonetheless give a sense of depth. The copy is decorated using transfer-prints which are then painted over in thin enamel, giving a dull, flat appearance. The black outline of the print can be seen in the illustration. Second, the gilding, which also follows a printed matrix, lacks dimension and has a somewhat brassy glitter to it, a characteristic of most mass-produced gilded porcelain or pottery from the end of the 19th century onwards. Third, this jug is opaque, which is not surprising since it is made of earthenware, whereas a Worcester specimen would be translucent, having a greenish tint in transmitted light. Fourth, the glaze on the original has a slight bluish or greenish look and is generally ''pegged'' (i.e. a narrow band of glaze is wiped away from the interior of the footrim leaving the body exposed). The copy, which is a dead white, is not pegged but glazed all over. Finally, although the shape is passable it lacks the more sinuous, elegant lines of the original, and the handle, which is formed from one thick piece of rolled clay, should have been much slimmer and grooved.

The plate (*Ill. 2*, overleaf) is a French hard-paste copy of a Worcester Neoclassical piece dating from the 1770s. The original is characteristically thinly potted with a greenish glaze ''pegged'' inside the footrim and with a slightly convex base. This copy is on the contrary more heavily moulded and with a smoky cream glaze. As has been mentioned elsewhere the coloured enamels applied to a soft-paste body tend to fuse with the glaze, presenting a more harmonious picture, and the gilding has a much softer mellow look. On the later hard-paste plate, the somewhat crisper enamels float on the surface and the gilding is a lot more metallic or brassy. On the back of the French plate there is a paper label inscribed ''Old Chelsea 1745''—wishful thinking but not uncommon.

③ A Booth's silicon china copy of a First Period Worcester jug (early 20th century).

④ A Samson copy of an early Worcester silver-shape sauceboat, late 19th or early 20th century.

Among the most appealing of English porcelains are the early chinoiserie blue and white wares made at Worcester in its first ten years. They are painted in a greyish underglaze cobalt blue which fuses perfectly with the body under an off-white slightly greenish glaze that is often speckled with minute black grains. The painting on this copy is tentative and slightly wooden, and the cobalt has a purplish hue under the very glassy bluish glaze.

## Lowestoft

The Lowestoft factory, which was established in 1757, is noteworthy for a considerable number of commemorative or inscribed pieces. These wares date from the early 1760s and are often painted in underglaze blue (enamels were introduced at Lowestoft in 1770).

The mug (*Ill. 3, 4*, opposite) is inscribed and dated on the base "Abrm. Moore, August 29th 1765" and is a fake, probably produced in France at the end of the 19th or the beginning of the present century. The original was from a set of three and it is worth quoting Geoffrey Godden on the appearance of these early wares: "The 1764 and later pieces are normally of a new lighter body, which I describe as 'floury' as it appears open rather than compact, but the reliefs are now not so sharply defined as those made from the earlier compact body, often being quite blunt. The covering glaze is now almost perfect and clear, not blued, and the early tendency to bubbling has been corrected. This new body and glaze would seem to have been first introduced in about 1764 and was universally employed from about 1768."

The forgery has been painted in a runny underglaze cobalt blue, exaggerating the slightly blurred appearance found on some of the earlier Lowestoft wares. The glaze on this hard-paste copy is also crackled, a characteristic never found on phosphatic soft-paste porcelain.

After 1770 coloured or enamel decoration was introduced at Lowestoft and the factory continued to supply inscribed pieces. The cylindrical form of tankard superseded the bell shape from around 1775, the shape and restrained decoration being more in keeping with the Neoclassical style current in the last quarter of the 18th century.

The interest shown by late Victorian and Edwardian collectors encouraged a number of French factories to copy these porcelains. Godden cites an advertisement of 1914 by Paul Bocquillon, the Paris manufacturer, which includes a plate bearing the inscription "A Trifle from Lowestoft".

## Plymouth

William Cookworthy, a Plymouth chemist, spent many years searching for the right materials to produce true or hard-paste porcelain in England. He eventually obtained the correct ingredients, and his experiments proved satisfactory enough for him to take out a patent in 1768, a year before the French were able to produce hard-paste at Sèvres.

His earliest efforts were not particularly successful, largely because of the intractability of the clay and its tendency to warp in the extreme heat of the kiln. And he also encountered difficulty with smoke staining from his coal-fired kiln, which gave some pieces a decidedly burnt ivory patina.

Richard Champion, a fellow Quaker (who was later to take over the factory when it had moved to Bristol), notes in a letter to Caleb Lloyd dated 7 November 1765 during the period of

1 *above*
A ribbed cup and saucer. A bone-china copy or replacement for a Worcester original, probably painted in the studio of James Giles around 1770. This pure glassy white type of porcelain was only invented in the 19th century and contrasts with a greenish steatitic original. The palette is also incorrect: the Brunswick green was never used on early Worcester. It is interesting to note that both pieces are speckled and blackened on the foot, indicating that they have themselves been later decorated.

2 *above*
A forgery of a Lowestoft Abraham Moore mug, late 19th century.

3 *right*
The base of the forged Abraham Moore mug, (*Ill. 3*).

4 *left*
A copy of a Plymouth tankard, made around the turn of this century in France, almost certainly by Emile Samson.
These bell-shaped tankards were copied in some quantity, probably because the originals were extremely scarce collectors' items. It is painted in the late French Rococo style in the manner of the mysterious Monsieur Soqui, who was employed as a painter at the Plymouth factory. However, it is painted with the copyist's usual hesitancy and in a palette which differs from the Plymouth colours. The colours are generally far too bright and the puce is too "clean".

5 *left*
Another forgery of a Plymouth tankard, even less convincing than *Ill. 4*
The shape is not quite correct: it lacks the elegant curves and good proportions of the original. The glaze has a fine "orange-skin" texture, but the Plymouth glaze is quite smooth. In transmitted light the original appears white, whereas the copy is a dull orange. The brushwork here is far too clumsy and insensitive. Apart from the very poorly written mark, the footrim is too neat and with no adherent grit or dribbled glaze.

6 *above*
A hard-paste porcelain shell sweetmeat dish (late 19th century). This type of dish was made by Bow, Derby, Plymouth and Worcester. This piece, modelled by Tebo, was probably intended to pass as Plymouth, but the enamels are incorrect and the brushwork crude.

7 *above*
A reproduction of a Lowestoft tankard (*c.* 1900).

8
A more elaborately decorated reproduction of a Lowestoft tankard (*c.* 1900). This mug is made of hard-paste porcelain, on which the enamels do not "marry" to the glaze quite as well as they do on Lowestoft.

experiment that preceded the official opening of the Plymouth factory, "... . But in burning there is a deficiency; though the body is perfectly white within, but not without, which is always smoky."

Characteristic of Plymouth—and for that matter Champion's Bristol and Newhall factories, which were related in their use of very similar material—is a tendency to show the potter's throwing contours, known as "wreathing". This is most noticeable when looking at a vase or bowl held at a slight angle to the light.

[1] *above*
A Samson hard-paste figure of a flowerseller.

[2] *above*
A Samson hard-paste copy of a Derby frill vase.

[3]
A Samson hard-paste figure of a sheep.

## Nineteenth-Century Chelsea and Derby Copies

Samson's flowerseller (*Ill. 1*, left) was copied from one of a pair modelled by Joseph Williams of Chelsea, probably after an engraving by Sebastian le Clerc. These were almost certainly the "Gardener and his wife sitting with baskets" itemized in the Chelsea Sale Catalogue of 1755. Apart from the very obvious difference between the red anchor period soft-paste porcelain and the French hard-paste variety, this figure fails simply because the repairer has failed to smooth off the mould seams. These are never evident on Chelsea or on most 18th-century figures.

Samson's copy of a Derby pot-pourri vase of about 1765 on the other hand (*Ill. 2*, below) is reasonably accurate in both form and size, but there would normally be butterflies and other winged creatures in the spaces between the floral ornamentations. The base is marked with the ubiquitous Chelsea gold anchor so beloved of Samson and every other European manufacturer at the end of the last century.

## Twentieth-Century Chelsea and Derby Copies

Samson's sheep (*Ill. 3*, below), thinly potted by the slip-casting method, is after a Derby model, itself based on a Meissen original which was probably made by Kändler in the 1750s. Both the Meissen and Derby examples would be much heavier, modelled by press-moulding with unglazed bases, the former being flat with a small vent hole, the latter probably hollow with an irregular interior surface.

The interesting pair of birds (*Ill. 4*, opposite), reproducing 18th-century Derby originals, was made in Torquay around 1950. One is very lightly slip-cast, but the other is much heavier although taken from the same mould. The forger, perhaps realizing that the first was too light to pass as an early figure, allowed the second to stay longer in the mould, thereby making the sides much thicker and heavier and the whole figure consequently more convincing. The glaze is glassy and quite milky, not too dissimilar to early Chelsea, but the pastel pink flowers are too weak. On the base there are incised numerals, just like the ones that can be found on the right figures.

The Torquay hare is the last in a long line of figures stretching back to the Meissen original modelled by Johann Joachim Kändler in about 1745. It was copied at Chelsea during the red anchor period, i.e. between 1752 and 1757, contemporaneously in Staffordshire salt-glaze and finally at Torquay. The Torquay model is attempting to copy the Chelsea version, since the detailing is less sharply defined than one would expect on Meissen. The Torquay paste has a quite primitive look, which goes a long way towards explaining its success in beguiling one into thinking that it is very early and experimental soft-paste porcelain from either Chelsea, Bow or Derby. It is open-grained, grey and dry, most closely resembling either Bow of the 1750s or perhaps even early 19th-century Derby. The slightly dirty crackled glaze adds to the confusion. A careful examination when the hare is placed alongside his earlier colleagues will highlight his inadequacies however, the most obvious being the absence of applied flowers and the poor modelling of the paws.

## Welsh Porcelain

Arguably the finest porcelains produced in the first half of the 19th century in the British Isles were from the Welsh factories at Swansea and the closely related works at Nantgarw.

Nantgarw was founded by William Billingsley, the celebrated flower painter, in 1813, but the entire concern was moved to Swansea in the following year. It is therefore not surprising that the early porcelain from Swansea is very similar to that from Nantgarw. The Swansea formula was changed, however, since the Nantgarw body was prone to vitrify suddenly, causing the silicate to fuse with the kiln-furniture and resulting in considerable loss (90% in one recorded firing).

Early Nantgarw porcelain is slightly thicker than the succeeding Swansea porcelain. It is translucent and appears a pure white in transmitted light. Features of Nantgarw porcelain are the patches of iridescence noticeable on the base inside the foot. The glaze is thick and silky with no obvious rippling, such as can be found on the thinner glazed porcelain of later Swansea.

Later Swansea variations are the so-called "duck-egg", "trident" and "glassy" porcelains. The first and probably most famous of the three is highly translucent and very thinly potted with a slight suggestion of green, which is obvious in transmitted light.

The great majority of the output of both factories was composed of dishes, plates and shallow wares. More ambitious pieces such as ice pails and vases were made only in small numbers, almost certainly because of their extreme vulnerability in the kiln. Much Welsh porcelain was sent "in the white" to be decorated in London. When Nantgarw or Swansea wares were not available, the London enamellers used wares from other factories such as Coalport, Davenport or even some of the Paris factories. In the past this has led to

4 *above*
Torquay soft-paste porcelain finches (*c.* 1950).

5
A Torquay porcellaneous model hare (*c.* 1950).

6 *below*
The long line of hares, from the Meissen original on the left, through Chelsea and Staffordshire salt-glaze versions to the 1950s Torquay forgery on the right.

[1] a, b *above*
Two fake Welsh porcelain plates, thickly constructed, relatively opaque in transmitted light and covered in characterless white glaze. The painting is flat and insensitive and the gilding is dull and brassy.

[2] a, b *above*
The undersides of the two plates in (*Ill. 1*). Both are impressed "Nantgarw", but not in the conventional neat manner. One has far larger lettering than normal and space between each letter, unlike the usual mark where they are close together. The first is also inscribed in an amateurish way "Swansea" in red enamel, as if to give greater credence to a Welsh ancestry.

some quite erroneous attributions, since it is quite easy, for example, to assume mistakenly that an ice-pail surrounded by Nantgarw plates decorated in the same hand is also another Welsh piece.

Closest to the Welsh is contemporary Spode porcelain, but there is often confusion also with Grainger's Worcester, Davenport and Coalport. It should be noted that plates moulded with floral cartouches similar to those at Nantgarw and Swansea were also made at Derby, Davenport and Coalport around 1820. The Welsh plates with this decoration can be recognized quite simply—literally with one's eyes shut. It is easy to feel the contours of the mould on the backs of the Welsh pieces but not on the English versions.

## Modern Studio Pottery

At the time of writing the author is unaware of any forgeries of Studio pottery except the now celebrated attempts by inmates of Featherstone Prison near Wolverhampton to copy the works of Bernard Leach. These fakes first appeared on the market in 1980 and fooled both auction houses and dealers alike, and it is worth quoting from an article which appeared in *The Sunday Times* on 10 January 1981. ''By last summer there was a notable rise in the number of 'rare' Leaches on the London art market. A London dealer and ceramic specialist, Richard Dennis, was one of the first to spot that there was something 'rather wrong' with a number he had bought. For example, at Bonham's last October he successfully bid £600 ($900) for one, a stoneware bottle vase.

''Dennis finally became suspicious after buying a handsome and unusual green-glazed dish at Christie's. 'When I went over to Phillips I saw two more and they, too, had the same peculiar green glaze,' he said. 'When I saw so many dishes like that I thought there was something wrong.' ''

This illustrates perfectly the common mistake of putting too many objects on the market in a short space of time. If the ''master-potters'' of Featherstone Prison had been as sophisticated in their marketing as in their potting, they would probably still be enjoying the revenue from their efforts during Occupational Therapy hours.

The work of Shoji Hamada, Hans Coper, Lucie Rie, William Staite Murray, Michael Cardew and other leading 20th-century potters has to my knowledge not yet received similar flattery, but doubtless it will in future.

[5] *left*
A Bernard Leach fake, made by inmates of Featherstone Prison, Wolverhampton.

# 13 : QUILTS

INTEREST IN QUILT COLLECTING developed in the United States over ten years ago and spread gradually to Japan, West Germany, France, England and Scandinavia, where there are now major collections. In the past five years collectors from these areas have had a major impact on the market, driving prices for better examples to new highs.

The major source of period quilts is the United States, where they have been made since at least the 18th century. Canadian quilts, which closely resemble American examples, are of

[1] *left*
Crazy or silk quilts, which were widely made in both the United States and the British Isles during the late 19th century, are extremely fragile. Watch for repairs that may have involved simple patching or the removal and replacement of an entire block. On the other hand, the complexity of these pieces and their relatively low market value make it unlikely that they will be faked at present.

similar vintage. English quilts date only from the late Victorian period and are almost entirely of the silk and satin so-called "crazy" quilt form.

Collectors' interests are clearly differentiated. Early and fine examples are treated as folk art or paintings and displayed on walls beneath protective glass — only mediocre quilts are used today as bed coverings. Demand for the finest pieces outstrips the supply, but ordinary or damaged examples raise little interest and remain abundant. It is only the best examples that are liable to be faked: the amount of time and degree of skill required ensure that only a piece that will bring a substantial price will be altered or reproduced.

## The Valuation of Quilts

Several elements go into the valuation of a quilt, and the importance of each varies according to a collector's attitude. For a small but highly sophisticated group the important thing is the quilting — that is, the stitching that holds the back of the piece together and supports the inner batting. Connoisseurs look for elaborately designed quiltings: hearts, vines, floral groupings and, in rare cases, human and animal forms. They will also pay a premium for the closest stitching. The more stitches per inch a seamstress achieved the more highly thought of her work is. Solid white quilts, of little interest to most enthusiasts, are snapped up by this group if the

[2] *above*
Relatively recent (c. 1930–1940) quilts like this one are seldom faked. At present there are plenty of originals available and at reasonable prices. But as with all quilts beware the scalloped or shaped border: these are much less common than straight borders and may indicate recent reworking to "improve" upon the original design.

stitchwork is of the finest. Since quilting of this quality is time consuming and beyond the ability of all but a very few people, it is not likely to be faked.

A major group of collectors seeks strongly graphic quilts with bright colours and bold designs. Many of these resemble abstract paintings and they are displayed as such by their owners, who often have no interest at all in other antiques. Some of the major problems with faking and reproduction occur in this area. Because they are often of geometric pattern these quilts are not hard to put together, and since would-be purchasers frequently have little knowledge of or interest in quilting or early fabrics they are more easily gulled than individuals in the previous groups. Moreover, as the time and skill involved in faking are modest and the prices that can be obtained for the more spectacular examples are quite high, the fakers are naturally drawn to this area.

While there are collectors most interested in extremely early quilts or those that are dated, signed or have some authentic historical association, these pieces form such a tiny proportion of all existing quilts that they offer little inducement to the faker. However, all names and dates should be regarded with suspicion and examined closely to make sure that they are of an age and style appropriate to the quilt on which they appear.

## The Types Most Likely to be Faked or Reproduced

Robert Bishop, Director of New York's Museum of American Folk Art and the author of the leading book in this field, *America's Quilts and Coverlets*, notes that the three major problem areas today are Amish quilts and similar graphic geometrics; crib quilts; and Baltimore "album" quilts.

The Amish quilts are a particularly difficult area because Amish women were among the first to use sewing machines, not only to bind the edges of a quilt but also to piece it. Consequently, the general guideline that machine stitching in a 19th-century quilt is a danger sign might not apply. Note, however, that the Amish always hand-stitched their quilting, which was often quite complex. But Amish quilts are so sought after at present because they are composed of relatively large, geometric units of bold colour, and this type of construction is much more easily and quickly duplicated than that of a detailed quilt such as the Postage Stamp variety or a complex appliquéd quilt.

It should also be borne in mind that many women of the Amish sect are still making quilts in the traditional manner. Some of these are done in acrylic fibres and can therefore be quickly recognized as contemporary, but a quilt in traditional wool or cotton may be very hard to recognize as recent.

Age is not usually regarded as important in Amish quilts, since the look is what sells them. In fact, many of the most spectacular period examples date only from the 1920s and 30s. On the other hand, no one wants to pay $2,000 for an Amish quilt in the belief it was made 50 years ago, when in fact it was produced only last year.

1 *above*
Simple quilts such as this zig-zag form can be reproduced easily. Here one must examine not simply the pattern but also the stitching, the fabric and the batting. New batting and backing may indicate a recently quilted top. Machine stitching may also, though not always, indicate that a piece lacks age.

2 *above*
This star variation quilt combines patchwork and appliqué. Examine such pieces to be sure that the appliqué, particularly if it is a border as here, has not been added recently to enhance the value of the piece. Differences in colour, fading and stitchwork are the things to look for.

Crib and doll quilts are smaller versions of full size bed coverings. The former are usually about 3 feet (lm) square, while the latter can be as small as 12 x 18ins (30 x 45cm). Both types may be faked. The usual procedure is to cut an appropriate section out of a damaged full size quilt. Some crib quilts are completely made up or reproduced, but Bishop notes that ''. . . the modest prices to be realized in this field have served as a brake to any major faking . . .'' Nevertheless, the convenient wall hanging or display size of these fabrics makes it likely that they will continue to be made.

Remember that a crib quilt is a true miniature, not a piece of something else. That means that the same balance and symmetry that are to be expected in a full size quilt should be

3 *below, left*
Offered as a crib or doll's quilt, this silk and satin piece is actually a pillow sham. Misrepresentation as to the nature of a quilt may be deliberate, but more often it simply reflects the dealer's lack of knowledge of the particular piece.

evident here. Borders should run all round the quilt: missing borders on two sides usually mean that the smaller quilt was cut from a corner of a larger one. A central motif or medallion should be in the centre and it should be properly balanced on all sides by design elements. Always check the border and binding. A new binding or elements of new binding on some sides may indicate recent cutting. Patterned quilting should terminate within the body of the quilt — a quilted rose, for example, that runs to the binding with some of the leaves missing is almost a guarantee of reworking.

During the past few years prices paid for album quilts, particularly those made around Baltimore, Maryland, during the mid-19th century, have increased sharply. A fine example will now bring upwards of $10,000 and charlatans have been quick to note this. An album quilt consists in most cases of many separate quilt blocks, each of which is carefully appliquéd in a different design. Flowers, hearts, human figures, houses, trees and animals are among the favourite devices, which are pieced together (the more common method) or laid down on a solid piece of fabric. These bed

4 *above*
Among the most valued of textiles, album quilts command high prices. If, as here, the elements of the design have been appliquéd to a single solid ground, repairs and alterations can be spotted readily. Beware, though, of album quilts made from individual blocks. Fakers may substitute especially appealing blocks (flags, ships, people and the like) for more ordinary ones. New stitching and fabric variations are the things to look for.

[1] *above*
Crib quilts present particular problems for the collector. Fakers may make up a crib quilt by cutting sections out of a damaged or less valuable full-size example. Be sure that all elements of the quilt balance, as here, and that borders do not show recent needlework.

[2]
Patchwork quilts in popular patterns such as schoolhouse are always prime candidates for faking. Examine the quilting. Does it show the skill and technical sophistication appropriate to the period of the textiles used? Do front and back appear to be originally joined? Does a stain on the front show on the back? These are the little clues that may provide an answer.

coverings were usually made as gifts and frequently bear signatures, dates and other mementoes.

Bishop says that skilled seamstresses are taking known Baltimore quilt patterns and either duplicating them or altering them slightly, employing old fabrics appropriate to the period. Such deceptions are particularly hard to spot. One thing to look for, Dr Bishop suggests, is new thread. Even if the faker has dyed the thread with tea or some other stain, a knowledgeable conservator can recognize modern thread used in the stitchwork. Conservators and others familiar with the textiles used in a given historical period can also provide information about whether or not the cloth in a quilt is appropriate to its design and suggested date. However, one must bear in mind that textile remnants for use in quilts were often kept for years or even decades before being incorporated into a bedcovering. It is entirely possible for a legitimate quilt to be made from fabrics or to incorporate fabrics dating from 20 or 30 years before it was worked.

## Restoration and Repair

The earlier and the more valuable a quilt is, the more likely that it has been restored. Damage from tears, insects, the dissolution of the fabric due to certain dyes used to colour it — all these as well as stains can seriously affect the appearance and value of a bed covering. There are many skilled conservators capable of repairing damage or replacing whole sections of a quilt, and there is, of course, nothing wrong with buying a restored fabric so long as you know that work has been done on it and the price reflects this fact. Depending on its nature and extent, restoration can decrease the value of a quilt by between 30 and 70 per cent.

When considering a purchase always look a quilt over with minute attention. Do all sections or blocks show equal wear, fading or discolouration? Is the stitchwork essentially identical throughout? Is the same thread used and in the same way? Any sections made from cloth of a different pattern or period from the majority should be closely scrutinized. The quilter may just have run out of fabric, but the odd section may also be a later repair. A stain that ends abruptly at the edge of a square may mean that a more seriously stained adjacent square has been replaced. Does the pattern maintain its original symmetry? If the design seems less developed in one direction or the quilt seems lopsided that may be because a worn end has been removed. Checking the binding for uniformity of wear and material may verify this suspicion.

It is unlikely that all these points will be found on one piece, but if several apply it is likely that it has been restored.

**Buying** The field of quilts is a subtle one, and all but the most expert may be fooled by some fakes or some repairs. Your best protection against an unfortunate purchase is to deal only with reputable sellers who are knowledgeable in the field and who will guarantee their merchandise.

# 14: SCIENTIFIC INSTRUMENTS

COLLECTING SCIENTIFIC INSTRUMENTS is a recent phenomenon: during the last hundred years, very few people recognized their significance. Most instruments had little commercial value, so collections were formed at small cost and were freely given or loaned to national museums. However, some instruments were always eagerly sought after, not for their historical interest, but for their intrinsic beauty and quality of workmanship, as objects for the *vitrine* or *Kunstkammer*.

When instruments became popular and prices soared, museums began to question collections that had remained dormant for so long. There was a time that a caller would leave a curious item with the museum for identification, then probably give it to them. Not now. Museums are besieged by earnest collectors, anxious for reassurance about the authenticity of their expensive purchases. In some cases, curators are having to admit that until further research establishes secure parameters, no final answers can be given.

Genuine period instruments are not necessarily of the first quality. Many instruments were made in the provinces of England, France and Germany, and also in places where there was no tradition of instrument making, such as Dublin or North America. Because the engraving is not fine and the workmanship poor it does not necessarily mean that the instrument is not a period one.

[1]
An astrolabic clock dial, French, 18th century, signed "Brulat & Thouret à Lyon". Size of square 10.3in (26.2cm). Apparently intended as the dial of a clock, the absence of attachment marks on the back of the plate suggests that the instrument was never so used. The variations in the quality of the engraving, especially noticeable in the zodiac signs and pictorial symbols, suggest that it was not made by professional instrument makers, but by two gentlemen amateurs of science as an exercise.

When new instruments were invented, they were described and illustrated in books for the benefit of other scholars. Instruments were often made from these instructions either by the scholars themselves, if they were handy with tools, or by a local tradesman. This accounts for the number of signed "amateur" instruments that still exist. The market value of such a piece would depend on whether it was contemporary with the book or later (and how much later), as well as the reputation of the scholar and where he worked.

## Outright Fakes

Fake instruments were sometimes made at the same time as genuine ones. The popularity of Islamic astrolabes encouraged contemporary engravers to make "nonsense" instruments of high quality for the patrons who did not wish to use one, only to own one for its aesthetics and metaphysics. The maker is sometimes unaware that the web is intended as a star indicator, and that the little pointers should bear star names, used in conjunction with the latitude plates. There is a continuous tradition of astrolabe making in the Middle East and India — some marvellous instruments were made in India in the 19th century, while the quality of those from Persia and North Africa declined. They are being made in the Middle East for tourists at the present time.

European astrolabes are just as dangerous, for they are so collectable. They were not made in great quantity, so the temptation to forge them must be irresistible. When western

1 *below*
A Persian astrolabe, back and front, signed "Made by the poor man Khalil Muhammad" and "Decorated by Abd al-a'imma". It is brass, early 18th century and 6.5in (16.5cm) in diameter. This is a genuine Islamic astrolabe of fine quality, but do not let the skill of the maker confuse you, as many instruments were made of even finer workmanship that are not genuine.

Unfortunately there is no substitute for experience or the reputation of the vendor when it comes to distinguishing the rogue from the genuine in this category.

2 *left*
A Spanish type astrolabe with a fake plate; the mater and rete are possibly genuine but come from different instruments.

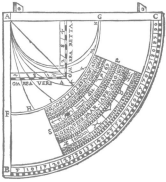

3 *above*
A quadrant with a cursor from G.P. Gallucci's *Della fabrica et uno di diversi strumenti di astronomia et cartographia*, Venice, 1598. This was the inspiration for the fake quadrant (below) made by Williams.

4 *right*
Williams's quadrant with a cursor, after Gallucci's design (above, right) published in 1598. This example dates from the 1970s. A medieval quadrant in the Museum for the History of Science at Oxford is a rare example of this type.

technology outran the astrolabe in the 18th century they were discarded, but were found again when they became collectors' items. Odd parts were assembled to make an instrument, but they can only serve as relics. This is a particularly specialized area of collecting, so you really should know what you are doing or get good advice.

What of the countless pocket sundials signed "Butterfield", sometimes spelled with one "t"? We are faced with a similar situation. Butterfield died in 1724, but these pretty little dials with their adjustable bird gnomons were made throughout the 18th and into the 19th century. They were very popular, and were no doubt pirated by small workshops. Quality varies considerably. The same is true of Dollond telescopes, spelled "Dolland". Reputable makers' marks were exploited by others under their very noses. By changing one letter in the signature, they could get away with it, just as the Bow factory intended to deceive when in the 1750s they called their building "New Canton" so that customers would think their porcelain was Chinese.

To satisfy wealthy collectors like the Rothschilds and Sir Richard Wallace, the 19th-century Paris art dealer Frédéric Spitzer employed highly skilled engravers to embellish plain old specimens and make new ones. A Nocturnal in the Science Museum, London, has been identified from this source.

There have been many forgeries since about which we know little, such as those of a Dutchman in the 1920s who is credited with Dutch and Flemish copies. We know considerably more about the fakes made by Lloyd Williams in the 1970s, whose output is recorded by the London police. A gun engraver, Williams made some incredibly beautiful instruments that rocked the art world. The owners of many of them would not release them for the inquiry, but they will emerge again. The possibilities available to the forger came as a shock to the guardians of our public collections who, to their credit, are instigating several detailed studies.

Why is an original instrument worth so much more than an exact copy? One could argue that if it looks the same with the same quality of workmanship and aesthetic appeal it should have the same market value as the original. This is what the forger thinks, but it is morally wrong. It may be a private joke to someone that a national treasure is a fake, but in reality it is not funny at all. The original piece has all the historical backup, which no copy could replace. Instruments of impeccable pedigree compare with any other work of art; their value enhances with time. Questionable instruments are always much cheaper, and their price fluctuates with demand. These look-alikes are frequently sold to unsuspecting tyros as "19th-century copies" by unscrupulous or ignorant dealers.

There is no fast, easy way to detect a fake scientific instrument. Each clue has to be detected, studied and evaluated. Generally speaking, it is only valuable instruments that have attracted the attention of the forger, but many small, relatively unimportant items have been made for fun, for devilment, or just to try to put one over on an expert.

## Replicas

Replicas play an important role in public collections, especially for educational purposes. Copies of rare, archaic navigation instruments provide valuable information on how early explorers found their way around the oceans. Made for the purpose, they are clearly marked and could never be confused with an original. However, some instruments are so accurately reproduced that they send shivers down the spine, reminding us to be ever vigilant. They are utterly honest replicas now, but if their provenance is forgotten or disguised in the future, their quality could well make them deceptive.

With the intention of sharing the joy of ownership of their own collection, Replica Rara published a handsome catalogue of 20 period microscopes which they proposed to replicate in limited editions. As far as I can discover, only three models were made before the project was abandoned.

Two models were stamped with their logo. These were the Cuff type, signed *J. CUFF Londini. Invt. & Fecit* and a ''Wilson'' screw barrel type signed *Culpeper fecit* both on the stand and on the barrel. The Cuff had a piece of iron inserted in the body so that it could be detected with a magnet. It was supplied with a mahogany case and was optically correct. The screw barrel was made with an ivory eyepiece and supplied with a fishskin

**1** *above*
A quadrant with Rojas type orthographic projection, surrounded by a four quadrant degree scale, with its O on an east–west axis. On the limb, a degree scale (0–90) reading to halves. This type of projection can only be read with a sighting arm, which this instrument lacks. Note the discoloration. Another fake by Williams.

**2**
The diestamp of Replica Rara.

① *above and below*
A European astrolabe with orthographic Rojas projection. The rarest form of astrolabe, this example embodies features expected from reference books, but the engraved lettering does not conform to any known style and is too thin to relate to broad nib techniques. The difference in colour under and around the sighting arm (see the detail, below) was explained by the seller's claim that it had lain in a vault in Germany for 80 years, but it was later discovered to be chemically induced. Modern copy.

case. Fifty numbered examples of each were made. Four unmarked replicas were made of George Adams' "New Universal Double Microscope" *c.* 1750. These were signed *Invented and made by GEO. ADAMS at Tycho Brahe's Head in Fleet Street LONDON*, and supplied with green shagreen cases. One of these was retained by the makers, Culpepper Instruments Ltd, two are in museums and the fourth is in private hands.

Replica garden sundials made by Pearson-Page in Birmingham, England, before the Second World War still plague us. They usually bear the names of famous makers and a date and they might also bear a homily such as "time is fleeting". They are well documented in the makers' catalogue, copies of which seem to be found only in museums. It is in fact unusual to see a period sundial with a date and a "message". Other instruments have been and will continue to be replicated. Barometers are extremely popular furnishing items in the western world, so they too are being reproduced.

## Design

Made before the dictum that form follows function, early scientific instruments were works of art which conformed to the spirit and fashion of their age. They were influenced in part by the location of manufacture, an extreme example of which would be the recognizable differences between oriental and occidental art forms. Also, compare a particular 18th-century instrument made in London with another from Paris, Augsburg, or Rome. Each has a different personality, yet all fulfil the same function.

Fashion in art is influenced by social and economic events and the imprimatur of every age is stamped on the output of artists. Their work reflects and is reflected in all other contemporary art forms. Instruments were not made in isolation; not only would the instrument maker have incorporated the latest scientific developments, he would also have reflected contemporary taste in his manner of execution. Instrument makers were forever advertising that they were offering the latest whatever on the market. Provincial makers were naturally a bit behind the times for their customers were less demanding, but they still conformed to the spirit of their age. A familiarity with the styles of the decorative arts is therefore essential for accurate dating.

## Patina

Having decided that the piece under consideration is of the design and style of a particular period, we now turn to the patination. Similar patination and oxidization should cover the whole instrument. False patina can be produced by using a form of sulphur, for it is the sulphur in the air that causes genuine tarnish. This is more successful on silver, but on brass or bronze, which naturally develops a green or brown patination, it forms an ugly blackish tint. If paint or pigment has been used, it will peel off in curls: real oxidization has to be scoured or scraped off. Chemical techniques can produce convicing patinas and burial in cow dung is reputed to be particularly successful.

A word about gilding. Like ormolu furniture mounts and candelabra, some instruments were gilded. The finish should be a mellow gold, possibly worn in places from handling. Modern gilding cannot reproduce the effect of mercurial gilding, which was abandoned in the 19th century when it was superseded by electro-chemical technology. Only experience will enable you to spot the difference.

## Engraving

The "decoration" of scientific instruments is quite different from that on all other works of art: however tastefully ornamented a piece may be, the main purpose of the engraving is to supply information to the user.

Engravers work with a burin and the design of the burin has changed with time as has the manner in which it was used. The techniques of the many schools of engravers at different periods have been the subject of much study, the result of

[2]
A mariner's astrolabe, possibly Portuguese, signed with a maker's mark and dated 1555. This is the earliest surviving dated mariner's astrolabe of wheel type with base ballast. The scale is graduated for zenith distances. A mark made up of five circles has been interpreted by Marcel Destombes as the sign of Lopo Homem, a Master of Nautical Instruments in Portugal, 1517–1565. The reverse is stamped "ANDREW SMYTON 1688". Smyton (Smieton) was a Dundee shipmaster. Compare this with *Ill. 1* overleaf.

1

A mariner's astrolabe. Modern fake. At first glance the age and patination of the metal together with the style of the punched numerals and the early date intimate authenticity, but the 1535 date precedes all other known instruments of this type, so further investigation is required. Curious oval indentations suggest an implement associated with the user, such as a signet ring. However, the microscope reveals that some of the numerals were stamped over the indentations, proving that the metal had been deliberately damaged before completion to simulate wear. The similarity of the design of the maker's logo to the much publicised "Dundee" astrolabe (*Ill. 2*, previous page) made comparison inevitable and the fraud was discovered.

2 *below*

A genuine English Gunter quadrant signed "J (ohn) Marke" (successor to Henry Sutton who died in the Plague), *c.*1670. The limb bears a degree scale (0–90) and hour scales. There is an engraved table of the times of rising of five stars. Note the simplicity and soft aspect of the engraving.

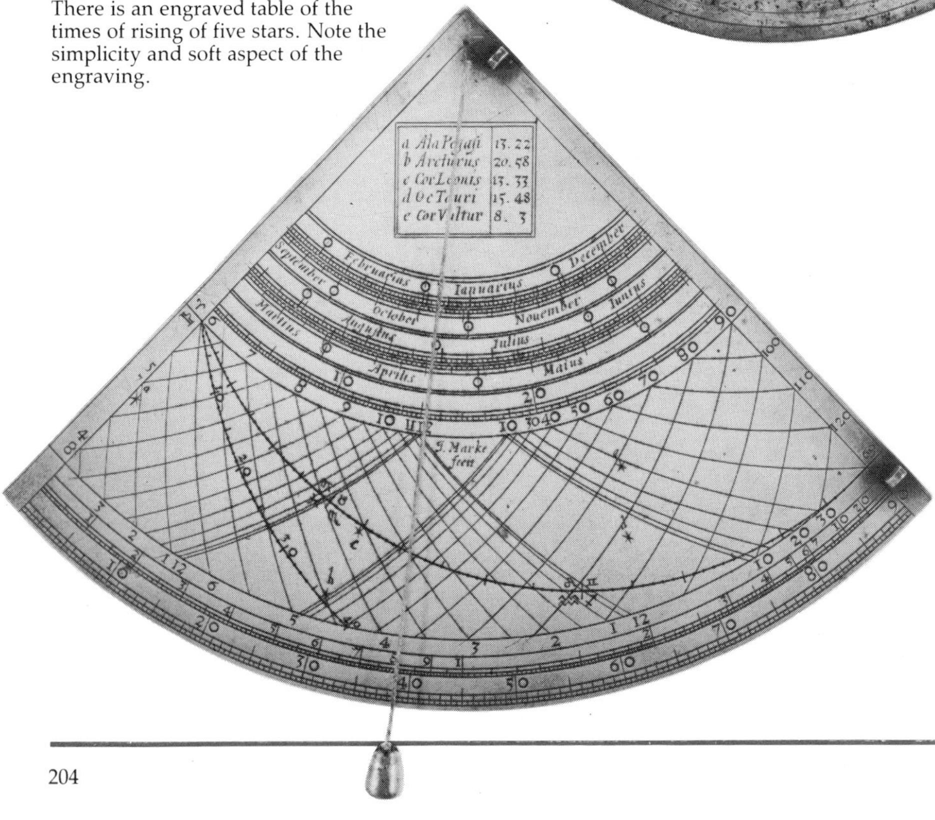

which is a large bibliography. Art historians can add something from their special experience in certain instances.

When the burin cuts its groove a burr is formed on one or both sides of the cut. If the burr is left untouched it is a sign of new workmanship, so a forger will usually polish it off. Should the new engraving be a signature, for example, then the polishing will also remove adjacent scratches and other marks of wear and tear. If the old scratches stop short of the signature and start again a tiny distance away, then it is a sure sign that they existed before the signature was added.

Look at the burin marks through a magnifying glass or a microscope. New lines will cut through pitting and will be smooth below the level of the pitting on the original surface. Old engraving will normally have pits in the vertical walls of the cuts and along the bottom. New cuts will be smooth, even if the forger has rubbed dirt or lampblack into the lines to hide clean surfaces. Old marks are soft and smooth to the touch while hard, sharp edges are an immediate sign of new work. To hide all the evidence, the forger would have to remove and polish the entire surface, thus destroying all the patination. Smooth, highly polished old instruments are therefore dangerous and should arouse suspicion.

## Lettering

The history of letters is a part of the history of style. Good lettering is perfect in function as all good design should be. Good calligraphy comprises living designs that are subject to the blunders as well as the creative efforts of the master-craftsman and have lasting aesthetic value. It is important to remember that letters originated in a broad pen style of writing; they should be studied first as a broad pen product and then as a type design and back again. A familiarity with type styles of the relevant periods and locations is essential, as one of the commonest faults of the forger is to use a style that is not properly compatible with the purported date of the instrument.

The forger's most formidable task is to re-create the spirit behind the original instrument maker's burin. It was his inability to do so that betrayed Williams. He was very fond of adding serifs in an idiosyncratic manner to his s's. When several instruments with different signatures were compared, this similarity in every piece pointed to the work of a single engraver.

Apart from the burin, a set of punches was used for small numerals and letters on a calibrated scale. They too have a personality which can be allotted to period and place.

## Brass

A comparatively new technique called spectrographic analysis exists which can specify the percentages of the constituents of brass without damaging the instrument. As the composition of brass changed over the centuries an approximate dating can

**3** *above*
A perpetual calendar in silver, dated 1689. An interesting piece that serves to show contemporary punched lettering. This is genuine, but as many silver instruments are not, be vigilant.

**4** *above*
Detail of the signature "Hauser in Wien" — an example of Williams's workmanship.

**5** *above*
Le Maire — a fake signature; note the formation of the "s".

**6**
Le Maire — a genuine signature.

be arrived at using tested documentary pieces as benchmarks. The molecular structure of brass is irregular, so — the metal is not a homogeneous blend. Thus different results can show from various parts of the same piece, making it necessary to perform several tests. The service is therefore costly and anyway it is largely restricted to museums.

On their own, positive results from spectrographic analysis are insufficient proof of authenticity. After all, anyone could take a piece of old brass and make an instrument with it. Its true value is its corroboration of other evidence. So where does the collector start? The obvious test would be to check the thickness of the metal with a micrometer. If it conforms to a modern metric or a standard wire gauge size, you need look no further. There were no standard sizes until the 20th century.

Significant reduction in the thickness of early brass was achieved by hammering one or both sides in conjunction with annealing. If a sheet was to be engraved, only one side would be annealed. The variation in grain size across the sheet and the larger grain on the underside, which had been exposed to the fire, can be observed under a microscope.

Early pieces were hammered with great care and only when necessary. Brass pieces will show marks of the hammer, and each mark will have a purpose. This is an important feature to remember, as forgers have been known to get carried away with their own exuberance. The hammer marks are shallow and softly rounded dents. On a convex surface a series of small flats and facets can be seen, not a pock-marked pattern of dents. Rolling sheet brass to make it thinner was not done until the 17th century, and can be recognized by the striations it leaves in the metal.

Cast pieces of brass were often finished on a lathe, which left a series of concentric rings. By 1850 a stamping technique was common and these rings disappeared. These rings should not be confused with similar rings caused by the spinning technique introduced for holloware after 1850. Early "dished" articles were made of two or three separate pieces, soldered or brazed together, or hammered out of a single sheet.

## Restoration

There is a continuous debate concerning the restoration and polishing of old scientific instruments. Customers expect to see brass instruments gleaming like beacons, so it is tempting to polish them bright. The oxidized finish on sextants and theodolites gets removed because the customers dislike it, together with the khaki paint on First World War army instruments. In doing so we are destroying part of their history, which will not please later generations. It is a great mistake to machine buff an engraved brass article, for like the butlers of old who zealously polished out the marks on the family silver, you will have removed all the data that makes an instrument more than just a pretty face.

An instrument that has lost a few small parts is a ready candidate for repair. There are still a few good restorers about,

An armillary sphere. The measurements taken of all the metal parts indicate that they are all modern metric sizes with small differences resulting from polishing and buffing. The equatorial circle was cast with names of the winds, but their typography is early 20th-century. The signs of the zodiac were executed in a poor fashion, and the lettering used does not conform to any period style. This is a 20th-century fake.

whose empathy with instruments prevents them from desecrating them, but they are outnumbered by the ignorant vandals who do. We have discussed the dangers of buying polished instruments. There is nothing to be gained in making a good item look like a fake, so when new pieces of brass have been used for repairs do not disguise them by buffing the whole piece. New parts should ideally be diestamped with their date of manufacture, or at least left in their natural new colour so that repairs can be seen.

There is nothing wrong in repairing an instrument which would otherwise be unusable, for instruments were constantly repaired in their time, and that is part of their charm and history. But incomplete instruments are sold in the salerooms that reappear later in immaculate condition. Unless new parts are pointed out, it can be extremely hard to detect them. There is a regular traffic in instruments of this sort and no-one should underestimate the skill of present-day restorers. They have old lathes and hand tools with which they

A pair of table globes. The stands and calendar plates are 19th-century. The globes are covered in freshly cut, 17th-century gores which have been recently coloured.

can make any small parts. Some dealers boast that their ''chap'' can do wonders with wrecks.

Paper conservation is a specialist job. However, many paper restorers are unable to deal with globes, which are another speciality altogether. Terrestrial and celestial globes are usually in a bad state after years of neglect, and have more than likely already undergone some degree of restoration. How much restoration should be permitted before the globes become unacceptable?

The most interesting parts of globes are the printed papers covering the entire surface; they are extremely difficult to restore. These mathematically contoured wedges, called gores, were once printed in flat sheets, and sometimes bound into books. Some survived, and old-time restorers could replace missing pieces with facility. If a present-day restorer also has access to these, you can be sure that he will use them. If he does not, he will have to cover the damage with plain paper and draw in the missing data. A small area neatly repaired and sympathetically redrawn would be acceptable; large areas are not.

On the flat top of the stand, which represents the horizon, there should be an applied paper which bears a calendar scale. These are usually the worst affected by misuse, and the most likely to be restored or even replaced. As legitimate wear and tear has ruined most calendar scales, replacements are generally acceptable. It is possible to remove the papers and photocopy the better of the two, but unless great skill is exercised when the photocopy is glued onto the stand it can stretch, extending over its assigned area.

Beware of globes that are covered in dark varnish. This does not signify great age. It implies that the restorer could do nothing with them as they were too far gone. If the stands are early and in good original state, then the furniture buff would be pleased to have them, hoping that other globes of the right size and period would turn up. Whether you find this acceptable depends on what you expect from your collection.

We are moving away from the times when authenticity, age, and untouched condition were of vital importance to collectors. Because there is a diminished supply of period goods, the look-alike is becoming acceptable. The vast numbers of decorators who scour our countryside are more interested in the look than in reality, for they serve an ignorant public. Do not let this attitude seep into your collection, or you will have more than a few items to embarrass you later on.

Scientific instruments are different from other works of art. They were never intended to be placed on pedestals, solely for admiration. They are living tools, not quite perfect from the toll taken by usage, with their history written all over them. It is a matter of choice which aspect you wish to cultivate, for creating a collection of art objects is an art in itself.

Wherever you choose to buy your instruments, remember that in the last analysis a reputable dealer accepts responsibility for the authenticity of the articles he has sold.

# 15 : SCRIMSHAW

THE COLLECTOR OF SCRIMSHAW runs into an immediate problem: exactly what is it that he is collecting? The word defies accurate definition and can cover as narrow a group of objects as those produced by American sailors from whale teeth during the first three-quarters of the 19th century to anything made by sailors from whale, fish or other sea animals and stretching as far as prisoner-of-war work in bone, engravings on ostrich eggs and elephant ivory.

We are concerned here with forgeries produced on whale bones, walrus tusks, turtleshells and baleen (the fibres in the mouth of the baleen whale, often referred to as whalebone but actually keratin, the same material as finger nails).

Whalers were away on voyages that lasted three to four years—on occasion, eight. One of the most serious dangers came not from storm and tempest or a harpooned whale wrecking the boat, but from the utter boredom of waiting for weeks on end for a whale to appear. Scrimshawing (or scrimshandering in the USA) filled in time for all hands from the captain down. It was executed with the most primitive tools—the seaman's knife and sail needles figuring prominently.

**Subjects and Sources** Subjects tend to reflect the daily life of the whaler, the life he left behind on dry land (or an idealized version of it) and contemporary events. Thus ships and whaling boats, whales spouting, whales harpooned and overturning boats, the whalers themselves, anchors, ladies dressed in finery or less commonly without it, homesick doggerel verses, political figures, flags and American eagles were common. Occasionally the recipient's name appears, more rarely the name of the carver and exceptionally a date, a ship's name, a record of whales caught on the voyage. A combination of two of these themes is not uncommon, three is unusual and more rare indeed. And herein lies the downfall of the scrimshammer, as we shall refer to this forger of sailors' items. In an attempt to generate the maximum from his effort he goes too far.

The scrimshammer is also let down by poor research. His sailing ships have faults to the rigging that no sailor could possibly conceive; he engraves lettering from one period while his style is of another.

The sailor, while he had endless time to concentrate on his work, was rarely an artist. Had he been he would have been unlikely to sign on for the poor rewards usually accruing from a whaling trip. He therefore turned to images he knew at first hand or used illustrations in books or magazines as reference material. Until the 1840s and 1850s these would have been copper or steel engravings, which make up the image from numerous finely engraved lines and dots. Thus genuine early scrimshaw reflects this source material and is finely engraved. From the 1850s to the 80s and 90s wood engraving was the common method of reproduction. The picture here is made up of heavier, blacker lines of varying thickness. Still later examples would reflect the photomechanical processes that reproduced pen drawings. By the end of the century a great

1 *above*, 2 *below*
Two genuine whale tooth scrimshaws, 6 in. (15.2 cm). Note the finely engraved lines and, particularly on Miss Woodham, the naïve handling. The lettering is typical of the middle of the 19th century.

deal of the charm had been lost and later scrimshaw lacks invention, merely reproducing blindly someone else's work.

Prior to the turn of the 19th century, inscriptions would be in flowing script or with copies of printed letters, which at that time all had serifs. At the beginning of the 19th century ''fat face'' letters with exaggerated thick and thin strokes were prevalent. Capitals without serifs are extremely unlikely before 1880. Naturally, styles afloat continued long after changes had taken place ashore, but they do provide a way of discounting some fakes.

The human figure is the downfall of even the most skilled scrimshawer, even when copying an illustration. He therefore frequently resorted to pricking round the figure in one of two ways: either through onto the tooth, joining up the pin pricks (which can still sometimes be distinguished), or pencilling through the holes. The scrimshammer may ape these pin pricks but will probably not be able to resist the temptation to overdo them. There is also a world of difference between an untutored hand striving to make the best possible reproduction of an illustration and a third party attempting to reproduce a naïve reproduction. Anyone doubting this should try copying a child's drawing.

The majority of forged engravings on whale teeth of modern origin are in the style of the very late 19th century and have been copied skilfully from books of the period. The collector should be extremely hesitant about buying any work in which the design is a very dense black and in a naturalistic, pictorial style. Perspective is rare and limited to seascapes with ships and whales, but even here there is a childlike, cut-out or theatrical quality in the genuine article that is very hard to recreate. What is often apparent is a natural skill at pattern making, zig-zags, diamonds, hearts and borders. These, particularly in the American examples, bear an affinity to quilts and are instinctively well balanced.

The faker (as distinct from the forger, the former altering a piece, the latter making something new in imitation of the old) has been at work on scrimshaw. Take a tooth with a perfectly genuine but somewhat unexciting ship, add an American flag or a date and hey presto, you double your money in minutes.

The collector has to be on his guard and examine every detail of the engraving, looking for variations in depth, width of line, staining, hesitancy (the faker has a lot at stake and the result is often an unsure line) and plausibility.

A warning might be added here of the distinct possibility of producing on a blank tooth an exact reproduction of a genuine design by photographing an original, sensitizing the tooth and etching the line. While this is entirely possible, an examination of the line through a magnifying glass should reveal irregularities where the acid bit inconsistently.

1 a, b *far left and left*
Front and rear of a genuine whale tooth scrimshaw, 6 in. (15.2 cm). Note the fine line engraving and the convincing naïveté.

2 a, b, c
Three modern forged scrimshaws, 5 in. (12.7 cm), 4.5 in. (11.4 cm) and 5.5 in. (14 cm). Note in the top example the heavy lines and outline: the swag appears stiff as if cut from card. The capital letters of ''Liberty'' are ill proportioned and the serifs are not all present. The script lettering on the banner could not predate the late 19th century and is more akin to the 1920s or 30s. The script on the other two is again obviously anachronistic.

A raw whale tooth is ridged and rough and considerable time must be spent in smoothing and polishing before engraving can begin (the polishing instrument was sharkskin stuck to a wooden handle). An exposed surface of tooth, be it elephant, whale or walrus, develops a patina which is impossible to reproduce. The new tooth—not that there is much likelihood of new teeth appearing on the market as most countries now respect the ban on whaling—is fresh white with irregular staining. The overall creamy colour appears with age and no amount of heating or staining can simulate it.

Reproductions are available on the market from such respectable retailers as the shops in British and American museums in moulded plastic taken from flexible rubber moulds and picking up every minute detail of engraving, pitting and cracking. They are extremely well coloured to reproduce the original and the weight is realistic. While there is no suggestion that such sources are in any way irresponsible, the fact is that these reproductions are appearing in auctions, trade fairs and antique shops all over the country. In some cases the auctioneer or dealer may be ignorant of the fact that he is handling a reproduction, but in most cases this must be a generous assessment. Always ask for a written receipt stating the material and the date of the piece.

Another source of modern copies is an American manufacturer who has an enormous variety of plastic scrimshaw—whale bone, turtleshell, walrus tusks—on offer but, presumably through ignorance, has chosen to reproduce nothing but forgeries. There is also a continuing tradition of scrimshawing in the Azores on new teeth engraved with traditional motifs. These are let down by the newness of the tooth and the poor, rather than naïve, quality of the workmanship.

1 *above*
The subject here is far more complicated than would normally be tackled even by the most skilled carver, and the scrimshammer has made a disastrous attempt. The whole engraving is too dense and black and the anatomy and handling are bad rather than naïve. The lettering has been taken, as has the whole, from a late 19th-century illustration.

2 *right*
A modern resin turtle carapace with moulded ''engraved'' decoration, approximately 24 in. (61 cm). This reproduction has been taken not from an original but from a forgery.

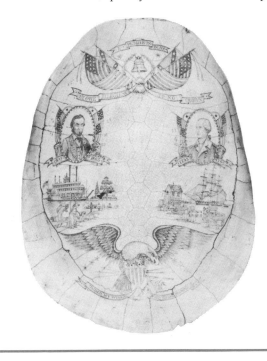

# 16 : TOYS

IT IS UNDERSTANDABLE — indeed, to be expected — that forgeries should exist in the long established collecting fields such as silver, furniture and porcelain, where prices have been high for many years. It may come as a surprise to many, however, to learn that the collector of toys must be just as rigorous in his assessments as a collector of drawings trying to decide whether the Samuel Palmer pen-and-ink he is considering is an original or a Keating pastiche.

Across the wide field of toy collecting the production of modern copies, designed to deceive, is being encouraged by the high prices at which toys change hands in shops, at auctions and privately. Since most collectable toys are constructed from either pressed tinplate or cast-iron, both expensive methods to recreate, copies are either produced in large quantities by a parallel to the original manufacturing process, spreading the high cost of "tooling-up", or alternatively they may be hand made to simulate the work of a machine. The latter method is obviously much more laborious and is used only to construct highly desirable and correspondingly expensive toys, with which a good return can be made on the time invested in production.

Today some highly skilled craftsmen construct their own interpretations of early toys. These are sold as reproductions by the manufacturers, but in years to come, when they have acquired a patina of age, it is possible that the unscrupulous or the unknowing will pass these on as authentic early toys.

## Restoration

Restoration can be as detrimental to the desirability and value of a toy as a repair to a piece of porcelain, since any restoration undertaken removes the toy further from its original state of manufacture. Most collectors dream of finding a toy in mint condition within its original box and restored acquisitions tend to stay in an established collection only until an unrestored example can be obtained. Restoration includes repainting, the manufacture of missing pieces and the marriage of original and non-original sections to recreate a complete toy. In some cases a maker's trademark or label is added to a toy which is either wholly unoriginal or is one which would be worth considerably more if it could be identified as the product of a particular manufacturer. A trademark on a toy may also mislead the amateur enthusiast by persuading him to buy a piece about which, in other respects, he might have been doubtful.

## Teddy Bears

The media has expressed its astonishment at the prices realized by discarded teddy bears at auction. Prices exceeding £2,000 ($3,000) are now commonplace, and it was to be expected that the fakers would cash in on this bonanza.

Teddy bears were made by a number of factories, but the best and most sought after examples come from the German company of Steiff. The Steiff company was established in 1882

[1]
A genuine Steiff teddy bear, c. 1905; 23 in. (60 cm) high.

**1** *left*
A modern copy of a Steiff teddy bear, 17 in. (43 cm) high. It has a Steiff rivet in its left ear, but a seam runs down its nose and the pile of its fur does not run downwards as it should; nor are its facial features those of an authentic Steiff product.

**2** *below*
The Steiff company trademark: a rivet fixed to the left ear of genuine Steiff teddy bears, and to many bears of altogether different provenance.

as a family firm and the original plush bear was designed by the nephew of the founder in 1903. These bears were used as table decorations at the wedding of Theodore Roosevelt's daughter, Alice. Theodore Roosevelt had refused in 1902 to kill a young bear cub when a hunt for a grizzly bear had proved fruitless. Cartoonists rapidly represented him as a friend to bears and the plush toy bears that adorned the tables at his daughter's wedding were nicknamed "Teddy's Bears" after this hunting incident.

The Steiff trademark is a small nickled or steel rivet found in the left ears of their bears. Since the mid-1980s these original metal rivets have been found in the ears of bears that are modern fabrications. The bear illustrated on p. 213 is an original by Steiff; the muzzle is stitched either side, rather than having a seam running down the centre; he is worn, but in the places where you would expect the fur to have been eroded by affection; his eyes are similar to boot buttons, although they can authentically be brown and black glass; and he has a metal Steiff rivet in his left ear.

The teddy bear illustrated above is one which, to the amateur, may appear almost identical. He is made from light coloured plush fabric but this bear has a seam running down the front of his muzzle; his ears are a slightly different shape to those of the authentic bear and his facial features are obviously lacking in similarity to the other. Although the fur of this bear is in extremely good condition the pile of the fabric does not run downwards as on authentic bears but appears to be without any definite direction. In addition, there are some examples on the market that have been worn in the most unlikely places — they are obviously reconstructed from the pelts of cannibalized toys of the correct date.

The limbs of authentic teddy bears should be swivel jointed, with the flat edge of the shoulder and hip joints butting against a flattened body surface. In the case of copies, the limbs are simply stitched to the body with thread without this swivel facility. The fake bear opposite has a Steiff rivet in his left ear (a copy of the original), but it is there only to persuade the dubious collector that this bear is an authentic example.

## Trains

Toy trains are not widely copied but, with prices inflated to the £28,000 ($42,000) realized by a 1909 toy train at Sotheby's in 1984, reproduction trains will surely appear in greater numbers. One such facsimile is illustrated above right; the original toy, dating from c. 1905, is shown with a tender, carriage and box lid below.

The benefits of side-by-side comparison are obvious in this case since the reproduction is cunningly wrought. Quality of manufacture is one important guideline when judging the authenticity of a piece; although toys were mass produced by machine, the complexity of the machining and tooling as well as the finish of the paintwork are useful indications as to the date of manufacture.

The original was made by Ernst Plank of Nuremburg, a company founded in 1866 and renowned particularly for its locomotives, steam accessories, cars and boats until production ceased in the 1930s. The train has spoked wheels of cast metal, a painted oscillating cylinder driving the wheels, delicately modelled smoke stack, buffers, whistle and shaped cab. The copy is of entirely different construction, with drilled brass wheels, a brass oscillating cylinder and crudely modelled details; in addition, the brass boiler is very poorly constructed and roughly soldered and would not be steam-proof under pressure. The locomotive should also have a spirit burner to heat the boiler from below, but it is apparent from *Ill. 5* that there has never been a spirit-firing mechanism beneath this particular locomotive. Both toys have the nameplate "Vulcan" and the copy actually has a reproduction maker's trade label applied to the body (*Ill. 6*).

## Steam Cars

One of the most convincing fake toys produced during the last ten years has been a copy of a 1902 steam-driven toy car, originally produced by the Nuremberg company of Gebrüder Bing. The authentic toy has been highly rated by collectors for many years and as early as 1978 an example in almost mint condition and with its original box was sold for £3,400 ($5,100) at Sotheby's.

Modelled on a full-sized vehicle of the same period, the toy is of pressed and hand-painted tinplate. After application the paint was baked on a low heat to give the finish a hardened enamel-like quality which is difficult to reproduce today. With a padded front seat, delicate suspension and large headlamps

**3** *above*
A modern facsimile of a Plank locomotive: its altogether cruder construction should cause the buyer to be wary.

**4** *above*
An original 3-in. gauge tinplate trainset by Ernst Plank of Nuremburg, c. 1905. The wheels are cast and the modelling fine.

**5** *above*
The underside of the reproduction Plank locomotive. The originals were proper working models, their boilers heated by spirit burners underneath. The absence of any fittings for spirit-firing indicates that this is not an authentic model.

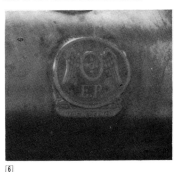

**6**
The presence of an Ernst Plank trademark is no guarantee of authenticity — this is from the reproduction shown above.

①
A tinplate steam car by Gebrüder Bing of Nuremburg, c. 1902. These toys are now so valuable that it can pay the faker to make them largely by hand as individual examples, rather than producing a run of them by machine. It can be very difficult to distinguish the copy from the original — signs of use, such as some blistering of the paint, are helpful, but of course these do not appear on mint originals.

the vehicle is powered by a simple, spirit-fired, single-cylindered steam engine at the back, linked to the rear axle and propelling the toy forward on its delicately spoked rubber-tyred wheels.

The copy is almost identical, making it extremely difficult for a knowledgeable collector, let alone an enthusiastic amateur, to recognize the slight differences without the benefit of direct comparison with the original.

Particular attention should be given to the quality and texture of the paint to judge whether it has the enamel-like finish of the original. In the case of a toy driven by steam (unless in absolutely unused condition in its original cardboard box) one would anticipate some signs of use: bubbling or blistering of the paint where it has been affected by heat from the steam engine, slight rust where steam or water from the tank regularly dampened the paint surface and, most difficult to recognize, wear to the propulsion cylinder. It would be extremely expensive to reproduce accurately the complex tooling required to mass produce the headlamps as made for the original toy; those on the copy are constructed from turned brass and nickel plated. This is a case where the price that such toys can realize makes it financially viable to produce the pieces almost entirely by hand.

## Cast-Iron Toys

The production of cast-iron toys involves separate casting of a number of different pieces that fit together to make the finished toy. This is an expensive process for the manufacture of a small number of toys, but highly profitable when many thousands are produced. The original cast-iron toys were made largely in America from the 1870s. Here manufacturers of cast-iron farming, commercial and household equipment, such as J. & E. Stevens Co. of Cromwell, Connecticut, and H. L. Judd Co. of Wallingford, Connecticut, soon learned that a smaller amount of raw material could reap greater profits for the company if made into a toy or a money bank.

In the last century these toys were painstakingly cast and assembled so that each piece aligned exactly against the next; the crack at the join of the two sections is practically unnoticeable on the original examples. The surface was smoothly finished and colours were applied and baked, creating a hard enamel-like finish which chips rather than peels if damaged. Each of the different designs was registered at the American Patent Office and cast-iron toys and money banks will have the patent-granted date stamped clearly on the underside. The mechanisms in original money banks are well finished and operate smoothly when a lever is pressed down — any stickiness in the action can normally be remedied by the application of a little oil.

**Reproduction Money Banks** Over the last 15 years cast-iron money banks have been reproduced in enormous quantities in Taiwan and are exported worldwide. These banks were not made to deceive, however, and all examples are stamped with the name of the country of origin in capital letters on the underside. It has only been in recent years that the unscrupulous have either ground out the name or filled it in to mislead the public.

These reproduction money banks are usually roughly cast rather than smoothly finished and are crudely painted in bright, harsh colours without detail. The original hues should be mellow with a dulling patina of age. To try to reproduce this patination modern banks are often buried underground for a period. This certainly makes them dirty and encourages rust, but cannot really mislead if the collector is aware that this practice exists. The Taiwanese do not reproduce clearly the patent date stamped on the underside of a bank and often this may be the only way to judge the authenticity of a toy which in every other respect may appear to be of the correct date.

"Trick Dog" banks illustrate the differences between the authentic and the modern admirably. *Ill. 2* (above, right) shows a bank produced in the 1890s in America. The quality of the casting can easily be judged from the detail of the costume and the facial features. The bank has been painstakingly decorated, with attention given to painting the hoops on the barrel and the trimmings on the costume. The bank in *Ill. 3* however shows a fierce, knock-kneed figure who lacks both detail in the casting and in the painting — the casting is rough and the finish dull.

Originally sold in shops as reproductions for a few pounds, banks such as that illustrated now often appear on market stalls and in general auctions, where they realize prices of £60 or £70 ($90-$100), albeit probably believed by the traders to be authentic examples. Each design of bank has a different name stamped clearly on the front of the toy. Certain banks, such as the "Trick Dog", "Uncle Sam", and "Punch and Judy", were originally made in large numbers; others such as "Dentist", "Magician", "Jonah and the Whale", "Indian and Bear" and "Boy Scout" are scarcely seen as original examples outside America; if one is found it is almost certain to be Taiwanese.

## Modern Facsimiles

Advertisements now appear regularly in specialist magazines from companies selling modern copies of old toys. In some instances (*Ill. 4*, for example) these copies have been produced from the original moulds and have no features to distinguish them from the 1930s originals. Today, of course, they are bought as obvious reproductions, with their gleaming tinplate and bright lithographed colours. But in 20 years' time, when their tinplate is dulled and their clockwork motors have rusted, will the toy collectors of the next century be fooled into buying a fake?

Perhaps reproductions will, by that time, have acquired their own mystique, and collections may be formed that spurn the original in favour of the example which so accurately illustrates the ingenuity of 20th-century man.

2 *above*
An original cast-iron "Trick Dog" mechanical money bank by Hubley, late 19th century. The casting and finish are both finely detailed.

3 *above*
A Taiwanese reproduction "Trick Dog" money bank. Superficially similar to the Hubley model above, it is not refined in its details. An honest example will have its place of origin stamped on the underside but there are dishonest pieces on the market with the stamp erased.

4
A modern toy aeroplane, illustrated in a contemporary magazine; originally produced by Paya in the 1930s.

# BIBLIOGRAPHY

☐ CLOCKS

**ALLIX, Charles and BONNERT, Peter,** *Carriage Clocks: Their History and Development,* Antique Collectors' Club, Woodbridge, 1974

**BAILLIE, G. H.,** *Watchmakers and Clockmakers of the World,* volume 1, NAG Press, London, 1974

**BRITTEN, Frederick James,** *Old Clocks and Watches and Their Makers,* Spon, London, 1933

**CESCINSKY, Herbert C. and WEBSTER, Malcolm, R.,** *English Domestic Clocks,* Spring Books/Hamlyn, London, 1969

**DAWSON, P. G., DROVER, C. B., PARKES, D. W.,** *Early English Clocks,* Antique Collectors' Club, Woodbridge, 1982

**LOOMES, Brian,** *Watchmakers and Clockmakers of the World,* volume 2, NAG Press, London, 1976

**ROYER-COLLARD, F. Bernard,** *Skeleton Clocks,* NAG Press, London, 1969

☐ DECOYS

**EARNEST, Adele,** *The Art of the Decoy,* Schiffer, Exton PA, 1982

**MACKEY, William J.,** *American Bird Decoys,* Dutton, New York, 1965

**STARR, George Ross, Jr,** *Decoys of the Atlantic Flyway,* Winchester, New York, 1974

☐ AMERICAN FURNITURE

**HECKSCHER, Morrison,** *American Furniture in the Metropolitan Museum of Art,* Knopf, New York, 1972

**KIRK, John,** *American Chairs, Queen Anne and Chippendale,* Knopf, New York, 1972

**MONTGOMERY, Charles F.,** *American Furniture, The Federal Period,* Viking, New York, 1966

**MOSES, Michael,** *Master Craftsmen of Newport,* MMI Americana, New York, 1984

**NUTTING, Wallace,** *Furniture Treasury* volumes 1, 2 and 3, Macmillan, New York, 1928

**SACK, Albert,** *Fine Points of Furniture,* Crown, New York, 1950

**STONEMAN, Vernon C.,** *John and Thomas Seymour* and *Supplement,* Special Publications, Boston, 1959

☐ CONTINENTAL FURNITURE

**HAYWARD, Helena (ed.),** *World Furniture,* Hamlyn, London, 1965

**KREISEL, H.,** *Die Kunst des Deutschen Möbels,* C. H. Beck, Munich, 1973

**LEDOUX-LEBARD, Denise,** *Les Ebénistes du XIXe Siècle,* Editions de l'Amateur, Paris, revised edition 1985

**PAYNE, Christopher,** *19th Century European Furniture,* Antique Collectors' Club, Woodbridge, 1985

☐ ENGLISH FURNITURE

**BLY, John,** *Discovering English Furniture,* Shire, Aylesbury, 1976

**CHINNERY, Victor,** *Oak Furniture: The British Tradition,* Antique Collectors' Club, Woodbridge, 1979

**EDWARDS, Ralph,** *The Dictionary of English Furniture* (3 volumes), Country Life, London, revised edition 1953

**SYMONDS, R. W.,** *English Furniture from Charles II to George II,* The Connoisseur, London, 1929

**SYMONDS, R. W.,** *Furniture Making in 17th and 18th Century England,* The Connoisseur, London, 1955

*The Journal of the Furniture History Society,* The Department of Furniture and Interior Design, The Victoria and Albert Museum, London, 1965–

☐ GLASS

**BICKERTON, L. M.,** *English Drinking Glasses,* Barrie and Jenkins, London, 1971

**BROOKS, John,** *The Arthur Negus Guide to British Glass,* Hamlyn, London, 1981

**CHARLESTON, Robert J.,** *English Glass and the Glass Used in England c. 400–1940,* George Allen and Unwin, London, 1984

**KLEIN, Dan and LLOYD, Ward,** *The History of Glass,* Orbis, London, 1984

**NEWMAN, Harold,** *An Illustrated Dictionary of Glass,* Thames and Hudson, London, 1977

**SPIEGL, Walter,** *Glas des Historismus,* Klinkhardt and Biermann, Braunschweig, 1980

☐ AMERICAN SILVER

**BOHAN, Peter and HAMMERSLOUGH, P.,** *Early Connecticut Silver, 1700–1840,* Wesleyan University Press, Middletown, 1970

**BUHLER, Kathryn C.,** *American Silver in the Museum of Fine Arts, Boston,* New York Graphic Society, New York, 1982

**BUHLER, Kathryn C. and HOOD, Graham,** *American Silver in the Yale University Art Gallery,* Yale University Press, New Haven and London, 1970

**CARPENTER, Charles H., Jr,** *Gorham Silver 1831–1981,* Dodd, Mead, New York, 1982

**ENSKO, Stephen,** *American Silversmiths and Their Marks* (3 volumes), Ensko, New York, 1937

**FALES, Martha G.,** *Joseph Richardson and Family, Philadelphia Silversmiths,* Wesleyan University Press, Middletown, 1974

**PLEASANTS, Jacob Hall and SILL, Howard,** *Maryland Silversmiths, 1715–1830,* Lord Baltimore Press, Baltimore, 1930

**RAINWATER, Dorothy T.,** *Encyclopedia of American Silver Manufacturers,* Crown, New York, 1975

☐ ENGLISH SILVER

**BARR, Elaine,** *George Wickes, Royal Goldsmith,* Studio Vista/Christie's, London, 1980

**CLAYTON, Michael,** *The Collectors Dictionary of the Silver and Gold of Great Britain and South America,* Antique Collectors' Club, Woodbridge, 1985

**CULME, John,** *Nineteenth Century Silver,* Antique Collectors' Club, Woodbridge, 1977

**JACKSON, Sir Charles James,** *An Illustrated History of English Plate,* Macmillan, London, 1905

**JACKSON, Sir Charles James,** *English Goldsmiths and Their Marks,* Dover, New York, revised edition 1965

## ☐ BASE METALS

COTTERELL, Howard, *Old Pewter: Its Makers and Marks*, Batsford, London, 1968

FEILD, Rachael and GENTLE, Rupert, *English Domestic Brass*, Elek, London, 1985

HORNSBY, P. R. G., *Pewter of the Western World*, Schiffer, Exton PA and Moorland, Ashbourne, 1983

LAUGHLIN, L. I., *Pewter in America*, Crown, New York, 1981

LINDSAY, J. Seymour, *Iron and Brass Implements of the English House*, Tiranti, London, 1970

LISTER, Raymond, *Decorative Cast Ironwork in Great Britain*, George Bell, London, 1960

MICHAELIS, Ronald Frederick, *Old Domestic Brass Candlesticks*, Antique Collectors' Club, Woodbridge, 1978

PEAL, Christopher Arthur (ed.), *More Pewter Marks*, Norwich Print Brokers, Norwich, 1979

WILLS, Geoffrey, *Collecting Copper and Brass*, Mayflower, London, 1970

## ☐ SHEFFIELD PLATE

BRADBURY, F., *History of Old Sheffield Plate*, Northend Press, Sheffield, 1968

FROST, T. W., *The Price Guide to Old Sheffield Plate*, Antique Collectors' Club, Woodbridge, 1971

HUGHES, G. B., *Antique Sheffield Plate*, Batsford, London, 1970

VEITCH, H. M., *Sheffield Plate, Its History, Manufacture and Art*, George Bell, London, 1908

WALDRON, Peter, *Price Guide to Antique Silver*, Antique Collectors' Club, Woodbridge, 1985

## ☐ NETSUKE

BUSHELL, Raymond, *Collectors' Netsuke*, Walker/Weatherhill, New York, 1971

BUSHELL, Raymond, *Netsuke Familiar and Unfamiliar*, Weatherhill, New York, 1975

DAVEY, Neil K., *Netsuke*, Sotheby's, London, 1974, revised edition 1982

KINSEY, Mirian, *Living Masters of Netsuke*, Kodansha, Tokyo, New York, San Francisco, 1983

MASATOSHI, *The Art of Netsuke Carving*, Kodansha, Tokyo, New York, San Francisco, 1981

## ☐ POTTERY & PORCELAIN

ATTERBURY, Paul (ed.), *The History of Porcelain*, Orbis, London, 1982

BRITTON, Frank, *English Delftware in the Bristol Collection*, Sotheby's, London, 1982

BRUNET, Marcelle and PREAUD, Tamara, *Sèvres, Des Origines à Nos Jours*, Office du Livre, Paris, 1978

CHARLESTON, Robert (ed.), *World Ceramics*, Hamlyn, London, 1968

FOUREST, Henry-Pierre, *Delftware: Faience Production at Delft*, Thames and Hudson, London, 1980

GARNER, Sir Harry, *Oriental Blue and White Porcelain*, Faber, London, third edition 1973

GIACOMOTTI, Jeanne, *French Faience*, Oldbourne Press, London, 1963

GODDEN, Geoffrey, *British Porcelain*, Barrie and Jenkins, London, 1974

GODDEN, Geoffrey, *British Pottery*, Barrie and Jenkins, London, 1974

GOMPERTZ, G. St G. M., *Chinese Celadon Wares*, Faber, London, 1958

JENYNS, Soame, *Japanese Porcelain*, Faber, London, 1965

LUNSINGH SCHEURLEER, D. F., *Chinese Export Porcelain, Chine de Commande*, Faber, London, 1974

RACKHAM, Bernard, *Catalogue of Italian Maiolica in the Victoria and Albert Museum*, HMSO, London, 1940

WALCHA, Otto, *Meissen Porcelain*, Studio Vista/Christie's, London, 1973

## ☐ QUILTS

BISHOP, Robert and SAFFORD, Carleton, *America's Quilts and Coverlets*, Dutton, New York, 1972

GREENSTEIN, Blanche and WOODARD, Thomas K., *Crib Quilts and Other Small Wonders*, Dutton, New York, 1981

KHIN, Yvonne M., *The Collector's Dictionary of Quilt Names and Patterns*, Acropolis, Washington D.C., 1980

## ☐ SCIENTIFIC INSTRUMENTS

PETERSON, Harold L., *How Do You Know It's Old?*, George Allen and Unwin, London, 1977

TAYLOR, E. G. R., *Bostock, Hurt and Hurt. An Index to the Mathematical Practitioners of Hanoverian England*, Harriet Wynter, London, 1980

TURNER, Gerard L'E., *Collecting Microscopes*, Studio Vista, London, 1981

TURNER, Gerard L'E., *19th Century Scientific Instruments*, Sothebys, California, 1983

TURNER, Gerard L'E. and WYNTER, Harriet, *Scientific Instruments*, Studio Vista, London, 1975

## ☐ SCRIMSHAW

FLAYDERMAN, E. Norman, *Scrimshaw and Scrimshanders*, Flayderman, New Milford CT, 1972

FRERE-COOK, Gervais (ed.), *The Decorative Arts of the Mariner*, Jupiter, London, 1974

RANDIER, Jean, *Nautical Antiques for the Collector*, Barrie and Jenkins, London 1976

## ☐ TOYS

HILLIER, Mary, *Teddy Bears: A Celebration*, Ebury, London, 1985

LEVY, Alan, *A Century of Model Trains*, New Cavendish, London, 1984

NORMAN, Bill, *The Bank Book*, Accent Studios, San Diego, 1985

PRESSLAND, David, *Art of the Tin Toy*, New Cavendish, London, 1976 ·

# INDEX

# ACKNOWLEDGEMENTS

The following have rendered valuable assistance, material or moral, to the General Editor, the Contributors or Cooper Dale in the preparation of this book. Their help is gratefully acknowledged:

Gareth Abbit; Christopher Bangs; Michael Bass; Margaret Baxter; Dr Robert Bishop; Joe Black; Caroline Blacker; John Brooks; David Bryden; David Buchan; Bobby and Andrew Burns; Iona Cairns; Sam Camerer Cuss; James Chambers; Caroline Chapman; James Collingridge; John Culme; Sandra Davison, The Conservation Studio; Alan and Paul Freeman; Philippe Garner; Linda Glasgow; Col Robert Alan Green; Judith Harris; Christopher Hawkings; Jeanette Hayhurst; Bridget Heal; Charles Hearn; Roger Hearn; Malcolm Higby; Michael Hill; Michael and Stephanie Hine; Sue Hurt; Eric Knowles; Kay Lambert; Lady Victoria Leatham, Burghley House; Michael Lipitch; Annie Lurie; David Mallott; Tracy Mead; Christopher Meehan; Kevin Morris; Martin Mortimer, Delomosne & Son; Dora Papasolomontos, Lalique Ltd; Peter Peetoom; Roger Pring; Promises Ltd; Toni Rann; Philip Reynolds; Joe Robinson; Rachel Russell; Christopher Shepard; John Smith, Aspreys; Neil Smith; Kenneth Snowman; Eta Spencer; E. S. Tett; Kevin Tierney; Laural Wade; Kenneth M. Wilson, Henry Ford Museum, Dearborn, Michigan; Perran Wood.

## Picture Sources

p. 9: Strike One; p. 10: *1* Strike One; p. 11: Christie's; p. 12: *2* Christie's; p. 13: *3* Christie's; pp. 15-16: Strike One; p. 17: Christie's; p. 18: *1* Christie's; *2* Strike One; p. 19: *1* ESTO Photographics; *2, 3* Chun Y. Lai/ESTO; *4* Schector Lee/ESTO; p. 20: *1* Schector Lee/ESTO; *2* ESTO Photographics; p. 21: Schector Lee/ESTO; pp. 22-7: Israel Sack Inc.; p. 29: Sotheby's; p. 30: *1* Victoria and Albert Museum; *2* Sotheby's; p. 31: Victoria and Albert Museum; p. 32: Christopher Payne; p. 33: *3* Christopher Payne; *4* Sotheby's; p. 34: Sotheby's; p. 35: *5* Sotheby's; *6* Victoria and Albert Museum; p. 36: *1* Sotheby's; *2* Christopher Payne; pp. 37-8: Israel Sack Inc.; pp. 39-40: Collection Pierre Lecoules; p. 41: Victoria and Albert Museum; p. 42: Christopher Payne; p. 43: Sotheby's; p. 44: *1* Sotheby's; *2* Christopher Payne; p. 45: Christopher Payne; p. 46: Sotheby's; p. 47: *3* Christopher Payne; *4* Sotheby's; p. 48: Dickson of Ipswich; pp. 49-72: John Bly; p. 73: *1, 2* Burghley House; *3* John Bly; pp. 74-9: John Bly; p. 80: *1* Collection C. Shepard; *2* Corning Museum of Glass; p. 81: *3* Broadfield House Glass Museum; *4 Glas des Historismus* by Walter Spiegl, Klinkhardt and Biermann; p. 82: *1 Glas des Historismus* by Walter Spiegl, Klinkhardt and Biermann; *2* Broadfield House Glass Museum; *3* Ashmolean Museum; p. 84: Collection J. Hayhurst; p. 85: Broadfield House Glass Museum; p. 86: Collection J. Hayhurst; p. 87: Stuart Crystal; p. 88: *1* Collection J. Hayhurst; *2* Collection J. Brooks; p. 89: *3* Broadfield House Glass Museum; *4* Delomosne & Son Ltd; *5 left and centre* Collection J. Hayhurst; *5 right* Collection J. Brooks; p. 90: Broadfield House Glass Museum; p. 93: Collection C. Shepard; p. 94: Broadfield House Glass Museum; p. 95: *3 left* Broadfield House Glass Museum; *3 right* Collection J. Hayhurst; *4 left* Broadfield House Glass Museum; *4 centre and right* J. and P. Pacifico; p. 96: *1* Charles Hajdamach; *2* Broadfield House Glass Museum; *3* Sotheby's; pp. 97-101 Broadfield House Glass Museum; p. 102: *1* Broadfield House Glass Museum; *2* Lalique Ltd; p. 103: The Hot Glass Information Exchange; p. 104: *1* P.R.G. Hornsby; *2* Robin Bellamy; pp. 105-6: Robin Bellamy; p. 107: *2* Robin Bellamy; *3* Witney Antiques; *4* Robin Bellamy; p. 108: *1, 2* Andrew Cross; *3* Robin Bellamy; p. 109: *4* Charles Smith Ken; *5* P.R.G. Hornsby; pp. 110-14; Robin Bellamy; p. 115: *2, 3* Colin Greenway; *4* Robin Bellamy; *5, 6* Colin Greenway; p. 116: *1* Witney Antiques; *2* Colin Greenway; p. 117: P. R. G. Hornsby; p. 118: Robin Bellamy; p. 119: *3* Robin Bellamy; *4* P. R. G. Hornsby; p. 120: *1 History of Old Sheffield Plate* by Frederick Bradbury; *2* Phillips Son & Neale; *3, 4* and p. 121 S. J. Shrubsole Ltd; p. 123: *8* Christie's New York; *9* Museum of Fine Arts Boston; p. 124: Museum of Fine Arts Boston; p. 125: Brand Inglis; p. 126: Christie's New York; pp. 128-32: Sotheby's; p. 133: *1* Christie's New York; *2* The Worshipful Company of Goldsmiths; pp. 134-92: Sotheby's; p. 193: *1* Chun Y. Lai/ESTO; *2* Schector Lee/ESTO; pp. 194-5: Chun Y. Lai/ESTO; p. 196: Schector Lee/ESTO; p. 197: Private Collection; p. 198: Harriet Wynter; p. 199: *2* Trustees of the National Maritime Museum; *3, 4* Whipple Museum; p. 201: *1* Harriet Wynter; *2* Trustees of the National Maritime Museum; p. 202: Harriet Wynter; p. 203: Dundee Museums and Art Galleries; p. 204: Harriet Wynter; p. 205: *3* Harriet Wynter; *4, 5, 6* Photo-bibliothèque Alain Brieux; p. 207: Photobibliothèque Alain Brieux; p. 208: Harriet Wynter; pp. 209-13 Sotheby's; p. 214: *1* Christie's; *2* Sotheby's; pp. 215-16: Sotheby's; p. 217: *2, 3* Sotheby's; *4* Hilary Kay.